D0847748

PR
5075
.C34

1-10162

DATE DUE			

Texas Woman's University
Library
Denton, Texas

THE PASTORAL VISION OF
WILLIAM MORRIS

SOUTH ATLANTIC
MODERN LANGUAGE ASSOCIATION
AWARD STUDY

Blue Calhoun

The Pastoral Vision of William Morris:

The Earthly Paradise

Athens:
the University of Georgia Press

Library of Congress Catalog Card Number: 74–14054
International Standard Book Number: 0–8203–0354–2

The University of Georgia Press, Athens 30602

© 1975 by the University of Georgia Press
All rights reserved

Printed in the United States of America

PR
5075
.C34

FOR MY MOTHER AND FATHER

1-10162

contents

acknowledgments

I wish to express appreciation to the South Atlantic Modern Language Association and the Georgia Press for sponsoring publication of this book. Kenneth Cherry and Barbara Reitt of the Press have been particularly helpful. I am indebted to many friends for their encouragement and suggestions at various stages of writing. I am especially grateful to Fred C. Thomson for providing patient and confident direction when this study began as a dissertation for the University of North Carolina; to George M. Harper, who showed me the pastoral possibilities of Yeats and Morris; to George O. Marshall, Jr., for his careful reading of the manuscript; to Lillian Newman of the Agnes Scott College Library and Peter W. McGoran of the William Morris Gallery, Walthamstow, for their assistance in research; and to Sir Basil Blackwell, whose keen sense of the poet's world sharpened my own vision of William Morris.

ILLIAM MORRIS was one of the most thoroughly attractive figures of his age. Gifted and articulate, he was admired by his contemporaries for the diverse activities that issued from his credo: "Apart from the desire to produce beautiful things, the leading passion of my life has been and is hatred of modern civilization." [1] The procession of beautiful things was endless, of course, including the designs of the firm in homes, churches, and public buildings all over England; over twenty volumes of poems, stories, and translations from four languages; and the books splendidly designed and printed by his own Kelmscott Press. Committed also to "more complete civilization," Morris fought to preserve the continuity of the English heritage in the crafts of the individual workman, in the old buildings doomed for "restoration," and in the natural legacy of woodlands like Epping Forest or the waters of the Thames. An energetic and creative man, even his hatred was constructive. An engaging man as well, he has been the subject of numerous memoirs, appreciations, and biographical studies. [2] Although a good many of these are early, often based on Mackail's monumental *Life of William Morris* (1899), others show continuing critical discovery from about the time of the Morris centenary. [3] For writers of the last decade, preoccupied with the crises of modern culture, Morris has assumed the stature of cultural hero, a prophet concerned with the quality of life, the dignity of labor, and the fundamental relationship of man to the earth. Recent studies thus augment past scholarship to insure what C. S. Lewis foresaw in 1939—the "rehabilitation" of Morris as a craftsman, socialist, and a man of complex dimensions. [4]

If Morris has escaped obscurity, however, his poetry has not. Lewis complained that as a writer Morris was the victim of "misleading labels." These labels have not been altogether abandoned. The temptation, even among astute critics, is to

take Morris quite at his word about the ease of weaving tapes-
tries and verses simultaneously, or about his pose as the "idle
singer of an empty day." The complexity of character that his
recent biographers are at pains to reveal is emphatically limited to his personal relationships and his activities in crafts and
politics. As a writer, William Morris is still considered an
escapist.[5]

The critic's attempt to rescue Morris from the land of the
lotos-eaters is often foiled by the poet himself—in the great
mass of the poetry, the location of settings in the distant past,
the neutral style, and the invocation of the atmosphere of
dream. Nowhere does he seem so insistently mild-eyed and
melancholy as in *The Earthly Paradise*, the poem that established his reputation as both a popular story-teller and escapist.[6] Published in three volumes between 1868 and 1870, then
later in four, the poem is a collection of twenty-four ancient
tales within a medieval frame narrative. This story relates the
misadventures of fourteenth-century mariners who fail to find
the fabled Earthly Paradise; tired and nearing death, these
Wanderers pass their time by telling stories from alternately
classical and European sources. These tales are then "gathered" and introduced by a narrator who proclaims himself "an
idle singer of an empty day" and a "dreamer of dreams, born
out of my due time." Whatever his motive, the poet seems
undeniably certain in his choice of dreamland and the aesthetic distance it implies.

The Earthly Paradise thus seems an important place to begin
a critical assessment of Morris's poetry and its relationship to
a career of social commitment. Whether the poem lends itself
to explication is not so much the question as whether it helps
us see the beginning of a pattern in Morris's writing. Read in
context with the early poetry, the lectures, and the late
utopian romances, *The Earthly Paradise* suggests that the deliberate stance of the narrator, the choice of the past as setting,
and the use of dream as an impersonal aesthetic vehicle all
contribute to a unified social vision.

There is critical consensus that *The Earthly Paradise*, like a good deal else that Morris wrote, is a response to his age. Yet it is generally considered to be a retreat from Victorian ugliness and from growing domestic unhappiness. There can be no denying the existence of "bewildering care" in either area, but retreat seems an inappropriately negative label. It overlooks Morris's simultaneous engagement in other areas, such as his energetic involvement in two of the new firm's most important projects, the Green Dining Room at the South Kensington Museum and the Armoury at St. James's Palace. It further implies that the emotions Morris may have evaded in his business he channeled into melancholy verse. This view of Morris as a romantic *poète maudit* is incongruous with his vehement rejection of such a posture: he insisted, "I abominate introspective poetry." [7] Labels of retreat and escape ultimately pose more problems than they solve.

A more appropriate term is provided by Morris himself when he describes "idleness" in an 1886 lecture entitled "The Aims of Art." Here he acknowledges the "influence of two dominating moods, which for the lack of better words I must call the mood of energy and the mood of idleness: these two moods are now one, now the other, always crying out in me to be satisfied." Both moods he finds to be natural, universal, and complementary, but the tenor of one is active, the other contemplative. Although each is a kind of restlessness, physical activity is the response to "the mood of energy," and "the mood of idleness" is associated with memory, vision, and dream: "When the mood of idleness is on me, I find it hard indeed if I cannot rest and let my mind wander over the various pictures, pleasant or terrible, which my own experience or my communing with the thoughts of other men, dead or alive, have fashioned in it" (*CW* 23:81).

Literally, the terms illuminate the distinction between the activity of the craftsman and the poet. *Energy* directs the work of the hand; *idleness* makes other aesthetic response meditative or evaluative rather than prescriptive and suggests that the proper work of the writer is visionary. Symbolically, however, energy and idleness take on broader connotations in the body of Morris's work. In the lectures he began in the late 1870s he would speak of the "blind energy" of the middle-class capitalists, exactly the terms applied by Arnold to the Philistines, whose Hebraic obsession with deeds contributed to the confusion he called anarchy. Thus in Morris's developing social philosophy, energy suggests the feverish but insignificant activity of the marketplace and its "heroic" literature, the sort Shakespeare called "the public means which public manners breeds." The very intensity of this apparent energy requires a counter-image of a totally different sort. Idleness, an ambiguous and even ironic term, provides the compensatory vision in a style that absolutely rejects heroic motion and a philosophy that redefines energy as sensuous, individual activity in a simple, natural world.

Finally, the most significant implication of energy and idleness is that they remind us of a striking quality in all of Morris's writing—its dialectical balance. Lewis called it an unresolved tension between opposing moods, a balance that "must not be mistaken for a debate between two doctrines." [8] The same quality was recognized by Morris's earliest modern admirer, W. B. Yeats, who called the older poet's art an "antithetical dream." [9] Yeats perfectly describes the work of the "idle singer" in *The Earthly Paradise* when he creates a dreamworld to counter the "snorting steam and piston stroke" of his empty day. Dreaming, an idle activity, is less escape than creation of a compensatory image, a kind of aesthetic activity with social significance. Although the response need not be conscious, i.e., rational, it is directed as much toward society as away from it. Explaining the unconscious relationship of the artist to his age, Jung could well be describing Morris's idleness: "Therein lies the social importance of art; it is constantly at work educating the spirit of the age, since it brings to birth those forms in which the age is most lacking. Recoiling from the unsatisfying present the yearning of the artist reaches out to that primordial image in the unconscious which is best fitted to compensate the insufficiency and onesidedness of the spirit of the age." [10] Morris's primordial image, according to Yeats, is the Green Tree, the symbol of a world that celebrates natural profusion, delight in the body, and simplicity of life. This "dream of natural happiness" is conveyed by a concrete descriptive style, and it is created in antithesis to the world of the Dry Tree, the symbol of sterile abstraction in science, religion, and poetry. [11] In the idle dream itself, its stylistic simplicity and its dialectical relationship with the poet's real world, we can see that Morris's aesthetic response is not escape, but a kind of writing often mistaken for escape literature—the pastoral. [12]

The pastoral has always been one of the most influential ancient genres. Its conventional form, created by Theocritus and Virgil, was absorbed into Western literature to serve thousands of writers for as many years. In England the genre flourished among the finest poets of the sixteenth and seventeenth centuries. By the end of the eighteenth century, however, the limits of this traditional version of pastoral had for the most part been realized. The structure of the idyll and eclogue, the rustic characters, and the artificial surface of the convention were revived—or at least continued—by a small number of Victorian poets. But with many more Romantic and Victorian poets, the pastoral impulse experienced a renaissance that shifted emphasis from the conventional formula to the broader concerns of theme and point of view. The change was appropriate to the epistemological bias of the age and to the cultural self-consciousness of Romantic and Victorian writers, who were equally attuned to the genre's main interest, the threat posed to the natural world by civilization. The pastoral practice of the nineteenth century has spurred a revival of critical interest in the subject in our own. Leo Marx, whose work on the pastoral in American tradition is definitive, examines "the motive that lies behind the form, and . . . the images and themes and even the conception of life associated with it." [13]

The primary motive of the pastoral is a vision of the natural world that sets it in evaluative juxtaposition with the civilized world that threatens it—the complexities of urban society in general, and in the last two centuries the problems of industrialization in particular. Every pastoral then is in some sense both "a green thought in a green shade" and an awareness of the world beyond. The pastoral also makes the green world a microcosm: a particular kind of society is implied. Finally, pastoral style is apt to be of a special sort as well, usually reflecting the simplicity of life within its garden. In the nineteenth century, each of these characteristics of the pastoral retains the universal motives of the genre with modifications appropriate to the age.

In the new pastoral of the nineteenth century a primary emphasis is perception. Its optics are complicated to make it a vehicle of vision, literal and symbolic. Since the vision is double, evaluative contrast is the main purpose. It juxtaposes city and country life, complex and simple responses to human problems, and in the broadest sense, heroic and meditative activity. John Lynen, analyzing the pastoral technique of Robert Frost, reminds us "that the contrast between country and town involves a recognition of two sets of values, and the pastoral does not simply eulogize the rural world at the expense of the great world beyond. . . . The pastoral poet's real power springs from his ability to keep the two worlds in equilibrium." [14] Thus we could say that antithesis is basic to the pastoral vision. Rejection of civilization is not enough, nor is celebration of the garden. The pastoral, a vehicle of comparison, requires a double vision of the relative merits of both kinds of life. This perceptive activity is facilitated by the use of a narrator. Although there is a certain sense of authorial presence in the ancient poems, there is no narrative persona. Morris's narrator complicates the dimensions of comparison and contrast by combining the self-consciousness of the romantic journeyer (like Wordsworth in *The Prelude*) with the classical disengagement of the idle singer (like Virgil or Spenser).

Second, the pastoral society undergoes redefinition, as does the stylistic treatment of the landscape, a third important element of nineteenth-century pastorals. In both these areas, there is almost a reversal of the earlier tendency toward idealization that began with Virgil. In the social vision the community of shepherds is retained somewhat to stress the importance of preserving English rural life, but it is extended to include the urban working classes who are victims of industry. For this proletarian society life is simple but not painless. It includes suffering and death, and it values labor. All three of these "realities" suggest the bond between man and earthly process. In landscape description the idealized, formulaic landscape is replaced with a real one. Many Victorians express a preference for Theocritus, assuming his descriptions to be more realistic. Like the Romantics before them, these writers are interested in real, particular natural phenomena and the real threat of their destruction by industry; thus natural description becomes more localized and particularized. The resulting style might be called romantic, in the sense that Wordsworth uses "a selection of the language really spoken by men," but I prefer the vocabulary of C. S. Lewis in describing Morris's style: "Those who are really repelled by it after a fair trial are being repelled not by its romanticism but by its classicism, for in one sense Morris is as classical as Johnson." That sense is Morris's language, which is "as earthy, as rooted, as Aristotle or Dr. Johnson. He is everywhere concrete." [15]

Now the pastoral "idleness" that emerges in *The Earthly Paradise* in 1870 is not the clear vision of *News from Nowhere* twenty years later. In the early work it is intimated in the narrator's character and tone; in the multiple comparisons of individual tales, of tales and framework, of framework and lyric interludes; in the calendar arrangement of the tales; in their idyllic frames and landscape description; and in the glimpses of life in a "now altered world" where "all folk dwelt in great simplicity." This idle vision is somewhat blurred because it coexists with the poetry of energy, the active, heroic mode that dominates *The Defence of Guenevere* (1858). In *The Earthly Paradise* heroic poetry is represented by the romantic quest of the frame narrative and many of the tales, but this search for permanence, perfection, and love is consistently undercut by reversing the symbols of the romantic journey, by recounting the Wanderers' adventure as antecedent action, and by interruption of the tales with idyllic frames. The open-ended structure of the journey is checked by the closed structure of the idyll. While *The Earthly Paradise* utilizes dual and simultaneous structures, the poetry of energy is ultimately submitted to the contemplation of idleness.

The mixed modes of *The Earthly Paradise* show us the tension between Victorian expectations and Morris's aesthetic beliefs, between an old and a new style, between a romantic and a classical view of the world. A good deal of the dialectic is confused rather than clear; and some of the escapist criticism is understandable. In many ways, however, Morris had already achieved the distance from his life, work, and world that is necessary to the double vision of the pastoral and that is characteristic of the poetry of commitment, not escape.

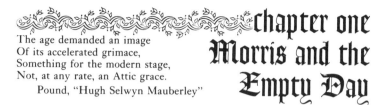

The age demanded an image
Of its accelerated grimace,
Something for the modern stage,
Not, at any rate, an Attic grace.
        Pound, "Hugh Selwyn Mauberley"

HE pastoral world is a civilized creation. Simple life in a green garden is necessarily the vision of a sophisticated writer, one who is committed by history and temperament to the complexities of city life but who questions its basic assumption, always the worship of some kind of power. In pastorals of pre-industrialized societies this force is apt to be martial or economic, personified in a tyrannical landowner who dispossesses the shepherd of his pastures. In pastoral response of the nineteenth century it is the impersonal power of the machine that threatens the natural environment and the quality of life it symbolizes. The garden of England—the figure used by Blake, Ruskin, and Morris—is invaded by "dark Satanic Mills," and the idol of riches is "set up where the green fields of England are furnace-burnt into the likeness of the plain of Dura." [1] But these writers, far from suggesting escape to the past, to primitive nature, or to a Palace of Art, use the pastoral contrast to evaluate the possibilities of life within what Morris calls a "more complete civilization" (*CW* 22:64). The purpose of the pastoral is not to wrest power from the machine but to question its ability to sustain life. Thus two worlds have dominated the pastoral from its inception to the present, the garden of the past or future and the city of the present where both the poet and his audience reside.

Theocritus, originator of the genre in the third century B.C., appears to have written his idylls about Sicilian country life from the civilized distance of the Alexandrian court, and Virgil could idealize memories of the Mantuan countryside where his father kept bees primarily because he was surrounded by a tottering Roman Republic unlikely to re-establish a Golden Age. William Morris, after a happy country childhood and before the discovery of Kelmscott by the upper Thames, wrote *The Earthly Paradise* in "the land of bricks and mortar called London," [2] the city that crowned Victoria's empire and by mid-century contained over half the population of a recently rural country.

Although he was born near London, Morris's early life sheltered him from the ugliness of the city. All three of the family homes in Walthamstow were near Epping Forest, where the young Morris memorized local birds, beasts, and trees. And not far to the north and east were the Essex marshes that he also knew intimately. The family life, as May Morris describes it, provided the security and pleasant ceremony of middleclass prosperity:

> The Morris family was brought up in an atmosphere of intelligent housekeeping of the old style—home-made beer and bread, real butter and real cream and the like; and the best of everything for home-consumption was bought carefully at special shops who knew their customers personally, sometimes at dark little shops in the City before which my Grandmother's heavy carriage-horses would stop now and then for enquiries and purchases. There were well-stocked gardens and orchards, horses and cows and pigs and poultry: the place, in short, a model of the "big house," the self-supporting unit of country life; though on a smaller scale and without the pretence of fashion. [3]

Later, at school in Marlborough and Oxford, Morris learned another face of the English landscape, the Wiltshire and Berkshire downs where great natural beauty surrounded the mysterious human monuments that Morris the lecturer would recall years later: prehistoric Avebury and Silbury Hill, and the White Horse of Uffington. The most recurrent pastoral images in Morris's writing, however, are drawn from the upper Thames valley where in 1871, one year after the publication of *The Earthly Paradise*, he would discover the Arcadian setting of *News from Nowhere*. Kelmscott Manor was "a heaven on earth." The farmhouse and its surrounding elms, water-meadows, birds, and the river echo through the works as the earthly paradise the Wanderers could never find. As a country retreat, Kelmscott provided Morris a spiritual center until his death in 1896.

Yet Morris was in fundamental ways bound to the city and modern civilization. Almost symbolically, his birth in 1834 was concurrent with the triumph of steam in English life. The transatlantic crossing of the steamboat *Royal William* in 1833 was quickly followed by the completion of the first railway to the capital, the London and Greenwich line, in 1836. And the source of plenitude in Morris's childhood was his father's success in business, wise investments in copper shares that gave his son a respectable education and secure entrée into the business world of London when Morris and his friends established the firm—Morris, Marshall, Faulkner and Company—in 1861.

The end of Morris's youth can be marked by this move to the city from Red House, the house built in Bexley Heath by Morris and his associates for the recently married Morrises. In 1865, after five years, he left this scene of idyllic merriment with his friends from the Oxford Brotherhood and apparently the only uncomplicated, happy days of his married life to go to Queen Square in London. Saddened by the loss of this paradise in "woody Kent," he refused ever to return when he went to join the "bugs of Bloomsbury." As much as he hated the city for "the squalor and ugliness that come of carelessness and despair," he remained there for most of his life, involved in what Yeats would call "the fascination of what's difficult." The energy that impelled him in the various projects of the firm, the organization of the Socialist League and indeed in his "idle" poems, required an urban setting, and he knew it. Surrounded even by the natural richness of Kelmscott Manor, he would say: "I rather want to be in London again, for I feel as if my time were passing with too little done in the country:

altogether I fear I am a London bird; its soot has been rubbed into me, and even these autumn mornings can't wash me clean of restlessness." [4]

Thus there are two central images in Morris's writing, London and Kelmscott, sometimes represented by the Thames. The first is the realistic center of a culture that cannot retreat "backward to the days before civilization," and the second is the pastoral garden. Within reach of the city, it provides a place and a subject for meditation. Each setting becomes a microcosm in a pastoral evaluation of the relative values of energy and idleness.

The antithetical symbols of city and country are evoked in all of Morris's major works, and in each the contrast aims to evaluate and purify the city locus, that familiar setting to which the poet must return. In the Apology of *The Earthly Paradise*, the "empty day" is associated with industrialized society that brings "The heavy trouble, the bewildering care / That weighs us down who live and earn our bread." The London setting is repeated in the opening lines of the Prologue:

> Forget six countries overhung with smoke,
> Forget the snorting steam and piston stroke,
> Forget the spreading of the hideous town.

The counter-image is provided, as it is in all these passages, by the Thames in a simpler, more natural city. The reader is invited to "think" and "dream" of London "small, and white, and clean, / The clear Thames bordered by its gardens green." This juxtaposition of past and present visions of London, a leitmotif of the lectures, is initiated in *The Life and Death of Jason* (1867), where the narrator's apology to Chaucer, also a city poet, is framed in terms of pastoral contrast. The narrator's aesthetic ineptness—like the idle singer's—is associated with modern inhibitions: he is "meshed within this smoky net / Of unrejoicing labor," but Chaucer's clear, sweet song originated in "the rose-hung lanes of woody Kent" in the days when "Thames' stream scarce fettered bore the bream along / Unto the bastioned bridge, his only chain." The characteristic contrast recurs in *News from Nowhere* (1890) when utopian London is freed of mechanical fetters: "The soap-works with their smoke-vomiting chimneys were gone; the engineer's works gone; the lead-works gone; and no sound or riveting and hammering came down the west wind from Thorney-croft's." And the Thames flows through a city that is "a continuous garden . . . going down to the water's edge, in which the flowers were now blooming luxuriantly, and sending delicious waves of summer scent over the eddying stream." [5]

News from Nowhere demonstrates the extension of the double images into a comprehensive point of view. It is a double vision that requires a double structure. Essential to both the perspective and the structure is the narrator, exactly the sort Morris utilizes in *The Life and Death of Jason* and *The Earthly Paradise*. At the center of his narrative in *News from Nowhere* is the revelation of a utopia that epitomizes pastoral virtues: a classless society with an amiable hierarchy, aesthetic satisfaction in simple work, and the integration of man with his natural environment. The dynamic, sensuous quality of the latter relationship is shown in the trip up the Thames that structures the dream-story. Like a meditative journey into the symbolic kernel or "seed" of the pastoral experience, its culmination at Kelmscott Manor is also the celebration of the harvest season in an England that has evolved from a foul workshop to "a garden, where nothing is wasted and nothing is spoilt" (*CW* 16:72). Constantly interrupting this utopian vision and finally surrounding it is the contemporary setting of "modern civilization." The narrator remembers its sordidness in the midst of his dream-pleasures and recognizes its reality on his jolting return. The aesthetic power of the work is dialectic. It depends upon the narrator's painful double awareness, which is accentuated by the more innocent utopian characters who notice: "You have begun again your never-ending contrast between the past and the present" (*CW* 16:203). *News from Nowhere* reminds us then of several concerns shared by Morris and the "old pastoral poets" he recalls as narrator: the role of double vision, emphasizing the theme of innocence and experience; the double structure, with its simultaneous sense of simple and complex, future (modeled on past) and present; and finally, the importance of "civilization" to Morris and other writers in this tradition. His utopia, like all works in that genre, intensifies the finest traits of culture as he knew it and eliminates the weakest. It is a higher civilization, a result of the New Birth that the lectures anticipate. It synthesizes the city and garden settings by retaining the order inherent in both but by enduing the city with the natural vitality of the garden. The utopian vision is also an exaggeration. As Mackail says of *News from Nowhere*, "A pastoral, whether it places its golden age in the past or the future, is by the nature of the case artificial, and perhaps as much so, though not so obviously, as when it boldly plants itself in the present." [6] The artificiality, if we wish to call it that, is necessitated by the disparity between life as we know it and life as it might be. Thus in a pastoral utopia or any pastoral vision, synthesis is less apparent than antithesis.

Morris shares this dialectical perspective with few Victorian writers. Certainly there were those suggesting a return to nature or those damning the mechanical destruction of life, but the double vision essential to constructive pastoral was not a typical response. It does appear, however, and the works of Arnold, Hardy, and Ruskin provide fine examples. Arnold uses the pastoral construct consistently by literally surrounding the meditative experience with the threat of the city's disorientation, a juxtaposition that heightens the experience itself. The manipulation of contrasting settings and attitudes is most sophisticated in "The Scholar-Gipsy" and "Thyrsis," but it is used simply and effectively in "Lines Written in Kensington Gardens." A speaker, obviously a city-dweller, experiences the unique pleasure of a rural setting in the midst of the city. The constant sense of double setting provides the motive force of the poem. The source of delight is that "the lone, open glade" lies "amid the city's jar," within "the girdling city's hum," and close to "the huge world, which roars hard by." Within this civilized enclosure the scale of the natural world is reduced and intensified:

> Here at my feet what wonders pass,
> What endless, active life is here!
> What blowing daisies, fragrant grass!
> An air-stirr'd forest, fresh and clear.

The glade, "Screen'd by deep boughs on either hand," is animated also by birdsong, sheep-cries, and the voices of children. Finally, in this microcosm the speaker can observe the pastoral cycle as "all things in this glade go through / The changes of their quiet day." [7] Arnold perfectly illustrates the pastoral as lyric.

Hardy's version of pastoral reveals the cultural disruption created by the machine's appropriation of natural offices. His vision is more ironic. The occasion is provided by the harvest at Flintcomb-Ash Farm in *Tess of the d'Urbervilles*. In the episode the machine invades the harvest, a sacred season of the ancient poets. At dawn Tess and the other workers wait to begin a natural ceremony that is transformed to an unnatural one by the presence of the machine: "Close under the eaves of the stack, and as yet barely visible, was the red tyrant that the women had come to serve—a timber-framed construction, with straps and wheels appertaining—the threshing-machine which, whilst it was going, kept up a despotic demand upon the endurance of their muscles and nerves." The personified machine is associated with the underworld through its servant, the engineer. Like a "creature from Tophet," he is subservient to "his Plutonic master," and his devotion isolates him from all else: "He spoke in a strange northern accent; his thoughts being turned inwards upon himself, his eye on his iron charge, hardly perceiving the scenes around him, and caring for them not at all." With its incessant motion and penetrating hum, the machine separates those who operate from natural process, but it separates the engineer from even the other people. He has no identity save for his function: "He was in the agricultural world, but not of it. He served fire and smoke; these denizens of the fields served vegetation, weather, frost, and sun." The machine and its "supernatural" power portend the technological bias of the future; Hardy's preference, human labor, is an anachronism. Thus the tone of his pastoral contrast is elegiac: "The old men in the rising straw-rick talked of the past days when they had been accustomed to thresh with flails on the oaken barn-floor; when everything, even to winnowing, was effected by hand-labour, which, to their thinking, though slow, produced better results." [8]

This loss of the dignity of individual labor is the focus of Ruskin's contrast, which converts elegy to a radical call to action. Like Morris, Arnold, and Hardy, Ruskin loved the earth, its seasons, and its labors. Increasingly frustrated by its destruction, he reiterates the image of England as a ruined garden, stressing the contrast of past and present implied in the Edenic connotations and of nature and machine. All his late works develop this figure, but its strongest pastoral expression comes in *Sesame and Lilies* (1865) and *The Crown of Wild Olive* (1866), both published shortly before *The Earthly Paradise* and well before Morris's lectures and late romances. The conclusion of *Sesame and Lilies* prophesies an apocalyptic change in which the garden becomes a coal mine. Not only does the garden epitomize all that is vital in English country life, but the image of the mine summarizes the material idolatry and desecration of the earth that Ruskin associates with riches throughout his lectures. The sacred earth itself is pillaged and converted to a Cave of Mammon: "Suppose you had each . . . a garden, large enough for your children to play in . . . no more—and that you could not change your abode; but that, if you chose, you could double your income, or quadruple it, by digging a coal shaft in the middle of the lawn, and turning the flower-beds into heaps of coke. Would you do it? I hope

not. . . . Yet this is what you are doing with all England." [9]
Ruskin most anticipates Morris in his association of man
and the earth. The landscapes he admires throughout his
works are those that bear the mark of man's labor; by the same
token, he finds the prototype of all labor to be those very
pastoral tasks that are threatened by the machine. His basic
complaint is not that the machine deprives man of an income
but of dignified and sensuous work that keeps him linked to
the earth. In *The Crown of Wild Olive* he shows that agrarian
labors are prostituted to the machine: the farmer "has got his
machine made, which goes creaking, screaming, and occasionally exploding, about modern Arcadia." Or it invades the harvest, for Ruskin as for Hardy a symbolic occasion: "Do you
know that lately, in Cumberland, in the chief pastoral district
of England,—in Wordsworth's own home,—a procession of
villagers on their festa day provided for themselves, by way
of music, a steam-plow whistling at the head of them!" To
counter this profane image of modern civilization, Ruskin
envisions a higher civilization as one that will recognize the
necessity and dignity of human labor: "Hand-labor on the
earth, the work of the husbandman and of the shepherd;—to
dress the earth and to keep the flocks of it—the first task of
man, and the final one. . . . Hand-labor on the earth, and the
harvest of it brought forth with singing:—not steam-piston
labor on the earth, and the harvest of it brought forth with
steam-whistling. You will have no prophet's voice accompanied by that shepherd's pipe, and pastoral symphony." Ruskin's juxtapositions of garden and machine, like Morris's, finally issue in a vision of a new Eden: "All land that is waste
and ugly, you must redeem into ordered fruitfulness." [10] But
the new world is based on labor, and in Morris's case possible
only through revolution. At that point we definitely move
from poetry to politics, from vision to action. In all these
writers the primary concern, however, is perception. Their
pastoral juxtaposition of two worlds shows a concern that
ranges from despair to anger, but all resist escape and commit

themselves to the inevitability of civilization, hoping to guide its misdirected energy literally back to earth.

Their dialectical response dramatizes the gap between reality and potential, but more significantly it emphasizes the contradictions in reality as writers knew it in the last half of the nineteenth century. For a century "progress" had effected a subtle reversal of traditional priorities in the relationship of man, nature, and machine. With the advent of science and now with the perfection of the machine, mechanical power was endowed with the breath of life, while nature was reduced to mechanism. In the latter instance machines literally conquered nature, but more dangerous was the metaphoric view of the mind of the individual and society as an instrument "as delicate as that of a spinning jenny." [11]

The first stage in the development of the Victorian tradition of energy was the apotheosis of the machine itself, a rather primitive response to its mysterious force. While it is true that the romance of the machine had palled somewhat by the beginning of the Victorian period, the steam engine in particular still had symbolic appeal. Charles Tennyson Turner's apostrophe to "The Steam Threshing-Machine" was published in 1868, the same year as the first volume of *The Earthly Paradise.* Although Turner's allusions are pastoral, his evaluation is not. In his personification he praises the very powers that Hardy relegates to the regions of Tophet:

> Did any seer of ancient time forebode
> This mighty engine, which we daily see
> Accepting our full harvests, like a god,
> With clouds about his shoulders—it might be
> Some poet-husbandman, some lord of verse,
> Old Hesiod, or the wizard Mantuan,
> Who catalogued in rich hexameters
> The rake, the roller, and the mystic van;
> Or else some priest of Ceres, it might seem,
> Who witnessed, as he trod the silent fane,
> The notes and auguries of coming change,

Of other ministrants in shrine and grange—
The sweating statue, and her sacred wain
Low-booming with the prophecy of steam!

The personified machine was a concrete expression of
Macaulay's theory that mechanical progress was "natural"
and that the scientific tradition initiated by Bacon was bearing
"fruit." The use of organic imagery to suggest the process of
history or the nature of society was romantic, and it was sys-
tematically developed by Carlyle to affirm a kind of progress
that is natural, that is to say, marked by gradual growth, a
vegetable evolution that Morris also would associate with the
cycle of cultures—their seeds, blossom, harvest, decay, and
New Birth, the reiterative theme of the lectures. When the
organic metaphor was appropriated by the antiromantic
spokesmen for scientific progress, however, their claims were
more supernatural than natural. The Green Tree became the
magician's blossoming rod, or to borrow Wordsworth's figure,
the stone suddenly claimed the powers of the shell. As the
spokesman for utilitarian liberalism, Macaulay was also the
first important spokesman for scientific progress. As he ex-
plains in his 1837 essay on Bacon, Utility and Progress are the
key concepts in Bacon's philosophy—and more especially,
Macaulay's. Both principles concern man's practical control
of "that visible and tangible world" scorned by the philoso-
phers; and that practical control asserts sudden, stunning mastery of the environment in a way that accentuates the dynamic
quality of progress itself. The well-known encomium of scientific advance in the essay on Bacon gives progress as much life
as Turner's machine:

It has lengthened life; it has mitigated pain; it has extin-
guished diseases; it has increased the fertility of the soil;
it has given new securities to the mariner; it has furnished new arms to the warrior; it has spanned great
rivers and estuaries with bridges of form unknown to
our fathers; it has guided the thunderbolt innocuously

from heaven to earth; it has lighted up the night with the splendor of day; it has extended the range of the human vision; it has multiplied the power of the human muscles; it has accelerated motion; it has annihilated distance; it has facilitated intercourse, correspondence, all friendly offices, all despatch of business; it has enabled man to descend to the depths of the sea, to soar into the air, to penetrate securely into the noxious recesses of the earth, to traverse the land in cars which whirl along without horses, and the ocean in ships which run ten knots an hour against the wind. These are but a part of its fruits, and of its first fruits. For it is a philosophy which never rests, which has never attained, which is never perfect. Its law is progress.[12]

Striking in the passage is the enormous sense of power in this dynamic force—extinguishing, extending, accelerating, annihilating, penetrating, and whirling. And virtually all of the activity is applied to the conquest of nature, the great elusive mystery of which man had heretofore stood in awe.

Although many years had contributed to these modern marvels, mid-Victorian England reaped the harvest, to use Macaulay's term. The Great Exhibition of 1851 was an occasion of self-adulation as the empire realized in an instant its triumph over the mysteries of centuries. It was about this time that John Stuart Mill helped to dispel the romantic "maxim of following Nature." Although his essay on *Nature* was published posthumously in 1874, its composition dates from mid-century, just before *The Origin of Species* and after Tennyson, in the closing lines of *In Memoriam*, anticipates "the crowning race"

Of those that, eye to eye shall look
   On knowledge; under whose command
   Is Earth and Earth's; and in their hand
Is Nature like an open book.

In the essay Mill addresses himself primarily to the practical necessity of altering and improving nature. Many of the feats he calls "great triumphs of Art over Nature" echo the accomplishments admired by Macaulay: building bridges, draining marshes, erecting lightning rods, "the excavation of Nature's wells," and "the dragging to light of what she has buried at immense depths in the earth." The rationale of this conquest utilizes an equally aggressive vocabulary:

> But to commend these and similar feats, is to acknowledge that the ways of Nature are to be conquered, not obeyed: that her powers are often towards man in the position of enemies, from whom he must wrest, by force and ingenuity, what little he can for his own use, and deserves to be applauded when that little is rather more than might be expected from his physical weakness in comparison to those gigantic powers. All praise of Civilization, or Art, or Contrivance, is so much dispraise of Nature; an admission of imperfection, which it is man's business, and merit, to be always endeavouring to correct or mitigate.[13]

The machine provided the age its symbol of power; science provided the rationale for the conquest of nature; but when the Victorian writers wanted to celebrate the energy of the age, they usually mirrored it in its heroes. When the idle singer ironically disclaimed his skills against the "ravening monsters mighty men shall slay," he was only slightly exaggerating the exaltation of heroic deeds that typified the Victorian age far into its twilight decades. The hero was a romantic legacy although his genealogy was less exotic than that of his ancestors. Fashioned primarily by Tennyson and Carlyle, he might derive his appearance from a Greek mariner or wear the medieval armor of "my King's ideal knight / Who reverenced his conscience as his king," but his motives were thoroughly English, and his admiration of force was thoroughly Victorian. Tennyson's admonition through Ulysses "to strive, to seek, to find, and not to yield" came in 1842, significantly the year between the publication of Carlyle's *Heroes and Hero-Worship* (1841) and *Past and Present* (1843). In these works Carlyle incarnated the kind of hero who would prove fit master to the machine. His response to the age is an admirable attempt to prove the efficacy of a romantic vision in a modern society; it is to the discredit of the age, not Carlyle, that his hero was a capitulation to the same Genius of Mechanism he condemned in *Sartor Resartus.* Only the writers of the last half of the century—Arnold, Ruskin, Morris—could see that the machine and its energy could serve no master.

In the lectures on *Heroes and Hero-Worship,* Carlyle revealed the need of the age for a dynamic hero, one whose supernatural force could counter the power of mechanism. The Great Man would be "a flowing light-fountain . . . of native original insight, of manhood and heroic nobleness." [14] The organic quality of the imagery, so typical of Carlyle's vision, suggests the compensatory function of the hero in the world of the machine. Yet a few years later, in *Past and Present,* in his attempt to accommodate his dream to the realities of Victorian England, Carlyle would create an empty hero derived from the industrial capitalist. Ironically, Morris, in a similar comparison of modern and medieval societies, would make an opposite evaluation of the leadership in both periods; in his view, the feudal ruler and the modern Captain of Industry shared "*mere* brute force" (*CW* 23:229) and "extinct brutality" (*CW* 22:11). Carlyle, fearing the same energy, admires it nevertheless. Despite his disclaimers, his modern hero emerges as a composite of Plugson of Undershot, John Bull, and the Captains of Industry.

Plugson is accorded a rough nobility, in spite of his "vulgarest" qualities: "But in this Plugson himself, conscious of almost no nobleness whatever, how much is there! Not without man's faculty, insight, courage, hard energy, is this rugged figure. His words none of the wisest; but his actings cannot be altogether foolish." [15] This emphasis on "hard energy" and

"actings" is also at the heart of the portrait of John Bull.
Although Bull is initially appraised "with a mixture of pity
and laughter," the narrator cannot resist feeling "wonder and
veneration" as well; for inarticulate as Bull is, his "bulk and
strength" invest him with a Promethean vigor.[16] He, in turn,
becomes a prototype for the Captains of Industry, whose
strength enables Carlyle to draw again on the romantic imagery of power and nobility. They are Teutonic gods and a
modern aristocracy who lead "your gallant battle-hosts" and
"noble Workers, warriors in the one true war." It is a war for
Work, to prove Carlyle's notion that "Deeds are greater than
words." It is then a war against chaos, idleness, and a mechanistic society, but the cause and the enemy have become inex-
tricably bound together in the cult of energy, with all the old
roots that go back past romantic heroism to the medieval romance and its dream of significant action: "No Working
World, any more than a Fighting World, can be led on without
a noble Chivalry of Work, and laws and fixed rules which
follow out of that,—far nobler than any Chivalry of Fighting
was." Finally, the leaders in this modern aristocracy, middle-
class mill owners, undergo an apotheosis that is a compelling
testament to modern energy: "Ye are most strong. Thor red-
bearded, with his blue sun-eyes, with his cheery heart and
strong thunder-hammer, he and you have prevailed. Ye are
most strong, ye Sons of the icy North, of the far East,—far
marching from your rugged Eastern Wildernesses, hither-
ward from the grey Dawn of Time! Ye are Sons of the *Jötun*-
land; the land of Difficulties Conquered." [17] Morris admired
Carlyle and claimed him as a mentor. Yet in 1885 he would
directly challenge the central claims of the author of *Past and
Present:* "The advance of the industrial army under its 'captains of industry' (save the mark!) is traced, like the advance
of other armies, in the ruin of the peace and loveliness of
earth's surface, and nature, who will have us live at any cost,
compels us to get used to our degradation at the expense of
losing our manhood, and producing children doomed to live

less like men than ourselves. Men living amidst such ugliness cannot conceive of beauty, and therefore, cannot express it." Carlyle's praise of abstract power may have prompted the comment attributed to Morris by Yeats: "Somebody should have been beside Carlyle and punched his head every five minutes." [18]

One stream of Victorian consciousness, then, exalts the energy of the "living" machine and imitates its motion as a model for life. The corollary trend is the reduction of nature, man, and society to machinery. Here are the origins of the modern figure of the wasteland, an image that dominates the poetry of Arnold and appears in Tennyson, Browning, Carlyle, Ruskin, and of course, Morris. At its inception, however, or at least its Victorian popularization, the notion of the world as machine carried with it an air of optimism. Like deism in the eighteenth century, it exalted rational control of natural mysteries, but reason for the Victorians was explicitly scientific. It was the scientists' dedication to theory and the reductive method of careful inquiry that gave the natural world and the human mind an abstract quality easily described in terms of mechanism. The exponents of science included Macaulay and Mill as well as practitioners influential throughout the period: Chambers, Lyell, Darwin, and the great popularizer, Thomas Henry Huxley.

In performing the valuable service of public education, Huxley also disseminated the mechanical vision. *On the Physical Basis of Life*, a lecture first published in 1869, makes wonderful use of concrete imagery to reveal the complexity of the simplest forms of life. Ironically, it is in the very attempt to vitalize his subject for his audience that Huxley invokes the reductive vocabulary. To explain the intricate "phaenomena" of living things, to anatomize their structures, he must temper technical jargon with homely images drawn from the now familiar urban world: "the wonderful noonday silence of a tropical forest is, after all, due only to the dulness of our hearing"; if our ears could hear the complex motions of the living cells "which constitute each tree, we should be stunned, as with the roar of a great city." [19]

If trees imitate the sounds of the city, so does the human mind operate with the precision of a well-crafted machine. In *Science and Education* Huxley describes the educated man: "That man, I think, has had a liberal education who has been so trained in youth that his body is the ready servant of his will, and does with ease and pleasure all the work that, as a mechanism, it is capable of; whose intellect is a clear, cold, logic engine, with all its parts of equal strength, and in smooth working order; ready, like a steam engine, to be turned to any kind of work, and spin the gossamers as well as forge the anchors of the mind." [20] The precision of the metaphor renders unto science and objectivity the force we have been tracing, but it dichotomizes the mind itself. Celebrating what Yeats calls "Grey Truth," it suggests, as his pastoral poem puts it, that for the scientists, "dead is all their human truth." The loss of human truth was the fear of Carlyle and of Arnold. Foreseeing the impact of the mechanistic philosophy on politics, Arnold described the terrible blandness of a world run by "machinery" in *Culture and Anarchy*, but it is in his poetry that he most eloquently evokes the vision of the wasteland created by the "gradual furnace of the world."

William Morris, aware of both the false energy of the machine and the resultant wasteland of the mind, rejected both as subjects for the writer. For him the inversion of traditional relationships implied by these two directions of Victorian thought would spawn an awful paradox: Morris's prophecy of "*mere* anarchy" anticipated Yeats's by almost forty years.[21] The lectures he delivered at regular intervals for most of his life show his growing preoccupation with these disturbing signs of the times.

Certainly he worried like Arnold and Ruskin about man's literal and symbolic bondage to machinery. He agreed with Marx, whom he claimed not to have read, that industrial capitalism makes the worker an appendage of the machine. The machine deprives him of pride in his work, and it turns what had been personal delight for the medieval guildsman into "joyless labour" (*CW* 23:108). It surrounds him with aesthetic ugliness in the cheap, "nasty wares" it proliferates for no purpose other than profit, which Morris like Ruskin or Dickens describes in the wasteland image of "a dust and refuse heap" where once was "a beautiful garden" (*CW* 23:114). It destroys nature and displaces it with "squalor" and "blank emptiness." And it infuses all of life with its mechanical quality: "The necessity which forced the profit-grinders to collect their men first into workshops working by the division of labour, and next into great factories worked by machinery, and so gradually draw them into the great towns and centres of civilization, gave birth to a distinct working class or proletariat: and this it was which gave them their *mechanical* existence, so to say" (*CW* 23:11).

"Mechanical" is a derogatory term that Morris applies to labor, to its products, to the life of the proletariat and the upper classes, to education, and to the arts, which he finds have become "trivial, mechanical, and unintelligent." Generally speaking, it is a concept that suggests to Morris the antithesis of sensuous pleasure in work and of natural simplicity. The horror of mechanism is its abstraction, token of its philosophical alliance with science. The wasteland for Morris then is an absence, a "dead blank," of the concrete apprehension of reality, of a concrete delight in work, of a particular perception of simple, natural beauty. Ironically, Morris was not an opponent of machinery per se. Much less reactionary on this subject than either Carlyle or Ruskin, he anticipated the perfection of machinery to create pleasant leisure in a perfectly balanced society that would enjoy "fearless rest and hopeful work" (*CW* 22:269). Yet he recognized man's tendency to be ruled by the machine. In "How We Live and How We Might Live" he refuses to ally himself with those who would abandon the machine: "I don't quite admit that; it is the allowing machines to be our masters and not our servants that so injures the beauty of life nowadays." He foresees "that the very elaboration of machinery in a society whose purpose is not the multiplication of labour, as it now is, but the carrying on of a pleasant life, as it would be under social order—that the elaboration of machinery, I say, will lead to the simplification of life, and so once more to the limitation of machinery." Morris's regret is that bondage to the idea of machinery prevents such a practical use: "It isn't possible now; we are not at liberty to do so; we are slaves to the monsters which we have created" (*CW* 23:24–25). Morris's reaction to the machine seems quite reasonable. It is also distinctly pastoral. He is bothered by the threat of the machine to people, to aesthetic experience, and to the earth.

His response to the tradition of energy is even more significant. If mechanical emptiness is experienced primarily by the working classes, energetic complexity, the worship of force, is attributed to its progenitors, the captains of industry. Energy also becomes the substance of heroic and didactic literature, the mainstream from which Morris deliberately dissociates himself. While the proletariat, the common people, received his lifelong sympathy, these so-called popular heroes, the industrialists, bore the brunt of his criticism. He held them responsible for "that shortsighted, reckless brutality of squalor that so disgraces our intricate civilization" and for the "increditable filth, disorder, and degradation of modern civilization." Totally countering Carlyle's view of these middle-class heroes, Morris states: "For my part I have never underrated the power of the middle classes, whom, in spite of their individual good nature and banality, I look upon as a most terrible and implacable force." [22] This terrible force, never admired though not really feared, is destructive but impotent; for satisfying, sensuous art cannot be produced by "all the heaped-up knowledge of modern science, all the energy of modern commerce." Industry's only contribution to society is to force on the consumer cheap goods "and with them a kind of life which that energetic, that aggressive cheapness determines for him" (*CW* 23:8). Finally, both legacies of the industrial society disturbed Morris because they threatened his "dream of natural happiness" and its roots in the common man and the earth.

The strong sense of continuity Morris values in the cultural heritage of the proletariat and in the repetition of earthly processes reminds us of the tenet asserted at the beginning of this chapter: Morris believed in civilization. The empty day which required an antithetical dream was simultaneously a wasteland and a culture infatuated with false energy. In the lectures and late romances Morris projects a vision for civilization that anticipates Yeats's cyclical theory of history. Utilizing appropriately organic figures, Morris prophesies an evolution that will culminate in a New Birth of higher simplicity. Describing contemporary decadence in art, Morris says, "This was the growth of art: like all growth, it was good and fruitful for a while; like all fruitful growth, it grew into decay; like all decay of what was once fruitful, it will grow into something new" (*CW* 22:9). The cyclical pattern, widely dispersed in the lectures, is applied to culture as well as the arts. From the "dead blank" of present society "the new seed must sprout," and from it a new harvest will come. But like Yeats, Morris foresees the New Birth as a violent exchange of gyres that inevitably issues from the self-destructive energy of the present civilization. In 1887 he says that the current system "is of its own weight pushing onwards towards its destruction. The energy and ceaseless activity which made its success so swift and startling, are now hurrying towards its end. . . . The commercial or capitalistic system is being eaten out by its own energy." The process of self-destruction, the moment of apocalypse, is also described organically: "it will be but a burning up of the gathered weeds, so that the field may bear more abundantly" (*CW* 22:9).

The New Birth that will follow the conflagration will become the "more complete civilization" that synthesizes the city and the garden. It will eliminate class oppression, revitalize labor, and reunite man with the earth. The false energy of the machine creates complexity, but the new society will celebrate simplicity: "Simplicity of life, begetting simplicity of taste, that is a love for sweet and lofty things, is of all matters most necessary for the birth of the new and better art we crave for; simplicity everywhere, in the palace as well as in the cottage" (*CW* 22:24). The role of *The Earthly Paradise* in projecting this vision is tentative and to some degree unconscious. We have seen that Morris sensed the separation of nature and civilization and reflected it in antithetical images. The images were at work long before the vision itself was articulated. Furthermore, Morris was probably personally uncertain about the relative values of energy and idleness at this point in his life when dialectical consciousness emerged. The biographical background of the poem shows that it was begun in an energetic phase and completed at a time when disillusionment was keen. Morris began it at Red House among the Brotherhood who had set out to wage a "Crusade and Holy Warfare against the age." In the *Oxford and Cambridge Magazine* he subscribed to the romantic dream of significant action that he had learned from Carlyle and Ruskin, who, Morris says, "gave form to my discontent, which I must say was not by any means vague" (*CW* 23:279). Although he never seriously shared Rossetti's affinity for a Palace of Art, he believed for a time that love, happiness, and beauty for all people might be realized with a vigorous campaign. The move to London, the loss of the dream represented by Red House, and the growing sense of personal failure became apparent during the period that he wrote *The Earthly Paradise*—aged thirty-five, removed from the "rose-hung lanes" of the countryside, and stunned by the perception that the modern world is "such a sordid loathsome place." Between two worlds, so to speak, Morris was hardly a happy man, but for the first time in his life his situation was perfectly conducive to pastoral contemplation. Painfully removed from a setting that epitomized romantic idealism and surrounded by the civilization he was irrevocably committed to, he could begin the process of evaluative contrast that would continue for a productive lifetime.

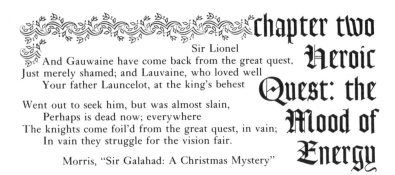

chapter two
Heroic Quest: the Mood of Energy

Sir Lionel
And Gauwaine have come back from the great quest,
Just merely shamed; and Lauvaine, who loved well
Your father Launcelot, at the king's behest

Went out to seek him, but was almost slain,
Perhaps is dead now; everywhere
The knights come foil'd from the great quest, in vain;
In vain they struggle for the vision fair.

Morris, "Sir Galahad: A Christmas Mystery"

EFORE the mood of idleness could emerge, the mood of energy had to be tested. *The Defence of Guenevere*, written when Morris was immersed in medieval art and history, shows the lingering appeal of romantic heroism. Read in context with *The Earthly Paradise*, the volume seems to affirm all that the longer work rejects—activity, complexity of character, and a dramatic mode of expression that creates scene and character with "keen, swift, and minute" detail.[1] Yet an elegiac note echoes through even the most vivid lyrics. The great romantic vision is lost, and the man of action is an anachronism: knights fail in their quest: "In vain they struggle for the vision fair." The valiant combat of the knight-at-arms repeatedly ends in betrayal, death, or bitter isolation. Power is increasingly associated with corruption; and the sword, often impotent in the hands of the good, serves those who would separate and destroy. It is significant that the volume begins and ends in the consciousness of a prisoner. The poet, who later characterized these poems as "exceedingly young . . . and very medieval," [2] was himself struggling between infatuation and disillusionment with heroic values.

The active elements of these poems are related to Morris's use of the quest, a symbolic mode firmly rooted in the ethos of heroic action and the search for value. As a narrative form, the quest adventure had served writers of ancient epics and medieval romances; for the poets of the nineteenth century, it also provided a theme and metaphoric structure for lyric poetry. All were part of Morris's tradition; all, however, did not share the same center of sympathy. The complete quest formula recognizes a hero, a supernatural otherworld, and an ordinary society. The romantic tradition, medieval and nineteenth century, stresses the hero and his adventures in the otherworld. The older epic like *Beowulf* values both the hero and his society, a sympathy we can call classical, to borrow Auden's sense of the term. The treatment of quest, literal and metaphoric, in *The Defence of Guenevere* reveals Morris's dilemma: as a romantic he wished to affirm the possibility of meaningful action, but he rejected the loneliness and social disengagement implied by both medieval and nineteenth-century treatments of the quest. Already he appreciated the communal dimension of life. Although he probably did not realize it at this time, his sympathies were more classical than romantic. He believed in civilization—its necessity and value. The romantic quest moves away from society and into enchanted wilderness. His Wanderers of *The Earthly Paradise* tried to be romantic and failed. Unlike the exotic nomads of medieval or nineteenth-century quests, they yearned for the communal order of the city. More and more after *The Defence of Guenevere* the characteristic pattern of Morris's journeys would be not away from but toward society.

THE QUEST TRADITION

The theme and structure of the quest can be found in the oldest narratives. Because it is a version of the adventure story, quest is structured in action that is sequential, episodic, and potentially endless; its continuity celebrates activity, conflict, and process. The feature that distinguishes the quest story from other adventures is its focus, however indistinct, on a goal. Whether the hero seeks the Holy Grail or destroys a particularly monstrous threat to human society or searches for self-fulfillment, he strives to achieve some ideal state. The quest myth thus asserts both the existential joy of activity and the belief that it pays significant dividends to the hero or his society.[3]

Joseph Campbell describes the quest "monomyth" as a circular structure in three stages, separation—initiation—return: "A hero ventures forth from the world of common day into a region of supernatural wonder: fabulous forces are there encountered and a decisive victory is won: the hero comes back from this mysterious adventure with the power to bestow boons on his fellow man." [4] Here in pure mythic form we see the basic elements of quest whenever it occurs: the presence of a hero with extraordinary bravery and perceptive potential; a series of events and landscapes which imply a supernatural reality subject to revelation and which provide the setting for combat; and in contrast to the otherworld locus, an ordinary society to which the transformed hero has some relationship—be it responsibility or alienation. Each of these elements contains interpretive potential and problems.

The hero is simultaneously Everyman and God. He represents his society but he is set apart from it. His splendid isolation derives from the fact that quest adventures, especially romances, are close to myth where "the hero is a divine being" and "superior in *kind* both to other men and to the environment of other men." Northrop Frye distinguishes: "If superior in *degree* to other men and his environment, the hero is the typical hero of *romance,* whose actions are marvellous but who is himself identified as a human being." [5] The line is very thin, of course, and the result is that many writers try to transform degree into kind, or man into god. For medieval romance in particular, the hero's distinguishing caste and class are associated with supernatural power. Insofar as he represents societal values, they are the values of the few, not the many. The romantic poets of the nineteenth century also celebrated the hero in a way that mixed the human and divine. Shelley's mythic god-heroes or Byron's "possessed" wanderers come first to mind, but the most important version of mythic man was the poet himself. He was set apart by his capacity for intense and unique experience. Wordsworth, his own hero in the quest of the imagination, described the poet's qualities as "nothing differing in kind from other men, but only in degree." Yet that distinguishing degree is greater sensibility, "a disposition to be affected more than any other men by absent things as if they were present; an ability of conjuring up in himself passions." Despite his insistence on the universality of aesthetic experience and his use of the "language really used by men," Wordsworth betrays a far greater interest in that "certain colouring of imagination" which is the sole possession of a poetic elect—those few in touch with the sacred mysteries. In short, the poet-hero has, in Wordsworth's words, a "more comprehensive soul than [is] supposed to be common among mankind." [6] Some heroes, however, are closer to Everyman than God. One such is Beowulf, a journeyer of the older, premedieval tradition. He is certainly a cultural hero with mythic dimensions, but he is most often defined in terms of his similarities to his fellows. He is an intensification of their best qualities, and he arrives and leaves Hrothgar surrounded by his troops and bearing gifts to his king. He must fight alone, but his center of interest is his men, the society of the Scyldings, and his own homeland. This older kind of hero would attract Morris repeatedly, in his own journeys to Iceland, in his translations of the Eddic sagas, Homer, Virgil, and finally, *Beowulf.* The first significant emergence of the "classical" hero would be in *The Earthly Paradise,* especially in the tales of volume IV.

The courage and perception of the hero are tested in an otherworld locus of conflict and discovery. To a significant degree, the myth locates reality in a distant realm which is both a supernatural and a psychological otherworld. In the medieval romance, it is external to the hero—a source of vital power that is independent and ubiquitous: "it yields the world's plenitude of both good and evil." [7] It awaits recognition and control by a perceptive hero who achieves stature by seizing mysteries denied the ordinary man. Thus the hero emerges often as a Promethean figure whose successful battle with the unknown forces elevates him within the society he redeems. On a psychological level, he enters a realm where opponents, episodes, and even landscapes symbolize the secret problems and potential of his own consciousness. Here his apotheosis is associated with complete self-knowledge. The first kind of meaning is characteristic of older adventures, while the second is more typical of nineteenth-century quests.

So far we have noted two elements of the quest that demand belief: the superior courage and insight of the individual hero, as well as the efficacy of his action; and the presence of value in the otherworld. We must now add the third element: the worth of society as a communal institution that deserves and supports the efforts of the hero. The traditional quest projects a messianic vision of the hero whose final "solemn task and deed therefore . . . is to return then to us, transfigured, and teach the lesson he has learned of life renewed." [8] It is reasonable to assume that changing historical contexts re-evaluate society, and as this happens, the meaning of the journey shifts.

In premedieval journeys a great deal of value is invested in society itself—so much, in fact, that journeys to the otherworld are necessary forays rather than quests for the ideal. Insofar as human nature can support it, the ideal is embodied in society. Beowulf's journey is brave and bold, and it surely reveals mysteries that reside in the distant, fabulous wilderness; but these mysteries are not associated with light, heavenly voices, or salvation. They are dark forces, and the light is associated with threatened society. Beowulf destroys a threat to civilization and assumes importance as a public figure. [9]

Much of the narrative action takes place in society. The battle with Grendel is in King Hrothgar's hall; the pursuit of Grendel's mother is a foray from the hall; and the tales of former personal and national exploits are reported—tales told within the confines of Heorot. For the heroes of older literature, society and its recurrent form, the city, are symbols of order and consequently of value. The unknown world beyond the boundaries is associated with chaos and disorder. The hero's battles serve to extend the boundaries of order—civilization. Heorot—place of light, music, and festivity—is the symbol of civilization. It has been created with sacred analogies to the creation of the world and is defended by the hero for what it is, a structure that encloses man's highest values. Mircea Eliade reminds us:

> The creation of the world is the exemplar for all constructions. Every new town, every new house that is built, imitates afresh, and in a sense repeats, the creation of the world. Indeed, every town, every dwelling stands at the "centre of the world," so that its construction was only possible by means of abolishing profane space and time and establishing sacred space and time. Just as the town is always an *imago mundi,* the house is a microcosm. The threshold divides the two sorts of space; the home is equivalent to the centre of the world.[10]

There are echoes here not only of the values of the Beowulf poet's world but of the late Victorians' as well. We recall Tennyson's interpretation of Camelot and the efforts of others to construct utopias on the basis of the city. Most significantly, we should remember Morris's later treatment of a pastoral society, his desire to transform England into a garden, his insistence on the home as center of aesthetic pleasure. Morris's interest in society as deliberately structured, self-sufficient, and oriented to human need is what Lewis Mumford has called a "classical" interest in the utopian city, which he says originates with the Greeks but remains "in open or disguised form, even in the supposedly more democratic utopias of the nineteenth century, such as Bellamy's *Looking Backward.*"[11]

It is a view that necessarily affects the meaning of the journey. W. H. Auden treats classical and romantic journeys as antithetical expressions in his book on the iconography of the sea. In classical literature, "The ship . . . is only used as a metaphor for society in danger from within or without. When society is normal the image is the City or the Garden. That is where people want and ought to be. As to the sea, the classical authors would have agreed with Marianne Moore. 'It is human nature to stand in the middle of a thing; But you cannot stand in the middle of this.' A voyage, therefore, is a necessary evil, a crossing of that which separates or estranges." [12] A belief in journeys seems incompatible with a belief in society, unless return is inevitable.

The age of medieval romance found real society not so interesting and invented a select one. Its heroes spent their time out of town and fed the fantasies of those who had to remain behind. According to Frye, "The social affinities of the romance, with its grave idealizing of heroism and purity, are with the aristocracy," and when we find in the romance the stylized landscapes and characters "which expand into psychological archetypes," [13] we can be reasonably sure that we are discovering the libido, anima, and shadow (hero, heroine, and villain, respectively) of the elite—not the masses. For on a narrative level, the romance emphasizes the "proving" of individual knighthood through a series of adventures; on a broader scale the romance attempts to "prove" knighthood and the feudal ethics it idealizes as a proper basis for culture. The effects of this flight from ordinary reality are seen in the focus of romance on the hero's journey itself and on the otherworld that is in essence closed to the ordinary man: the enchanted gardens, the Earthly Paradises, and even the dragons receive greater emphasis than before, and their delights give quest journeys a quality that makes home rather dull in comparison. Admittedly, the oft-sought Grail was to be a boon for society, but its elusiveness seems to have been its greatest narrative virtue. Erich Auerbach, commenting on the style of medieval romance, suggests that its failure to influence "the development of a literary art which should apprehend reality in its full breadth and depth" can be attributed to its perpetuation of a view of society that moves always away from "the connection with the real things of this earth to become ever more fictitious and devoid of practical purpose." [14]

Although the otherworldly qualities of the medieval romance excluded it from the realistic tradition Auerbach admires, this same exotic potential captured the imagination of many nineteenth-century poets. While they spurned the elite power embodied in feudal ethics, they sensed similar stultification in the "democratic" society of their day, and they responded like medieval knights: they took to the road in search of the ideal, or more often, to the sea. The otherworld enjoyed a revival. Auden summarizes "the distinctive new notes in the Romantic [as opposed to the classical] attitude" in the following way:

1) To leave the land and the city is the desire of every man of sensibility and honor.

2) The sea is the real situation and the voyage is the true condition of man.

3) The sea is where the decisive events, the moments of eternal choice, of temptation, fall, and redemption occur. The shore life is always trivial.

4) An abiding destination is unknown even if it may exist: a lasting relationship is not possible nor even to be desired. [15]

Many critics have discussed the romantic journey—its loneliness, its goal of self-discovery, its use of both narrative and lyric forms. Most relevant to Morris, however, are three points.

First, the hero is generally set apart from other men by his capacity for intense and unique experience rather than by physical endurance, prowess, or social status. Whether he is the poet himself or a persona, he seeks a kind of value-experience that is effect and cause of his special powers of insight. Most romantic journeys, then, are quests of the imagination for a unique and fully experienced perception and for the repetition of that blessed state when "we see into the life of things." Because the goal is a state of being and knowing that is dependent on a wide range of experience, the closure of society and its a priori demands must be abandoned. Thus the hero is deliberately alone. Because the desired state of being is continuous process, the journey is apt to be endless. Experience—the pleasure of the mind in excursive, kinetic activity—is quite literally the motive force of romantic journeys.[16]

Second, the locus of romantic journeys is an otherworld, but it is natural. The great chaotic flux of the sea is cited by Auden as the setting of self-discovery, and we are equally aware of the awesome presence of mountains, of storm, and of darkness and light—especially the "celestial light" of the visionary experience. But we are also aware of more commonplace phenomena, in various fields and vernal woods. The function of this natural locus is what gives it the supernatural aura of the traditional otherworld: its multiple mystery, chaos, beauty, and order are correspondent to the same qualities in man, and his fusion with nature, however temporary, is a sacred encounter.

Finally, the form of the romantic journey, for all its similarity to earlier quests, is also unique. Certainly there are instances of long narrative journeys. Endymion's quest for the ideal is an important example, as are the travels of Byron's heroes. This kind of quest story is the basic structure for many of the tales in *The Earthly Paradise*, including the framework story. The search for experience is embodied in narrative form and reflected in two shorter romantic forms which use metaphoric journeys to deal with the theme of cognition: the ballad and the dramatic lyric, especially the monologue. According to Morris, the mode he chose for *The Defence of Guenevere* was "more like Browning than any one else, I suppose,"[17] though the dramatic lyric was also a favorite form of Wordsworth and Coleridge, especially in their conversation poems: meditative quests that move toward revelation through particular observations at a particular time with a particular auditor. The ballad, suggested by other poems in the volume, emphasizes character less than monologue, but it similarly stresses dramatic progression and its concurrent revelation by indirection for the reader. Its strongly predicative structure and its "terminology of cognition and interaction," says Josephine Miles, produce a dramatic poetry which "admits conflicts and the difficulties of life, recognizes the low, even the hell, which may be on earth," [18] and which had direct influence on the dramatic monologue.

The meditative quest of the mind is seen in the conversation poems of Wordsworth and Coleridge, the odes of Keats, and in the most important "unfinished journey" of the period— *The Prelude.* These poems, in the opinion of Robert Langbaum, constitute the "poetry of experience." They are works in which "meaning is a movement of perception." By observing an object or situation that is both present and changing, the speaker "moves through a series of intellectual oscillations toward a purpose of which he is himself at each point not aware." The changing insight determines the organic structure of the poem, and the "final" conclusion, in terms of rational abstraction, is less important than the sense of shifting relationship between the observer and the object. The personal intensity gives the poetry its lyric force and shape, and the poet's creation of a speaker and often a listener gives it dramatic objectivity. Langbaum's argument is that these romantic poems are part of the evolution of the dramatic monologue, which he sees as the culmination of romantic form and sensibility.[19]

QUEST AND *THE DEFENCE OF GUENEVERE* ~~~~

In the light of all these comments about Morris's legacy of energy, *The Defence of Guenevere* presents a paradox. We can immediately sense the romantic idiom of the poems. The volume is written in a strongly active mode, and the characters are engaged in active conflict, mental or physical. Like the romantics before him, Morris is interested in the individual struggle for self-definition within the larger social context that seems variously dull, uncomprehending, and destructive. The positive appeal of "questing" is presented in two ways. The first is more or less literal, the quest for honor in the Arthurian Grail stories, and the quest for glory on the field of battle in the chronicles of Froissart. The second is the metaphoric search for self-realization and vindication. In this mode Morris explores the characters of Guenevere, Launcelot, Sir Peter Harpdon, Sir Galahad, and others.

The force of this romantic assertion, however, is checked by an even more powerful sense of failure. It is not the failure of the individual but of the society that destroys even the idealistic dream of action and deprives the hero of the bases of "experience." This vision of destruction comes in part from Morris's medieval sources, those works written later than the romances by men who shared Morris's belief that a vision of action is ultimately a social vision. In a fragmenting society, adventure becomes narcissistic; its energy is destructive rather than creative.

The medieval sources, especially Froissart's *Chronicles*, projected a theme of the dissolution of society and the failure of warfare. One critic has described the atmosphere of Froissart as a "*bildlichkeit* of widespread destruction, of blood and rapine lying just beneath the colourful and the fascinating and the legendary in the . . . account of the Hundred Years' War." [20] Malory's *Morte Darthur*, a second important source, was a product of roughly the same period,[21] and while it derives much in style and flavor from the French romances of chivalry, its overriding emphasis is on the rise and fall of a society and its ethical bases. Recent critics argue that the unity of the work depends on this theme of dissolution, specifically the revelation of the corrupt reality that underlies "the fair chivalric surface." [22] It is significant that the major Arthurian poems in *The Defence of Guenevere*, the first four poems of the volume, are based on events which come after the Grail quest in the

denouement of the narrative ("Defence of Guenevere" and
"King Arthur's Tomb") or events which emphasize failure in
the quest itself ("Sir Galahad: A Christmas Mystery" and
"The Chapel in Lyoness").

In short, Morris drew on sources or parts of sources in
which atmosphere was closer to realistic or "mimetic" concerns than idealistic ones,[23] and in doing so he made the Middle
Ages not so much a metaphor for the Palace of Art as for
contemporary society. The theme which emerges is the romantic theme of perception, but the poet does not see synthesis. Instead he sees the destructive disparity of purity and
force, of innocence and experience.

The title poem presents a situation that is typical of the
volume: in an attempt to vindicate unity of being, a character
is thwarted by hostile social circumstance. Based roughly on
Malory, Book XIX: chapters 1–9 and Book XX: chapters 1–8, the
poem dramatizes the trial of Queen Guenevere, who must
defend herself against charges of adultery with Launcelot in
order to avoid death by fire. Implicit in Malory's and Morris's
accounts is the notion that both incidents which provide evidence for the prosecution have been arranged by members of
a decadent society.

The poem plunges into the experience of the speaker at a
moment of intense conflict which is external and internal.[24]
She must literally defend her life against her accusers, whose
values emerge through her implications; but more important,
she must defend her integrity, values, and mode of being. To
do the first, she must cater to her audience; to do the second,
she risks the loss of sympathy of that same audience. Her
conflict as much as her situation wins the sympathy of her
second unseen audience, the reader. In terms of progression,
the second goal, an appeal for mercy, precedes the demand for
justice.

Broadly speaking, the content of Guenevere's defense falls
into two categories that parallel her goals. She talks about the
happy innocence (double implication—experiential and legal)

of her love with Launcelot, an experience that is primarily conveyed through natural imagery associated with spring, Edenic purity, and a safely enclosed garden world; and she dwells with equal vividness on the violence of the incidents of treachery. Here imagery is dominated by blood and instruments of war, especially the sword. It is the two worlds—of love and war, of nature and machine, of quiet lovers and martial groups, of innocence and experience—that dominate the consciousness of Guenevere. As her defense progresses, she realizes, as do we, how literally the second world has invaded and now surrounds the first. She sees herself as the lone survivor of the lost world of love—an isolated figure surrounded by a hostile crowd. Except for her prosecutor, Gauwaine, the unfriendly society of auditors are referred to only as "they," and their silent threat is mirrored in Gauwaine's gestures as Guenevere nervously acknowledges them. At the same time, we see another dimension in Guenevere's situation: proudly aware of her status as queen and as Launcelot's chivalric "prize," she is part of the world that accuses her.

In the first sixteen stanzas of the poem, Guenevere appeals directly to the positive emotions of her listeners. She is at first very aware of her audience, deferring to "knights and lords," and she seems in control of her argument. It is an object lesson to illustrate the basis of her actions, and it acknowledges both conscious choice and fate. The red and blue cloths are indeed objects of choice "of your own strength and mightiness," but because human limitation prevents foreknowledge, fate ultimately determines the meaning of the choice. This is Guenevere's first appeal to human complexity, as it is her first reference to the principles of fate and human passivity, which underlie the next sequence of the monologue. At this point, she senses failure, asserts her belief in her truth and Gauwaine's lie, and continues in another vein.

The next division (stanzas 21–48) is the core of the poem. Like the Wife of Bath's "digressions," it marks a descent—into the past through memory and into the deeper recesses of consciousness that evade the complete control of the speaker. We can never say that Guenevere loses awareness of her listeners, but Morris clearly intends a new phase that suggests immersion in her experiences. He implies her sincerity and loss of manipulative control when he describes her loss of shame now (*CW* 1:2), the "passionate twisting of her body," and later, the awkwardly handled suggestion that "I lose my head e'en now in doing this" (*CW* 1:5). The memory sequence takes on the improvisational intensity of all poems of experience as she relives the beginning of her love with Launcelot. The past has the vividness of the present and the resonance of a Wordsworthian spot in time:

> No minute of that wild day ever slips
> From out my memory; I hear the thrushes sing,
> And wheresoever I may be, straightway
> Thoughts of it all come up with most fresh sting.
>
> (*CW* 1:4)

One element of this section has special importance—the use of natural imagery. It suggests the natural necessity of the love encounter; it associates Guenevere with natural beauty; and it suggests the Edenic innocence of her relationship with Launcelot.[25] The first idea seems most conscious for Guenevere, who feels the force of fate in the events. She indirectly compares her state of mind to the seasons, whose progression is inevitable. Her life had progressed toward the autumnal emotions of death in life. In this state she was passive, a tabula rasa for those vernal impulses that "on that day" awakened her and pierced her to the bone. Here nature changes from metaphor of inevitability to direct cause. The second association, the psychological unity of Guenevere with nature, proceeds from the first. The atmosphere is both sexually concrete and mystical. Passively victimized by natural beauty, she experiences it in a way that suggests epiphany. She feels the union of body's beauty and natural beauty—her hand held "up against the blue":

> what would I have done
> If this had joined with yellow spotted singers,
> And startling green drawn upward by the sun? (*CW* 1:5)

She shouts and watches "trancedly" while the wind moves.

The third idea, the Edenic theme, is suggested by the "quiet garden walled round every way," and by the introduction of Launcelot in biblical rhetoric: "In that garden fair came Launcelot walking." His presence completes the perfection of paradise. The effect of this sequence is captured in Guenevere's word "bliss." The harmony of man, woman, and nature within the walled garden creates a universe of love. Its raison d'être is not the lusts of the blood—a kind of limited internal necessity—but the fulfillment of natural order, a larger necessity that Donne insisted belonged to a holy elect, not "dull sublunary lovers, . . . whose soul is sense." The ironic note in Guenevere's recollection is that her love-paradise, unlike Donne's, derives its appeal from the kind of innocence that is childlike, innocent of intent or control. She later states that she and Launcelot were like "children" (*CW* 1:9), and later also the green of the garden is associated with youth and hope.[26] It is significant—for her self-image as much as her defense— that she recalls only the initial event of their meeting (as does Launcelot in his similar reverie in "King Arthur's Tomb"), implying what she will never admit, a subsequent fall into consciousness. The implication is made explicit with the break in her narrative and her return to a more rational style.

As Gauwaine turns away, apparently unimpressed, Guenevere again directs her attention and method to her audience, abandoning the positive appeal for emotional integrity and adopting the negative tactics of her listeners—verbal force, destructive logic, and accusation:

> Ah God of mercy, how he turns away!
> So, ever must I dress me to the fight;
> So—let God's justice work! Gauwaine, I say,
> See me hew down your proofs.   (*CW* 1:6)

In this final section of the poem we move to events that are more recent and to a kind of verbal activity that reflects the interests of her audience. Guenevere attempts to discover the truth of the two incidents that are central in the evidence of the prosecution. The truth that she wishes to reveal is not in her actions but in the betrayal of Mellyagraunce first and then Gauwaine. The re-creation of events is no less vivid than before but more consciously controlled. Her chief tactics are to present the violence (associated with Mellyagraunce) and treachery (associated with Gauwaine) of her accusers and to contrast it with the quietness, loyalty, and openness of her relationship with Launcelot. In a sense she makes herself the champion of chivalry.

Mellyagraunce is protrayed as a "beast," by turns cunningly vicious and cowardly. He treats others as beasts as well—"setter of traps." He also is a victim of his emotions, but they are not the emotions of quietude and bliss earlier given Guenevere's blessing; they are the fluctuating moods of a man who has turned the potentially pure power of knighthood into "cursed unknightly outrage." The sword, traditionally the symbol of sacred heroic power, has become a profane surrogate for those who lack true courage and self-control. Armor conceals weakness when it should reveal strength. In both incidents designed to trap the lovers, Launcelot, "my knight" who embodies the old honor, is surprised unarmed. In the first incident he wins by using the strength of his hands and then by defeating Mellyagraunce in superior swordplay. He temporarily vindicates the old power of chivalry. In the second incident, the trap set by Gauwaine, Launcelot must escape.

Gauwaine is accused of a sin more dangerous than violence—guile. To Guenevere, his hyper-rational nature poses a greater threat than Mellyagraunce's thuggery. Guenevere dramatizes this point in the short sequence (stanzas 75–81) that separates her narration of the two incidents. In this self-celebration she again associates herself with nature and says that innocence is self-revealing. Illusion and duplicity, she implies, belong to the consciousness of a decadent world. Reality and truth are what can be readily seen. Such a view, however, assumes the purity of both observer and object. And at this point, we can assume neither.

The act of seeing has increasing significance in Morris's work. It is important to the multiple perspectives of *The Earthly Paradise;* it is important to Guenevere's monologue as well. Insight is a chief interest of monologue, and it is double: the insight of the character as he struggles through a particular experience and the insight of the reader into the character. The two revelations are often, as Langbaum says, in disequilibrium.[27] What we learn about the character is different from and more than what he learns about himself.

What Guenevere sees about herself is related to what she tries to show her audience. As she attempts to reveal her innocence and their duplicity, she realizes that the two ways of seeing are incompatible. "They" cannot see her as she sees herself: "Am I not gracious proof?" We infer that the case, arranged to accommodate a viewpoint already limited, is closed before and in spite of her defense. "There, see you," she says; "See me . . ."; "Look you . . ."; but she might well say that justice is indeed blind. She acknowledges defeat by breaking off her defense: "By God! I will not tell you more today, / Judge any way you will—what matters it?"

What the reader sees about Guenevere is more complex. As we said initially, her self-vindication is based on conflicting styles—the assertion of innocence that is unconscious and self-revealing and the use of highly conscious manipulative tactics. There is no indication that she perceives the paradox. Her intense immersion in the memories-of-love sequence is undeniable, but in the total context of her self-conscious performance, it takes on the quality of wish more than reality. We do not have to, and in fact cannot, sympathize with the limited vision of her audience, to see that Guenevere's humanity *is* her consciousness she would so like to discount. She

cannot avoid seeing on both levels. In this respect she transcends her auditors. Ultimately, then, the poem shows the
reader a contrast between complex human vision and a Cy-
clopian vision that is close to blindness.

It is clear that the poem's dichotomies are not an aberration
so much of character as of society. Frye and Auerbach point
out the medieval tendency to order experience according to
conflict of opposites—the forces of evil against the forces of
purity. By exploring character in realistic terms, Morris
shows the complexity of the results in the individual and culture. When the ideal decays—if it ever existed—there is a
"dissociation of sensibility." Guenevere's society sets innocence and experience in antithetical conflict rather than potential harmony. It associates truth and consciousness with obvious fact, legal evidence, and power, and reduces the once
powerful ideal of purity to childlike chastity. And it indicates
that salvation is possible only through force. Launcelot, his
horse, and his sword are the final instruments of justice. In
this case the sword is good as well as powerful, but we are
ironically aware of its double edge.

Morris's choice of Guenevere as heroine underlines the passivity that is one recurrent theme in the volume. Guenevere
is not the only lady who must be rescued by force or who
functions as the prize of the quest. Others who share the
dubious honor are Rapunzel, the damozels in "The Blue
Closet," or perhaps most notably, Lady Alice de la Barde in
"Sir Peter Harpdon's End." After hearing of her lover's death,
she mourns that she could not "go about with many knights"
and force the villain Guesclin to his knees:

> And then—alas! alas! when all is said,
> What could I do but let you go again,
> Being pitiful woman? I get no revenge,
> Whatever happens; and I get no comfort,
> I am but weak, and cannot move my feet,
> But as men bid me.   (*CW* 1:60)

Lady Alice, like Queen Guenevere and Jehane of "The Hay-stack in the Floods," is strong-willed, sensitive, and intelligent, but ultimately she is a victim of the system that pits force against weakness.

This negative passivity is more obviously associated with unconsciousness in "The Blue Closet." The measured simplicity of its form is especially appropriate to a situation and events that are as mysterious to the characters as to the reader. The poem, written in a ballad style, is on every level a song of innocence. It delights and mystifies the reader because the characters seem oblivious to the paradox of their situation: a world of simple security that is permeated by horror. The ladies, doubly enclosed in a room *within* a tower "*between* the wash of the tumbling seas," are arrested in their static, charming innocence. They sing "Let the children praise [the Lord]," and singing, describe past happiness and present reality with a wistful clarity that records details without judgment or understanding. Their sense perception juxtaposes the brilliant colors of the garments, the closet, and the harpsichord's gold strings with the deadly imagery of snow, the oozing sea-salt, and the gray lips of the dead Arthur. The dialogue, while it does move the vague narrative from life to death, another resolution by rescue, lacks the cognitive progression of the monologues. Instead it intensifies by repetition the mood and theme of helpless innocence. Death in life is simply transformed to death, and the dimension of cognition is subordinated to passive acceptance: Lady Louise, rescued to death, cannot *see* (*CW* 1:113). She must be guided by Arthur and her ladies. The song, sometimes a symbol of aesthetic permanence, ceases when the characters die because it has not been a vehicle for life at all—simply a means of enduring until the exchange of one unknown state for another.

The passivity of women in the volume is significant because it stands in contrast to the vital and "radical" innocence of the heroines who emerge in Morris's later works—beginning with Danae, Psyche, and Aslaug in *The Earthly Paradise* and culminating in the late romances with Ellen *(News from Nowhere)* and Birdalone *(The Wood beyond the World)*. In *The Defence of Guenevere*, however, the theme is expressed in the plight of men of war as well.

The antithesis of empty turbulence and static despair is a characteristic concern in the three poems concerning King Arthur's questing knights—Sir Launcelot, Sir Galahad, and Sir Ozana le Cure Hardy. In "The Defence of Guenevere" we saw Guenevere's reveries of innocence framed by the teeming world of martial reality. The irreconcilable conflict between modes of experience is explored in a different but complementary way in "King Arthur's Tomb," a kind of companion piece. Again the structure is dramatic, and the last meeting of Launcelot and Guenevere is handled as a turbulent dialogue. The central character, however, is Launcelot. It is his poem, as much as the first one was Guenevere's. His central consciousness is established by the poet's descriptive frame, and Morris makes it clear that the poem's dominant mood is the static and ironic despair which marks the end of the questing knight's career. It is in this sense a poem about abortive conclusions, separation, and spiritual death. The atmosphere is hardly comparable to Malory's, where both characters are sad but devoutly resigned to contemplative seclusion.

The melodrama of the confrontation is preceded by the poet's description of Launcelot and the setting of this final quest. It is primarily a night journey of a "dazed," "giddy," and "wearied" *(CW* 1:14) knight to the tomb of his king and to his lady, veiled and black-robed to signify rejection of the world Launcelot represents. For Launcelot this last journey back to the scene of past happiness and departures to glory reflects the collapse of society and of his own knightly control. With Arthur dead and the Round Table dissolved, his kinetic identity is lost:

> . . . whether good or bad
> He was, he knew not, though he knew perchance
> That he was Launcelot, the bravest knight

> Of all who since the world was, have borne lance,
> Or swung their swords in wrong cause or in right.
>
> (*CW* 1:11)

Like Guenevere in the earlier poem, he tries to vitalize the present with memory. In his attempt the central vision is Guenevere and "the old garden life" when she "loved to sit among the flowers" (*CW* 1:11). The sense of paradisal stasis is especially strong in two figures. He compares himself to Enoch translated:

> . . . her mouth on my cheek sent a delight
> Through all my ways of being; like the stroke
> Wherewith God threw all men upon the face
> When he took Enoch, and when Enoch woke
> With a changed body in the happy place. (*CW* 1:12)

Then he envisions Guenevere as a blessed damozel, "lily-like," under pale stars in the green sky:

> Because the moon shone like a star she shed
>
> When she dwelt up in heaven a while ago,
> And ruled all things but God. (*CW* 1:12–13)

In the same evening he recalls here, he woke from fitful sleep

> when before me one
>
> Stood whom I knew, but scarcely dared to touch,
> She seemed to have changed so in the night;
> Moreover she held scarlet lilies, such
> As Maiden Margaret bears upon the light
>
> Of the great church walls. . . . (*CW* 1:13)

Launcelot's memory creates a virgin Guenevere, just as her memory had in her defense. The idealization of his vision is made clear when he confronts the living woman—mad and "blighted" (*CW* 1:14) in such contrast to the vision that he is even more stunned. Just when he has created an Edenic image of Guenevere, she appears as fallen sinner to accuse him of

creating her present state. Then she too elegizes lost happiness
and finally accuses him of infidelity to Arthur and to chivalric
honor:

> Here let me tell you what a knight you are,
> O sword and shield of Arthur! you are found
> A crooked sword, I think, that leaves a scar
> On the bearer's arm, so be he thinks it straight. (*CW* 1:22)

Unable to cope with the dichotomies of vision, Launcelot protests weakly and finally faints, awakening on the tomb with
a sense of loss stronger than the one he felt on arriving.
Morris is clearly not interested in placing blame on either
Launcelot or Guenevere as independent, rational agents. He
is more concerned with the irrational excesses that are
released by circumstance and that show the simultaneous desire and incapacity of the mind to deal with contradictory
experience. The immediate circumstance is Arthur's death
and all that it evokes of fragmented order and lost ideals.
Unlike Malory, Morris reunites the lovers over the tomb itself.
Again unlike Malory, Morris intensifies the emotions of the
two, suggesting that each is mad—Guenevere violently and
Launcelot passively. The purity of the chivalric code has made
and unmade them, and neither can synthesize the poles of
innocence and experience. E. D. H. Johnson's comments on
the contrasting use of dream and madness in Tennyson are
relevant also to Morris: "Thus, dream usually appears in Tennyson's poetry as a condition in which the individual fulfills
inherent needs of his own nature; but madness is treated as
a disease brought on by overexposure to harsh circumstance
and expressing an inability to compensate. Through dreams
outer and inner tensions are equalized; madness results from
the failure to make any such adjustment." [28]
    The other two Arthurian poems concern the quest for the
Grail, and both suggest that its elusive idealism nourishes a
few while the many fail. In "Sir Galahad: A Christmas Mystery" the final arming and spiritual preparation of Galahad is
the topic, but the atmosphere emphasizes disillusionment. An-

other study in consciousness, the poem shows Galahad's human isolation just before he receives the final vision of the Grail and the promise of heaven. It is characteristically the isolation from love that induces his sadness, and his reaction is similar to Launcelot's at the beginning of "King Arthur's Tomb." Drowsy and weak, he is incapable of comprehensive vision. He stares at the ground feeling "heartless and stupid" (*CW* 1:24), like Rossetti's observer of the woodspurge, and he thinks of the promise of love allowed the more human and foundering knights.

In spite of the lengthy rebuttal of this longing and God's promise of life in the eternal garden, and in spite of the ritual arming for the final quest, the human dimension is reinforced at the end of the poem by the entrance of Sir Bors and his report of the world of reality: for all the others the vision has failed. The knights have been hacked, shamed, and foiled by the very same emblem endorsed by heaven—the sword of conquest.

"The Chapel in Lyoness" produces interpretive difficulty. Like "The Blue Closet," it suggests less narrative than atmospheric meaning. Curtis Dahl has offered a reading to support its narrative unity and to argue its relation to the Grail story. The latter notion has more grounds because of various Grail images—the bloodless spear, the red and white samite cloth, the mysterious chapel setting—and the references to Launcelot, "far away" and apparently lost on the quest. Although the exact meaning of Ozana's transformation, when he begins "to fathom it," is puzzling, a more important element is the dramatic use of three characters to present contrasting degrees of perception. What they see is less important than how they see it.

Dahl judiciously points out Ozana's heroic limitations:

In the Arthurian cycle Sir Ozana is of no great stature as a hero and is nowhere specified as one of those knights who sought the Grail. Usually he is mentioned only as one of a group. He fights in battles; he is smitten down in tourneys; he is captured while vainly guarding the Queen; he fails to heal Sir Urre; he is imprisoned; he serves before the King at table. Often he and his fellow second-rate knights of the Round Table are defeated and have to be rescued. More than once he is grievously wounded. He is one of the forty foolish knights who pledge themselves under Gawain to find the missing Launcelot or die in the quest. As King Arthur predicts, they are unsuccessful and therefore forsworn.

The constructed situation of the poem depends upon Ozana's heroic anonymity "as a typical, frequently unsuccessful knight of the Round Table, a man who can represent the ordinary unheroic person. Ozana is not Prince Hamlet, merely an attendant lord." [29]

In the poem Ozana lies mortally wounded, perhaps under circumstances he cannot understand. His struggle is the attempt to comprehend the meaning of his life as a knight, to try to "fathom" how he might be considered either "true" or "good." His initial failure in vision is implied by his feverish madness. Whether Ozana in his dark night begins to fathom his success or failure is not clear, but his movement in perception is obviously dependent on the presence of Sir Galahad, who brings calm. As he watches, Ozana's "madness" abates and the mysterious gold hair, associated with love-loyalty, assumes soothing significance. The implication is strong that Ozana is a "good knight" *because* of his human limitation and need for companionship.

Higher vision in the poem belongs to Galahad, whose "great blue eyes" stare at "strange things" inaccessible to the reader or Sir Bors. Again serving as the chorus to a "mystery," Sir Bors functions as the agent who sees and marvels at the extremes of perception presented in Ozana and Galahad—the ordinary and the extraordinary. His presence suggests a third kind of vision—like the narrator's in *The Earthly Paradise*—a middle vision that acknowledges human complexity. In this poem and the preceding one, it is as if Morris cannot see the Grail either. Like Bors, he is interested in this world rather than the next. Unlike the romancers, he prefers the ordinary society that the quester leaves behind.

Finally, we should notice the other men of action in this volume, the knights who seek honor on the field of battle. Most of these characters are drawn from Froissart and reflect the attraction and failure of warfare as a source of self-fulfillment.

"Sir Peter Harpdon's End" is the most successful of these poems. Its dramatic force reveals the character of the good knight and the brutal context that renders that character impotent. Sir Peter is the complete soldier. The opening dialogue with Curzon, his lieutenant, reveals his code and implies that the situation will soon test it. The imminent defeat lends force and poignancy to his convictions. Three ideals emerge in this conversation: the ideal of loyalty, the ideal of pragmatism in battle, and the ideal of the active pursuit of life and honorable death. The first is revealed in his attitude toward Curzon, "good lump" (*CW* 1:38), who is treated with brusque gentleness and good humor. The second is shown by his firm treatment of prisoners, whose treachery is recognized for what it is and who must be killed in spite of their masonry skills that Sir Peter badly needs. The third ideal, suggested throughout the poem by Sir Peter's vitality in the face of defeat, is stated first to Curzon to cheer him in these grim circumstances, which summarize the situation of the whole volume:

> . . . look you, times are changed
> And now no longer does the country shake
> At sound of English names; our captains fade
> From off our muster-rolls. At Lusac Bridge
> I daresay you may even yet see the hole
> That Chandos beat in dying; far in Spain
> Pembroke is prisoner; Phelton prisoner here;
> Manny lies buried in the Charterhouse;
> Oliver Clisson turn'd these years agone;
> The Captal died in prison; and, over all,

Edward the prince lies underneath the ground;
Edward the king is dead; at Westminster
The carvers smooth the curls of his long beard.
Everything goes to rack—eh! and we too.
Now, Curzon, listen; if they come, these French,
Whom have I got to lean on here, but you?
A man can die but once; will you die then,
Your brave sword in your hand, thoughts in your heart
Of all the deeds we have done here in France—
And yet may do? So God will have your soul,
Whoever has your body.   (*CW* 1:37)

Later Sir Peter defends his English loyalty to his cousin
Lambert, who will soon betray country and family for personal power. Sir Peter compares his situation to the Trojans',
whose losing cause was justified by belief and tenacious courage. Inspired by "fair Helen" and her acts of "great beauty,"
they fought "in a mad whirl of knowing that they were
wrong." He continues:

                                        Now
Why should I not do this thing that I think,
For even when I come to count the gains,
I have them on my side: men will talk, you know,
(We talk of Hector, dead so long agone,)
When I am dead, of how this Peter clung
To what he thought the right; of how he died,
Perchance, at last, doing some desperate deed
Few men would care do now, and this is gain
To me, as ease and money is to you.
Moreover, too, I like the straining game
Of striving well to hold up things that fall;
So one becomes great.   (*CW* 1:43)

It is the "straining game of striving well" that motivates Sir
Peter throughout his "end." It is also a belief in life—in the
value of love, companionship, and beauty—that sustains him
and gives him human dimension when he must die. The irony,

of course, is that he does not die in battle "doing some desperate deed" but by betrayal. The pettiness of Lambert, Guesclin, and even Clisson, makes them a brutal and mechanistic crowd, as inhumane as Mellyagraunce with his soldiers. We can hardly call Sir Peter an innocent, but we can call him a victim—the ordinary good soldier whose singular integrity is cut down by a bloodthirsty coalition.

His Lady Alice recognizes the anonymity of his death. No "men will talk" as he dreamed. She alone will remember and praise his deeds. So she eulogizes him, numbering his virtues which

> yet avail'd
> Just nothing, but to fail and fail and fail,
> And so at last to die.   (*CW* 1:60)

The lone individual against the crowd was introduced with Guenevere. It continues through the volume. Sir Peter is in his own way a triumphant example. More famous are Robert and Jehane of "The Haystack in the Floods." Or there is the narrator of "Concerning Geffray Teste Noire," whose shock of recognition on seeing two slaughtered lovers in the flowering wood shifts the legal tone of his report into elegy. In "Golden Wings" the paradisal plenitude of life in "a walled garden in the happy poplar land" is suddenly reduced to a single scene of ruin—natural and human:

> The apples now grow green and sour
>   Upon the mouldering castle-wall,
>   Before they ripen there they fall:
> There are no banners on the tower.
>
> The draggled swans most eagerly eat
>   The green weeds trailing in the moat;
>   Inside the rotting leaky boat
> You see a slain man's stiffen'd feet.   (*CW* 1:123)

This recurrent juxtaposition of the individual and the crowd, the innocent and the experienced, the natural and the brutal, and of love and war develops a thematic concern with the ironic disparities of life, the unnatural separation of the kinds of experience that make life whole.

A simple and powerful expression of this disparity occurs near the end of the volume in "Riding Together," a poem narrated by a lone survivor. He recalls the last ride with a comrade who was slain. He himself is a prisoner. The ironic tone of the poem is generally conveyed by the sudden destruction of peace and comradeship by massive slaughter. It is expressed in particular ways also. Morris sets the events at the time of a "ceremony of innocence"—our Lady's Feast. He uses a simple rhyme scheme and stanzaic form that employs incremental repetition of innocent elements, especially the weather. The weather—hot, bright, sunny, clear, and fresh —mirrors the freedom, joy, and innocence of the friends who ride steadily toward conquest in the East:

> And often as we rode together,
>   We, looking down the green-bank'd stream,
> Saw flowers in the sunny weather,
>   And saw the bubble-making bream.   (*CW* 1:135)

When their "threescore spears" are suddenly met by the "thick" ranks of the "pagans," the weather carries the force of the irony in its juxtaposition with death: "His eager face in the clear, fresh weather, / Shone out that last time by my side." In rapid action "the little Christian band" is "drown'd," "as in stormy weather / The river drowns low-lying land." And in the "lovely weather" his friend reels and dies and the narrator is bound and carried to prison, now heedless of "any weather" (*CW* 1:136).

In summary, we can say that the volume celebrates activity but questions its ability to achieve an ideal state in which all men's basic needs can grow in harmony. Most of Morris's characters seek peace, love, and simple, natural pleasures as much as they seek glory. Morris expresses doubt that peace or truth can be won by the sword. Its appeal is too negative

and its power too destructive. Activity, then, in its traditional
sense of adventure is an inevitable movement toward death for
the true seekers and toward self-indulgence for the insensitive
majority.

To return to the three basic elements of adventure, we see
the basis of Morris's reservations about the hero, the vision,
and the society.

The hero, as Morris sees him, is an ordinary rather than a
superior being. He is appealing in his failure. In his review
of Browning's *Men and Women* for the *Oxford and Cambridge
Magazine*, Morris especially praised "Childe Roland": "In my
own heart I think I love this poem the best of all in these
volumes" (*CW* 1:340). His interpretation shows his own desire
for affirmative action in the face of defeat: "for the poet's real
design was to show us a brave man doing his duty, making
his way on to his point through all dreadful things. What do
all these horrors matter to him? he must go on, they cannot
stop him; he will be slain certainly, who knows by what un-
heard-of death; yet he can leave all this in God's hands, and
go forward, for it will all come right at the end. And has not
Robert Browning shewn us this right well?" (*CW* 1:339) Morris's disillusionment with heroic quest is also reflected, however, for he notes the isolation of the hero: "Do you not feel
as you read, a strange sympathy for the lonely knight, so very,
very lonely, not allowed even the fellowship of kindly memories[?]" (*CW* 1:339). The alienation of the hero he could never
accept, and his most sympathetic characters are those whose
human needs exclude them from ultimate glory. Like Malory,
he prefers Launcelot, unsuccessful in the Grail quest, aware
of love and loneliness, yet perseverant in the face of personal
and cultural defeat. The anonymous song that concludes "Sir
Peter Harpdon's End" praises this humanity in the hero:

> Sing we therefore then
> Launcelot's praise again,
> For he wan crownès ten,
>   If he wan not twelve.

The ideal vision of the quest is placed in the distant forest and future only once, in "Sir Galahad." In all the other poems it is glimpsed through memory in the dream of past innocence. Here purity is associated less with goal than escape; yet its negative quality is imposed, not inherent. Paradise is lost because it was stultified. Nature, the romantic locus for the ideal, is often associated here with innocence, but it mirrors the plight of character more than it mends it. The failure of action in these poems is not only its inability to achieve the good but its power to deprive it of growth. Memory, elegiac language, and singing become a substitute for creative innocence. The narrator of "Concerning Geffray Teste Noire" does not elegize a perfect love that could never be but the willful destruction of natural love that could have flourished. And Lady Alice, of "Sir Peter Harpdon's End," when she hears the song of "Launcelot, and love and fate and death," is disturbed not by its theme of inevitabilities but by the ironic knowledge that her unsung knight died unnecessarily before love and fate were fulfilled. The principle of growth and fruition is essential to the unconscious realm of man and nature. Life by the sword —erratic, divisive, and abortive—denies natural process.

The society reflected in the poems clearly associates action with the values of medieval chivalry. Perhaps because they were the values of a few, their decay likewise meant that they were seized and distorted by an unholy elect whose violence gave them the quality of a mob. While the remaining true knights are frequently static, dreamy, or bound in prison, the nouveau knights are often depicted in turbulent phrases: grovelling Mellygraunce, the "setter of traps"; the "rascal" Sir Lambert, also a "filthy beast"; Sir Roger's "crafty" father; the "grim king" fuming at the council board and "blind with gnashing his teeth"; or "grinning" Godmar.

In his essay on utopias Lewis Mumford comments on the typical evolution of the city-society from ideal community to totalitarian regime: "a visible heaven on earth" easily moves toward "isolation, stratification, fixation, regimentation, standardization, militarization." [30] With means converted to ends and the central vision fading, we are then close to anarchy, a state of confusion in which old rituals are deprived of their original life and force. In *The Defence of Guenevere*, Morris depicts the plight of two select societies, two kingdoms of force—the medieval and the Victorian—in a way that foreshadows Yeats's apocalyptic vision of the modern world:

> Mere anarchy is loosed upon the world,
> The blood-dimmed tide is loosed, and everywhere
> The ceremony of innocence is drowned.[31]

For words alone are certain good:
Sing, then, for this is also sooth.

Yeats, "The Song of the
Happy Shepherd"

chapter three
Pastoral: the
Mood of Idleness

IDLENESS AS IMPERSONAL AESTHETIC

ASTORAL poetry is distinguished from the romantic lyric or narrative by its detachment. When the romantic describes a natural landscape, he "sees into the life of things." The more classical pastoralist maintains a certain distance from the object. Perception is the goal of both writers, but symbolic penetration of the subject is of less concern to the pastoral poet than comparative evaluation. Although Morris did not admire classical writers like Milton, his own aesthetic suggests a strong preference for both detachment and realism. If these principles did not make him a confirmed classicist, they did clearly establish his aesthetic beliefs as antiromantic. In describing her father's reaction to modern drama, May Morris noted his admiration of the Noh play and its use of masks to detach the actors and to universalize the substance of the drama: "The convention should be more marked, and people should once again act in masks, to simplify and detach the persons of the drama" (*CW* 22:xxvii). The pastoral mask that Morris himself assumes in *The Earthly Paradise* seems based on an impersonal aesthetic especially appropriate to his social philosophy.

Morris's aesthetic is not systematic, nor is it explicitly literary. His own affinity for crafts and his interest in the education of craftsmen limit his comments to practical concerns of the "lesser arts"—the "crafts of house-building, painting, joinery and carpentry, smith's work, pottery and glass-making, weaving, and many others"—all decorative arts which he distinguishes from architecture, sculpture, painting, and we might add, literature (*CW* 22:3-4). Undoubtedly his interest in the eye stems from this preoccupation with tangible objects. In another sense, however, his consuming interest in palpable art forms reflects an a priori belief that aesthetic experience is universally sensuous rather than intellectual. Several implications follow to suggest the work of the imagination, the nature of response for maker and audience, and the method of the artist.

First, Morris never seems interested in the imagination as the esemplastic power that isolates the romantic artist or his creations from common perception. In fact, the word "imagination" is used infrequently and cautiously in the lectures, as if Morris were acknowledging its lingering aura for those whose art is "an esoteric mystery shared by a little band of superior beings" (CW 22:133). The fascination of the mind with itself, and the resultant epistemological bias of romantic aesthetic theory, are unacceptable to Morris for at least two reasons. The first is obvious. The desire of Wordsworth, Coleridge, and Shelley, all admired by Morris for their poetry, had been to liberate man into self-confidence in his perceptive ability. For Coleridge the Primary Imagination is "the living Power and prime Agent of all human Perception, and as a repetition in the finite mind of the eternal act of creation in the infinite I AM." [1] Yet the simultaneous suggestion of special genius, previously noted, evolved into exclusive self-adulation in Morris's day. "The little band of superior beings," seldom named by Morris, were primarily the aesthetes and their works: "This would be an art cultivated professedly by a few, and for a few, who would consider it necessary—a duty, if they could admit duties—to despise the common herd, to hold themselves aloof from all that the world has been struggling for from the first, to guard carefully every approach to their palace of art." Thus one reason for Morris's rejection of romantic epistemology was understandably political.

More important, however, the romantic view of the imagination contained a built-in potential for dissociation of sensibility. Coleridge's notion of the primary and secondary imagination gave priority to the mood of energy in its synthetic, vital force: "It dissolves, diffuses, dissipates, in order to re-create; or where this process is rendered impossible, yet still at all events it struggles to idealize and to unify. It is essentially *vital*, even as all objects . . . are essentially fixed and dead." On the other hand, the fancy, given short shrift by Coleridge, was associated with idleness: "Fancy, on the contrary, has no other counters to play with, but fixities and definites. The Fancy is indeed no other than a mode of Memory emancipated from the order of time and space; . . . . But equally with the ordinary memory the Fancy must receive all its materials ready made from the law of association."

Although Morris at one point thinks wistfully of the days when "imagination and fancy mingled with all things made by man" (*CW* 22:9), we can see, when we compare Morris to Coleridge, that his aesthetic theory seeks to rehabilitate the work of the fancy, to defend the mood of idleness as the primary mode of aesthetic experience. For Morris, the imagination *is* the "aggregative and associative power" which Coleridge calls fancy. As Morris implies it, the work of "the faculty that creates beauty" is to associate—by letting the "mind wander over" concrete manifestations or "various pictures" of past and present experience—and to perceive the structure of the assembled and "fashioned" materials of the mind in a way that produces pleasure (*CW* 22:13; 23:81). The process of association is clearly mental activity; yet the induced state is slow, concrete, and contemplative. Intensity and excitement are less important than savoring. We might note that Morris frequently associates "rest" with aesthetic pleasure but takes care to distinguish it from sloth or enervation. This state, also related to "dream" or concrete "embodiment of dreams," is close to the contemplative-mystical moment attributed by Yeats to the effect of rhythm: "The purpose of rhythm, it has always seemed to me, is to prolong the moment of contemplation, the moment when we are both asleep and awake, which is the one moment of creation, by hushing us with an alluring monotony, while it holds us waking by variety, to keep us in that state of perhaps real trance, in which the mind liberated from the pressure of the will is unfolded in symbols." [2] The slow and sequential process of unfolding, the relation of sleep, contemplation, and insight, and the use of metrical monotony all remind us immediately of the "idle singer's" leisurely narrative, his dreams in a "sleepy region," and his "murmuring rhyme."

One other significant departure of Morris from the kinetic and subjective tradition of romantic imagination is his source of imaginative material. Insisting that originality is impossible, he deliberately returns to subjects and "forms used hundreds of years ago" (CW 22:7). He speaks of conventional forms as "windows to look upon the life of the past" (CW 22:7) and in his idle moments he not only recalls his "own experience" but enjoys "communing with the thoughts of other men, dead or alive" (CW 23:81). These considerations place Morris in a tradition that is both impersonal and communal. It is precisely the tradition that Jung calls mythical and extraverted in contrast to the personal tradition of the romantics.

Anticipating his preference for Morris's kind of work, Jung says, "Personal causality has as much or as little to do with the work of art, as the soil with the plant that springs from it." Speaking of the art-work, he says that "one might describe it as a being that uses man and his personal dispositions merely as a cultural medium or soil, disposing his powers according to its own laws, while shaping itself to the fulfilment of its own creative purpose." [3] Before discussing the creation of this kind of work, however, Jung describes its antithesis, the work of the romantic introvert: "He is the creative process itself, standing completely in it and undifferentiated from it with all his aims and all his powers." He continues: "The introverted attitude is characterized by an upholding of the subject with his conscious ends and aims against the claims and pretensions of the object; the extraverted attitude, on the contrary, is distinguished by a subordination of the subject to the claims of the object." Since the aims and sources of the impersonal artist are not in his consciousness, they must be accounted for elsewhere: "a hitherto unconscious region of the psyche is thrown into activity, and this activation undergoes a certain development and extension through the inclusion of related associations." This "hitherto unconscious region" is of course the "collective unconscious"—that "sphere of unconscious mythology, the primordial contents of which are the common heritage of mankind." Jung's theory of the archetype, the primordial image or set of images preserved in the "collective unconscious," is not of immediate interest here, but the idea of recurrent, communal forms does seem important to Morris's work. Morris might well be speaking when Jung says: "Each of these images contains a piece of human psychology and human destiny, a relic of suffering or delight that has happened countless times in our ancestral story, and on the average follows ever the same course." Compare Morris's statement: "For I suppose the best art to be the pictured representation of men's imaginings; what they have thought has happened to the world before their time, or what they deem they have seen with the eyes of the body or the soul: and the imaginings thus represented are always beautiful indeed, but oftenest stirring to men's passions and aspirations, and not seldom sorrowful or even terrible (*CW* 22:176). For both Morris and Jung the appeal of impersonal, extraverted art is its communal dimension. To a large degree Morris's work embodies one of Jung's archetypes, the "participation mystique." Art is sacramental because it unites men of all classes, races, and epochs in a kind of aesthetic feast—quiet but, of course, full of incident.

Finally we come to the sensuous element of Morris's aesthetic. Perhaps it seems incompatible with the contemplative elements, but it is not. The contemplative process literally embodies dreams by bringing to consciousness the residual unconscious interests of men and by directing them outward. The eyes, vehicles of sensuous and visionary perception, penetrate reality in a way that introspection cannot. As in the *Guenevere* poems, blindness is associated with hyper-consciousness, with thought too intricate to express. Seeing is associated with the perception of simple, sensuous, and eternal forms of man and nature—seeing "with the eyes of the body or the soul." In summary, we could say that the eyes perceive, the hand shapes in response, and the work of the artist assumes a voice. Morris devotes himself to "giving people back their eyes," the "healthy senses," because they see the natural loveliness that provides models for the shaping instinct of the artist: art *is* "the touching the imagination through the eye" (*CW* 22:427).

THE EARTHLY PARADISE AND PASTORAL TRADITION

In *The Defence of Guenevere* the poet immersed himself for the first and last time in the chaotic world of active experience—its subject and style. His dramatic exploration of character technically removed the poet from his material, but in a thematic sense it carried him into the turbulence of personal conflict in a hostile world. In his next venture, *The Earthly Paradise*, art is deliberately divorced from contemporary struggle, and its older, more impersonal voice is restored. Poetry provides neither intellectual nor political power; it conveys no "truth" in these realms. Its sooth is song, and the narrator as singer assumes a role that is both more distant and more comprehensive than the poet's role in the more romantic poems. The presence of the narrator, as we have noted before, is the single most important element of *The Earthly Paradise*. He provides a point of view that transforms a series of tales into an anthology, that structures the long work, and that conveys the aesthetic of pastoral vision. From the narrator, several meanings of idleness emerge. The first is disengagement from a heroic aesthetic.

In the opening lines of the poem the narrator immediately

invokes two traditions of song. One is bardic and the other is pastoral. Their difference is in their claims to truth-power. Milton, singing of Heaven and Hell, represents the first tradition. He is the bard, "the poet who sings about gods" and "is often considered to be singing as one, or as an instrument of one. His social function is that of an inspired oracle." [4] Morris is clearly aware of this role of the soothsayer, and he rejects it, ironically retaining its form for a kind of song that does not pretend to ease psychological or physical burdens, to strive toward solutions, or to slay dragons. Instead, this song can only regenerate memory, remind man of earthly beauty, and create dreams. Its source is not divine wisdom but folk wisdom, an ancient oral tradition that "folk say." This "ineffectual" song is pastoral, a mode that recognizes and values its limitations. The idle singer motif originated with Virgil. He did, of course, praise the "Arcadians, who are alone experienced in song," but he acknowledged the impotence of song in the world of power. In the ninth ecloque, a shepherd appropriately named Moeris protests, "But this poetry of ours, Lycidas, can do no more against a man in arms than the doves we have heard of at Dodona, when an eagle comes their way." [5] The eagle and dove represent the kingdoms of Rome and Arcady, but they simultaneously suggest two kinds of art. Morris uses the Arcadian idleness to disengage himself from the heroic tradition.

The awareness of limitation gives the pastoral narrator a special posture which is a self-deprecating (and therefore slightly satiric) inversion of the bard. This kind of narrator, frequently an anthologizer, speaks not as one elevated being to the masses but as one common man to another. He claims humility, artistic ineptness, and often, ignorance. Because he is in fact a sophisticated writer, his purposes are two—to demean the bardic pretensions preferred by the audience and to accentuate the virtues of the dove, Arcadia, and common life. His actual alienation from both gives him a sympathetic and speculative distance, but it is human rather than divine. The use of a calendar frame for his collection of eclogues or selections reminds him as well as his listeners of man's subordination to the inevitable rhythms of nature. We find prototypes of this kind of narrator in Spenser's *Shepheardes Calendar* and the "Maister Shepherde" of Spenser's suggested source, the old *Kalender of Shepherdes*, printed in various versions from around 1480.[6] The *Kalender*, much less sophisticated, is truly proletarian in its materials and audience. A rather haphazard combination of popular alamanac, encyclopedia of popular science, and handbook of devotion, it is directed toward the laboring lower classes. Like other medieval works of encyclopedic nature,[7] it varies in topic and tone, but it utilizes a calendar structure and its general orientation derives from Virgil's *Georgics*, which emphasize "the ways in which man can rely upon, and use for his own benefit, the phenomena of this world." [8] The *Kalender* is an elaborate explanation of seasonal signs and activities, and each month is assigned a lyric which personifies its character. The main function of the Maister Shepherde's introduction is to reassure his readers of natural stability and to remind them of the inevitable movement of life toward death. He thus provides a comforting overview and a warning. The motive is of course Christian, but the sources are pagan. In surveying the seasons, he introduces the old analogy of the four ages of man, an idea suggested also in Spenser[9] and to some degree in the progression of Morris's lyric interludes. The Maister Shepherde is careful to identify himself as "a shepherde kepynge his shepe whiche was no clerke ne understode no manere of scrypture nor wretynge but only by his naturall wyt," but his meditative posture gives him a certain distance from which to urge fellow "shepherds" to "lyve longe holylye and to dye well." [10]

Spenser's work is more sophisticated, and the pastoral mask serves a more complex satiric purpose, possibly because his sources can be more directly traced to Virgil's *Eclogues*, which embody less practical advice and more aesthetic pleasure. There are three narrators in the work—all created characters.

(I am assuming E. K. to be a persona of the poet rather than a historical person). They are the poet himself; E. K., who provides the introduction; and Colin Clout, the shepherd whose carefully arranged appearances in Eclogues I, VI, XI, and XII unify the work and establish the character of poet as singer, lover, and man subject to time. The parallels to Morris's narrator are striking, though probably indicative of shared tradition rather than direct influence.[11]

The poet himself is revealed most directly in the envois which begin and conclude the work. In the first, "To His Booke," he is conventionally apologetic, like Morris in his Envoi to The Earthly Paradise or his apology to Chaucer in Jason. Spenser signs: Immerito (the Worthless One). He releases his work to realize its own merit and portrays himself as its "parent unkent" and "a shepheards swaine" who "did thee sing all as his straying flock he fedde." [12] In his concluding envoi he admits the educational motive of the old Kalender: this "Calender for every yeare" is "To teach the ruder shepheard how to feede his sheepe." However he reiterates his humility in exactly the same terms as Morris. Both dedicate their efforts to a greater shepherd, Geoffrey Chaucer. For Spenser, it is primarily a matter of style: "Dare not to match thy pype with Tityrus his style." Morris admires both style and vision, hesitantly comparing his interest to Chaucer's similar love for "the pleasure of our eyes, and what our ears with sweetest sounds may fill" (CW 6:332). For both poets, disguise actually reveals motive: contempt for self-conscious didacticism and desire for artistic expression that is revealing in its simplicity.

The humble disguise is elaborated in E. K.'s dedicatory epistle and introductory "argument." The new poet is presented as "uncouthe, unkiste," and given to "naturall rudenesse." He has no sense of structure, and E. K. must apologize for his "disorderly order," a randomness that is echoed in Morris's suggestion of the source and arrangement of his tales, the "blossoms" that he chanced upon (they in his "footsteps lay," CW 3:81). Most important, the essential simplicity of Spenser's work must be forgiven: "his pastoral rudenesse, his morall wisenesse, . . . and generally, in al seemely simplycitie of handeling his matter, and framing his words: the which of many thinges which in him be straunge, I know will seeme the straungest, the words them selves being so auncient, the knitting of them so short and intricate, and the whole Periode and compasse of speache so delightsome for the roundnesse, and so grave for the straungenesse." [13] The exaggerated apology provides a good deal of humor at the poet's expense (as do the often misleading critical notes), but there is a serious satiric edge as well. Spenser is aware of the sophisticated preferences of his audience and his introduction of an old form that has a primitive aura. Thus E. K.'s apology and rehearsal of authoritative sources—Theocritus, Virgil, and others— seems to sanctify the work as proper art. Concurrently, however, the mask demeans the audience as well and questions their intellectual criterion of aesthetic truth. Morris was dealing with similar audience expectations, although he used his self-deprecation to question more generally cultural assumptions in a tone more meditative than Spenser's.

The character of Colin Clout also offers a narrator's perspective. He functions structurally like Morris's narrator in the monthly interludes by appearing at regular intervals to provide a sense of solitary lyric struggle, to individualize the theme of mutability, and to provide an overview. Colin's distance comes from the fact that more than any of the other characters, he fulfills the role of poet. He is known for his singing, and even in his absence his presence unifies scenes through his poetry. It is his song, sung by Hobbinoll, that dominates the April eclogue. His isolation is suggested by form and character. The first and last eclogues are monologues, and both are winter poems that emphasize lost love, mortality, and the inability of poetry-song to change the inevitable. In both poems bleak nature mirrors the singer: "Thou barrein ground, whome winters wrath hath wasted, / Art made a myrrhour to behold my plight." (I:19–20). In both poems he acknowledges the pleasure of song but abandons his pipe. His complex view of the role of singer is expressed in Eclogue VI for June, and it epitomizes the character of the idle singer:

> I never lyst presume to Parnasse hyll,
> But, pyping lowe in shade of lowly grove,
> I play to please myselfe, all be it ill.
>
> Nought weigh I who my song doth prayse or blame,
> Ne strive to winne renowne, or passe the rest:
> With shepheard sittes not followe flying fame,
> But feede his flocke in fields where falls hem best.
> I wote my rymes bene rough, and rudely drest;
> The fytter they my carefull case to frame:
> Enough is me to paint out my unrest,
> And poore my piteous plaints out in the same. (VI:70–80)

Two points in Spenser's use of Colin are especially relevant to Morris. One is Colin's growth in sensibility—though not necessarily happiness—as the year progresses. His final eclogue recognizes and accepts the ages of man, just as Morris's final lyric interlude (February), also a winter poem, acknowledges the bleakness of man, age, and nature in a kind of resignation that is not without optimism. The second point is Colin's pensive, melancholy character, a version of the shepherd heretofore unmentioned but important to the pastoral tradition and to Morris.

Yet another connotation of pastoral idleness is the poet's creation of a contemplative mood. The mood of meditation is conveyed by the "murmuring rhyme" of not only the tales he recounts but his Apology as well. The pentameter lines are carefully balanced; they employ structural repetitions; and syntax is formal. The stanzaic form here and in the lyric interludes is rime royal, a sound and sense structure that controls and subdues emotional intensity. Undoubtedly a tribute to his master Chaucer, the use of rime royal also establishes Morris's medium as old and conventional. Furthermore, we should recall its use by Chaucer in dream-vision poems, for Morris makes it clear that his rhyme, his archaisms, and his repeated tales are meant to induce a dream state in a "sleepy region." This connotation is suggested by one of two "Verses for Pictures" that May Morris assigns to the *Earthly Paradise* period:

> *The Pilgrim at the Gate of Idleness*
> Lo, Idlenesse that opes the Gates
> Where-through the wandering man awaits
> So many fair and gallant shows
> Born of the romance of the Rose.[14]

The allusion is to the lady Ydelnesse who keeps the gate to the garden in *The Romaunt of the Rose*, and it bears a striking resemblance to the Burne-Jones woodcut of the scene for the Kelmscott Chaucer. The narrator, dressed in pilgrim's weed, can just glimpse the wonders of the garden through a door held slightly ajar by Ydelnesse. The contemplative context in the poem, in Chaucer's version, is similar to Morris's method in *The Earthly Paradise*, where full perception is associated with entrance into a doubly enclosed space, symbolic of the dreaming mind and unlocked only by the contemplation of the poet and his readers.

Chaucer's association of contemplation and its proper setting suggests a third connotation of idleness. It is the deliberate provision of an aesthetic construct for meditation. In the poem Morris refers to three creations of the singer: the island, the garden, and the city. At the end of his introduction, his Apology, the idle singer says that he will "*build* a shadowy isle of bliss midmost the beating of the steely sea." It is something of an island built to music. The song orders nature, but more accurately, it reflects the order that is inherent in nature. As a singer, the poet participates as he structures. What he sings is the pattern he sees. As Leo Marx expresses it, "the woods 'echo back' the notes of his pipe. It is as if the consciousness of the musician shared a principle of order with the landscape, and indeed, the external universe." [15]

Closely related to the natural order of song is one other image of structure that Morris employs to describe his poem— the garden. In the Envoi, the singer tells his book:

> Then let the others go! and if indeed
> In some old garden thou and I have wrought,
> And made fresh flowers spring up from hoarded seed,
> And fragrance of old days and deeds have brought
> Back to folk weary; all was not for nought. (*CW* 6:333)

Earlier, at the conclusion of the Prologue, the narrator addresses his "listener" to identify his locus of meditation as "a flowery land, fair beyond words." It is from this distant place that he brings his tales, "blossoms that before my footsteps lay" (*CW* 3:81). While he attributes great natural beauty to the place, he makes clear that it is the imaginary, ideal garden where meditation is possible because all time and space are momentarily one. The figure repeats the vision of the Apology where the wizard—visionary—poet synthesizes time and space to create a seasonal tableau. From within the closure set apart from chaos and change, "the drear wind" of wintry reality, the wizard *shows* the variety of natural beauty. Morris equates his poem, his "isle of bliss," with this kind of contemplative locus and vision: he creates a place of retreat but shows that it reveals truth only in terms of its comparison with the antithetical locus and vision. It is "*midmost* the beating of the steely sea," the image of flux and locus of adventure:

> Folk say, a wizard to a northern king
> At Christmas-tide such wondrous things did show
> That through one window men beheld the spring,
> And through another saw the summer glow,
> And through a third the fruited vines a-row,
> While still, unheard, but in its wonted way,
> Piped the drear wind of that December day. (*CW* 3:2)

Morris's use of the garden as contemplative construct is as important as his use of the narrator in placing him in the pastoral tradition. The setting of the pastoral is its most distinguishing trait. The verdant enclosure of the garden gives pastoral its meditative symbol, but it also reveals the pastoral attitude toward nature, characterizes pastoral society, and illustrates the descriptive style of this classical mode. Our final survey of background material will summarize these implications of the garden. It is difficult to determine how much of this material might have been familiar to Morris. He admired Theocritus, tolerated Virgil, considered Homer and Hesiod "Bibles," and is known to have spent hours reading the garden lore of John Gerard, whose *Herbal* provided the Morris family with descriptions of "favourite plants" and "meditative notes." [16]

The symbol of the garden is old, and its origins and development have received much attention. [17] Because it is verdant, enclosed, and cultivated, the garden has long been associated with order, repose, and meditation. Whether it is a formal pleasance, a grove, or a meadow, the *locus amoenus* offers a place for retreat from the world of conflict. The degree of separation from the world, however, creates two traditions answering two aesthetic needs. One is the human longing to escape the bonds of time and space and to attain perfection and immortality. This desire creates the paradisal garden, the kind of place sought by Morris's Wanderers and the apparent source of his title. The longing is frequently based on romantic assumptions about the nature of man. The other view, more classical, accepts human limitation and creates a garden in which man is in harmony with nature but ultimately attuned to its rhythms of both life and death. This garden is pastoral. In *The Earthly Paradise*, Morris uses the two kinds of gardens as symbols of the views he contrasts; consequently his title becomes significantly ambiguous.

The paradisal garden has ancient sources. Even before Christian influence, the garden for some ancient writers was used as the *topos* of ultimate human pleasure and natural perfection. These paradises include classical Elysium, the Islands of the Blessed, the Hesperides, and the Golden Age. In Jewish and, later, Christian literature there is the garden of Eden, Heaven, the abode of the Blessed Dead, and the Millennium. In Christian commentary from early through medieval times there was in addition the concept of an earthly paradise "in some normally inaccessible part of the earth, which might become the goal of man's search and, in a literal as well as metaphorical way, the object of his dreams." [18] This is one concept Morris utilizes in the poem.

However fleetingly it was glimpsed by Homer, Hesiod, Pindar, or early Old Testament commentators, this kind of garden[19] shared certain traits that were to become conventions in later descriptions, including some pastoral ones: a constant temperate climate (usually eternal spring), beautiful and abundant vegetation, water (often fountains or springs), shade, bird song, fragrance, and balmy breezes—in short, a balance of sensory appeal. At the same time, the paradisal garden began with certain implications, intensified through the Middle Ages, that set it apart from the pastoral landscape. Despite some paradisal echoes of the Golden Age in pastoral, pastoral assumptions and style are generally antithetical to the tradition of the Earthly Paradise.

In every respect, the garden paradise is characterized by its separation from reality. First, it is always distant in time and space, and its removal suggests an existence that is impossible to attain in real life. It eliminates or softens painful aspects of earthly life and heightens pleasant ones. Consequently the temporal and spatial conditions, like all qualities of paradise, are constructed on analogues to ordinary experience. The treatment of time is especially important and has two aspects: the attitude toward time in present-tense experience and the location of paradise in the historical sense of time.

If change, aging, and death—the human results of time—are characteristic of life as we know it, then life as we wish it would eliminate time or de-emphasize its effects. The natural setting of paradise is eternal spring, emphasized both by the enumeration of spring's pleasant qualities and by negation of less pleasant seasons: "Snowfall is never known there, nor long frost of winter, nor torrential rain, but only mild and lulling airs from Ocean bearing refreshment for the souls of men—the West Wind always blowing." [20] Likewise there is the suggestion of eternal day in Homer, Hesiod, and Pindar, if only communicated by the apparent absence of night. The pastoral assumes a different attitude toward seasonal and diurnal change, though its setting employs many paradisal images of natural beauty. In both Theocritus and Virgil, there is a constant sense of diurnal time, of hour even, that in Virgil comes to emphasize that hour when human consciousness is most aware of time as transition and change—the elegiac evening and beginning of night. With regard to season, the pastoral acknowledges natural process, especially the changes that lead toward harvest time, with its sense of natural and human completion. As the pastoral is absorbed into the literature of more northern climates, it incorporates more references to the colder seasons—their activities and *topos*. Spenser is an example, as is Morris. The garden is momentarily transformed into the interior shelter of hearth, warm drink, tale-telling, and fellowship, but its sense of closure is preserved. And the recognition of seasonal process is implicit.

In both traditions seasonal time is thus closely related to human time. Paradisal literature emphasizes the absence of the processes of toil, aging, and death. In the first known reference to the Golden Age, Hesiod describes the "golden race of mortal men" who lived "without sorrow of heart, remote and free from toil and grief: miserable age rested not on them; but with legs and arms never failing they made merry with feasting beyond the reach of all evils." [21] Because they were mortal, the golden men died, but "it was as though they were overcome with sleep." In other words, life *and* death have the quiet tone of a dream, an idea expressed directly by Homer in a description of the Elysian Fields "where all existence is a dream of ease." The pastoral, on the other hand, values ease but it recognizes toil, age, suffering (though rarely physical), and death.

These are matters which will be explored separately, so it will suffice to mention here only that with respect to human time, the pastoral incorporates realistic attitudes not apparent in the paradise tradition.

In summary, the treatment of natural and human time within the pastoral garden emphasizes process in a way that reveals the stasis of the paradise garden. Stasis is merely suggested in these early references; it is expanded by later writers, notably the medieval and Renaissance poets Morris knew. As Giamatti shows at length, the true and false gardens of the Renaissance epic (including Dante, Tasso, Spenser, and Milton), with all their overtones of reality and illusion, of nature and artifice, were distinguished in part by their character of motion and stasis. The same is true for medieval romance. Important to Morris is the association of the paradise gardens with love. While there is the perfectly acceptable love-pleasance of Milton's Adam and Eve or of less famous lovers, there is the false paradise which descends from the Garden of Venus. An alluringly pleasant place, its landscape reflects its owner, known primarily for her powers of paralysis. Spenser's Bowre of Blisse is a well-known example. Artifice has paralyzed nature into tempting but boring submission, and Acrasia, "faire Witch," induces a similar effect in her victims. This false "love" of immortal "Enchauntresse" for mortal men takes the form of ultimate stasis, spell-binding. In Morris, we see many of these gardens, typified in the landscape and song of the sirens in the *Life and Death of Jason*, but we also see their "true" counterparts where man, woman, and nature participate in a kind of love that is vital—and pastoral.

Time has one other distinguishing role in the paradise garden, and here it is closely related to space. In the historical sense of time, an earthly paradise is always located in the distant past or future. Likewise it is distant in space, over the seas, often toward the West, at the end of the earth. It is considered a Golden Age or a Paradise Lost—a temporal separation from the present; or it is an island, mountain, or hidden valley—a spatial separation that makes it inaccessible. In contrast, the pastoral garden remains accessible via its "middle" location between city and wilderness, between familiar reality and paradise, between the lost past and the unattainable future. Its location in both time and space makes it a medial and transitional point between idealistic and realistic extremes: "The primitivist hero keeps going, as it were, so that eventually he locates value as far as possible, in space or time or both, from organized society; the shepherd, on the other hand, seeks a resolution of the conflict between the opposed worlds of nature and art." Marx says that in Virgil's first eclogue, "nothing makes the mediating character of the pastoral ideal so clear as the spatial symbolism in which it is expressed. The good place is a lovely green hollow. To arrive at this haven it is necessary to move away from Rome in the direction of nature. But the centrifugal motion stops far short of unimproved, raw nature." [22] And we might add, short of enchanted gardens or earthly paradises. Ultimately, the temporal and spatial implications of pastoral speak to the meaning of quest—its motive and destination.

One final difference between the two garden traditions should be noted. In addition to its unrealistic distance in time and space, the paradisal garden implies a social ethic that excludes the majority of men. Like the romance, one of its locations, the earthly paradise honors the aristocracy. This sympathy is suggested by the etymology of the word: both the Old Persian word *pairidaēza* and the Greek adaptation of the word into *paradeisos* mean a royal park or enclosure.[23] In the ancient sources we have mentioned, paradise is for the "golden race," for heroes who find just reward, or for the gods. Even Milton, whose garden combines pagan and Christian sources, makes Adam and Eve a royal pair, "God-like erect" and "lords of all." The garden created by the pastoral poets was peopled with more variety, and for the most part the aristocracy was represented by the power structure of the world just outside its borders.

When we concentrate on the pastoral garden itself, we are

aware of its natural harmony, its social structure, and the
pastoral style of description. The controlling theme in each
instance is order, and the source and end of order is human.
The garden, like the city, implies human society and acknowledges the value and necessity of human toil and companionship; ultimately, both city and garden—"civilized" places,
however natural—suggest that multiplicity requires structure. Thus Ruskin characterizes the classical landscape by "the
evident subservience of the whole landscape to human comfort, to the foot, the taste, or the smell." Ruskin's chief source
is Homer, not the pastoral poets, but his emphasis on human
orientation, on the usefulness of nature, is applicable to those
late writers as well. Ruskin's main point is that classical gardens—"flat bits," meadows, and groves—are generally more
domesticated than the wilder landscapes or terribly *over-*
ordered gardens of medieval writers who are more interested
in pleasure than utility. Even his lengthy analysis of the gardens of Alcinous in the *Odyssey* projects the pastoral balance
of pleasure and usefulness:

> If we glance through the references to pleasant landscape
> which occur in other parts of the *Odyssey*, we shall always
> be struck by this quiet subjection of their every feature
> to human service, and by the excessive similarity in the
> scenes. Perhaps the spot intended, after [Calypso's
> meadow], to be most perfect, may be the garden of Alci-
> nous, where the ideas are, still more definitely, order,
> symmetry, and fruitfulness; the beds being duly ranged
> between rows of vines, which, as well as the pear, apple,
> and figtrees, bear fruit continually, some grapes being
> yet sour, while others are getting black; there are plenty
> of "*orderly* square beds of herbs," chiefly leeks, and two
> fountains, one running through the garden, and one un-
> der the pavement of the palace to a reservoir for the
> citizens. Ulysses, pausing to contemplate this scene, is
> described nearly in the same terms as Mercury pausing
> to contemplate the wilder meadow; and it is interesting
> to observe that, in spite of all Homer's love of symmetry,

the god's admiration is excited by the free fountains, wild violets, and wandering vines; but the mortal's, by the vines in rows, the leeks in beds, and the fountains in pipes.[24]

Morris shares this preference for humanized nature. Nature's order not only inspires man; it reflects the mark of his hand. The kinetic harmony between man and nature is reciprocal. In the ideal society man's works live "amidst the very nature they were wrought into, and of which they are so completely a part" (CW 22:17). Nature gives man "possessions which should be common to all of us, . . . the green grass, . . . the leaves, . . . the waters, . . . the very light and air of heaven," and in return man orders the earth, "altering to human needs . . . the very face of the earth itself" (CW 22:70, 119). The "orderly beauty" which results is seen in city and town in "streets which are decent and orderly" and in the gardens of the populace (CW 22:130, 138). In the country man's control over nature is reflected in his physical labor, which Morris says "need not be by any means degrading. To plough the earth, to cast the net, to fold the flock—these, and such as these, which are rough occupations enough . . . are good enough for the best of us" (CW 22:45). These natural occupations, ancient in their pastoral connotations, domesticate the landscape and give it the human quality Ruskin called classical. "In all old civilized countries," Morris says, "even when we are in the country, out of sight of a single house, the aspect of the place is largely influenced by the work of man: the hedge-rows, the road, the lanes leading out of it, the trees which have all been planted by men's hands, the growing crops, the tame beasts and sheep, the banked and locked river, all these go to making up the loveliness which lies before us" (CW 22:428). Ultimately, man's touch gives the landscape "a certain something which we call 'character,' which does not depend on either bigness, or roughness, or richness; a something which means the expression of a human interest, the telling of a tale of life and incident, one may say, the touching the imagination through the eye" (*CW* 22:427). When the eyes are in fact open to this "character" of nature, the "flat and uninteresting country" is transformed, and Morris promises "to any one of you that goes with open eyes . . . into any unspoiled country-side, that you will find almost every field's end a paradise" (*CW* 22:427).

While the *locus amoenus* of the pastoral shares this typically classical preference for order and utility, its landscape, like all its other attributes, provides a mean between total symmetry and total wilderness. The garden is indeed "a green hollow" —neither an exotic formal garden nor untamed woods. Man's harmony with nature is reflected in wildlife that has a kind of homespun domesticity and familiarity. Alcinous' orchards and vineyards are replaced by the pasture and field, "the dense thornbrake," the "juniper thicket" and the "shelving bank." [25] The "pear trees, pomegranates" and "luscious figs" of the royal garden become the pine, oak, wild olive, sweet cedar, elm, and aspen. Typical pastoral flowers are wind-flower, dog-rose, and rock-roses. In the third idyll of Theocritus, the love-gifts offered Amaryllis by the shepherd include "half a score of apples," an ivy wreath of rosebuds twined with "fragrant parsley leaves," and a young white twinner-goat. The range of sensory appeal is elaborated in the spectrum of pastoral sounds. The nightingale is echoed by "the scritch-owl from the hill," and we hear the cricket's chirp, "prattling" locusts, and humming bees. In the air also are not only the fragrant aromas of "reeds and fresh-cut vine-strippings," but the smell of goats and shepherds. In Idyll v of Theocritus, Lacon tells Comatas: "Those buckgoat-pelts of thine smell e'en ranker than thou." The harmony of the pastoral locus depends on the variety and vitality of life within the boundaries of a garden world. The harmony is associated with the activity of both nature and man as he performs his daily tasks.

Perhaps the most famous Greek pastoral landscape descrip-tion occurs at the end of Theocritus' Idyll vii: The Harvest-

Home. There is a variety of natural detail as well as sensory appeal. There are the expected details of shade, shelter, and water. There are pleasant sights, sounds, and smells. All are in harmony, and all are associated with the time of year, late summer, that brings the harvest. Harvest time, a human time, is a reminder of pastoral man's economic self-sufficiency and daily activity. It is also suggestive of man and nature's fertility: "All nature smelt of the opulent summertime, smelt of the season of fruit."

The pastoral society contained in the garden, meadow, or pasture is like its setting, a conciliatory mean between primitive barbarism and civilized complexity, two kinds of chaos. Its order provides a model for harmony between man and nature and man and man. The simplified society, which Frye calls the basis of the pastoral convention, thus endorses an agrarian economy that utilizes natural plenitude but depends also on a kind of hierarchy that derives from the city.

Nature provides, but man must toil to convert its resources. In "Useful Work Versus Useless Toil" Morris stresses the idea "that the race of man must either labour or perish. Nature does not give us our livelihood gratis; we must win it by toil of some sort or degree" (*CW* 23:98). Poggioli says:

> Manna does not fall on pastoral soil, and the shepherd neither fasts nor feasts, but satisfies his thirst and hunger with earth's simplest gifts, such as fruit and water, or with the milk and cheese he gets from tending his sheep, which provide also the wool for his rustic garments. The shepherd does not need to grow wheat like the farmer, or prey on wild life like the hunter. He is a vegetarian on moral as well as on utilitarian grounds, choosing to live on a lean diet rather than on the fat of the land.[26]

Poggioli's rejection of "venatical attitudes" in the pastoral seems narrow, but it is true that the activities of shepherds, woodcutters, reapers, fishermen, or the hunters that *do* appear are presented as tasks that give men pleasure in nature while they "structure" its resources. Conventional duties are as-

signed to conventional characters, but there is also a sense of
shared responsibility that lends an air of equality and companionship. The qualities of humility and self-sufficiency produce
an attitude toward work that is similar to the spirit of the
medieval guilds Morris idealized. It is interesting that one of
Morris's most pastoral vignettes—aside from his extensive
portrait of society in *News from Nowhere*—describes the life of
ancient Icelandic tribes. It is his characteristically northern
version of pastoral, and it shows how the *comitatus* of the old
hierarchies provided motives superior to the power-pressure
of later feudal systems:

> As to the manners of these early settlers, they were
> naturally exceedingly simple, yet not lacking in dignity:
> contrary to the absurd feeling of the feudal or hierarchi-
> cal period manual labour was far from being considered
> a disgrace: the mythical heroes have often nearly as much
> fame given them for their skill as weaponsmiths as for
> their fighting qualities. . . . The greatest men lent a hand
> in ordinary field or house work, pretty much as they do
> in the Homeric poems: one chief is working in his hay-
> field at a crisis in his fortune; another is mending a gate,
> a third is sowing his corn, his cloak and sword laid by
> in a corner of the field; another is a great housebuilder;
> another a ship-builder: one chief says to his brother one
> eventful morning: "There's the calf to be killed and the
> viking to be fought. . . . Which of us shall kill the calf,
> and which shall fight the viking?" [27]

Although these comments were addressed to a socialist audience, they do not really imply a socialist society. They suggest
instead what Poggioli calls the pastoral economy—"the contained self-sufficiency that is the ideal of the tribe, of the clan,
and of the family." This simple and humane hierarchy reflects
both negative and positive values of civilized structure.

One of the strongest tenets is negative. Man's respect for
himself and for nature denies the acquisitive instinct of many
societies:

Foremost among the passions that the pastoral opposes and exposes are those related to the misuse, or merely to the possession, of worldly goods. They are the passions of greed: cupidity and avarice, the yearning after property and prosperity, the desire for affluence and opulence, for money and precious things. The bucolic considers the pursuit of wealth—*auri sacra fames*—as an error as well as a crime, since it makes impossible "the pursuit of happiness." [28]

On the other hand, the sense of hierarchy reflects the best and simplest uses of the order of the city: society rests on loyalty rather than power; furthermore, hierarchy recognizes a variety of human types, abilities, and interests that can exist in harmony without oppressive class distinction. Thus the shepherds, goatherds, reapers, landlords, old men, housewives, and young lovers suggest the possible variety of experience within a benign structure. They argue and sometimes complain, but they happily accept the limitations of their situation.

It is this rather conservative notion of limitation that accounts for the recurrent attitude of fatalism in the pastoral. Because he recognizes his limits in nature and society, man knows that he is subject to temporal change, failure in love, and even death. T. P. Harrison, Jr. in his analysis of the pastoral elegy, comments on the familiar melancholy note when youth is suddenly cut down and the poet invokes the "contrast between the cyclic course of the seasons from death to life, on the one hand, and the finality of human death on the other." [29] This recognition can lead variously to the solitary, introspective "pastoral of the self," [30] or to the elegiac softening of loss by Virgil, or to Milton's hope for "fresh woods and pastures new." But there is another, more realistic interpretation as well. As Erwin Panofsky has pointed out, the conventional epitaph *Et in Arcadia ego* was long misinterpreted through Virgilian influence to be the words of a once happy shepherd:

"They conjure up the retrospective vision of an unsurpassable happiness, enjoyed in the past, unattainable ever after, yet enduringly alive in the memory: a bygone happiness ended by death." This elegiac idealization, says Panofsky, is false. The words tell us instead that "Death is even in Arcadia"—an implication of "present happiness menaced by death." [31] This kind of truth is hard, but it is also a memento mori that is comforting in its clarity. John Lynen expresses well the pastoral appeal of fatalism: "Though the swain may not be master of his fate, he at least lives in a world where it is easily recognizable." [32]

Pastoral style involves two main principles: a simple, enumerative, and concrete description that conveys vitality and variety; and its enclosure within a framework that defines its theme and separates it aesthetically from the world of random, chaotic experience. The style of classical landscape description is clearly if impressionistically explained by J. A. Symonds, whose infatuation with Greek art was similar to Ruskin's. He is relieved to discover that in Greek landscape there is "no mystery of darkness, no labyrinth of tortuous shade, no conflict of contrasted form." [33] Instead he finds sunlight, purity of outline, and concrete detail. The landscape is alive, but its multiplicity of common forms makes it so: "rocks golden with broom-flowers, murmurous with bees, burning with anemones in spring and oleanders in summer, and odorous through all the year with thyme." Or he is attracted to "the silence of mountain valleys, thinly grown with arbutus and pine and oak, open at all seasons to pure air, and breaking downwards to the sea." Symonds's "imitation" conveys simple variety of detail, and his use of verbal adjectives suggests vitality. Both contribute to the style he calls classical: "Conciseness, simplicity, and an almost prosaic accuracy are the never-failing attributes of classical descriptive art." He comments on the virtues of the Greek idyllists: "The misuse which has been made of mythology by modern writers has effaced half its vigour and charm. It is only by returning to the nature which inspired these myths that we can reconstruct their exquisite vitality."

The general effect of such "prosaic" description is what Symonds calls "definition." He admires the gestalt of order suggested by the arrangement of details. The pastoral poets themselves seem to have viewed definition in a more aesthetic and less philosophical way. Virgil is famous for his use of a framing device that separates his eclogues from ordinary experience. Each begins and ends in a way that establishes Arcadia as an aesthetic construct. Usually the end of day marks the end of the poem. In the first eclogue, where we see Meliboeus dispossessed of his land and threatened by the world of power beyond, and where so much of the dialogue is devoted to this consciousness of worldly reality, Virgil gives the closing words to Tityrus, who lends pastoral optimism and invokes the close-of-day motif: "Yet surely you could sleep here as my guest for one night, with green leaves for your bed? I have got ripe apples, and some mealy chestnuts and a good supply of cheese. See over there—the rooftops of the farms are already putting up their evening smoke and shadows of the mountain crests are falling farther out" (Virgil I:79-83). This sense of aesthetic distance, so characteristic of Virgil, accounts for the fact "that his poems, unlike those of Theocritus, are not small clippings from the panorama of life, but well-constructed and rounded works of art. Each poem has its climaxes and its lulls; motifs light up and fade out again." [34] This kind of control is Virgil's way of acknowledging his sophisticated separation from the world he admires and creates. It may also account, however, for the nineteenth-century preference for the more realistic method of Theocritus, clearly admired by Morris for his "real ancient imaginative works" which had more appeal than the "archaeological value" of Virgil (*CW* 22:xiii).[35]

There is evidence, however, that Theocritus also used his sophisticated distance from shepherd life to explore the contrast between real and created worlds. Idyll VII, which we examined earlier, provides the example. The speaker, while he is a member of the group, also serves as a narrator. The idyll is related in the past tense, and its concluding description of natural harmony has the intensity of an experience which is both unique and past. The shepherd-poet recalls the scene that surrounded the reclining friends:

> High above our heads swayed many poplars and elms. The sacred stream close by gushed murmuring from the cave of the Nymphs. On the shady boughs the dusky cicadas chirped busily, while far off the tree toad uttered his cry in the dense bramble thickets. Larks and linnets sang; the turtledove sighed; yellow bees were flitting about the springs. All the air was filled with the fragrance of rich summer, the fragrance of the harvest time. There were pears at our feet, and by our sides rolled apples in profusion. The young trees were bowed toward the ground with the weight of their plums.

Then the friends drank together; and here the narrative is transformed into the present tense as the speaker wonders whether the perfection of the event will ever be recaptured. He uses words—song—to hold it before him for a moment in a series of mythical allusions and concludes: "On [Demeter's] heap of grain may I once more plant a great winnowing fan, and may she smile as she holds sheaves and poppies in her arms." The speaker, like Morris's narrator in *News from Nowhere*, stands simultaneously inside and outside the scene, and in this sense, the passage is a concluding frame that establishes the idyll for what it is—a short, intense narrative that is very much concerned with reality but set apart from ordinary experience.

Summarily, the idleness of *The Earthly Paradise* narrator shares several meanings with pastoral tradition—his ironic disengagement from the energetic aesthetic of heroism, his invocation of a meditative mood, the use of the conventional construct of the garden, and the creation of a realistic, impersonal style.

chapter four
The Quest of the Wanderers: the Uses of the Past in the Prologue

And therefore I have sailed the seas and come
To the holy city of Byzantium.
Yeats, "Sailing to Byzantium"

ETWEEN 1865 and 1866, two years before the appearance of the first volume of *The Earthly Paradise*, Morris wrote a complete version of the Prologue called "The Wanderers." Never published with the poem, it remained unknown until its inclusion in the *Collected Works* in 1915. According to Mackail, it "still laboured under the defeats of this earlier poetry; unevenness in transitions, a lumbering structure, awkward and often needlessly violent rhythm and diction." [1] It was, of course, these very "defects" that gave *The Defence of Guenevere* its romantic intensity, and their deliberate revival and abandonment here suggest Morris's intentions about both the meaning of romantic quest and the relative function of the framework narrative in the whole poem.

Several elements of the original "Wanderers" point up its contrast with the published Prologue. In the first poem Morris employs a ballad style that gives past events present intensity; he uses dialogue to produce a sense of character conflict; he creates a series of fabulous otherworld settings; and he gives the episodes clear definition and symbolic structure. In other words, his use of the quest is conventionally romantic. There is no doubt that the quest of the Wanderers is unsuccessful and foolish, but Morris's treatment is neither so ironic nor ambiguous as it is in the second version. Their voyage to find the ideal world is a symbolic romantic journey, with some degree of cognition as theme, and with a formula of casual choice leading to temptation, fall, purgation, and redemption that is characteristic of *The Rime of the Ancient Mariner*.

Morris's unpublished "argument" for this first Prologue suggests its symbolic structure:

> How certain knights of Norway, moved by a dream, sailed to find the Earthly Paradise and how they came first to land in the western sea and what happened to them there. How they came to land of the blacks and how they fought with them and how they escaped out of their hands. Of a storm and of the loss of the Fighting Man. How they came to the valley of the lions and of the damsels they saw there. How they arrived in the Land of Ladies and saw their queen. Of the King whom they fought with & slew, and how they lived long in the Land of Ladies. How when they were now getting old they sailed from the Land of Ladies on their quest. How they came to the city of the Stony Men and what happened to them there. How they escaped the Stony Men and sailing by strange places came at last to the land whereof they had dreamed and of what kind it was.[2]

In this completed quest there are two central adventures, the events in the Land of the Ladies and those in the city of the Stony Men. Then there are the initial exploits with the black men, which actually comprises a third adventure. The whole narrative is presented in five stages—these three adventures plus a beginning and conclusion, a plan not unlike Coleridge's. The first stage (*CW* 24:87–94), which sketchily describes the characters and elaborates the motivating event, Nicholas' dream, serves as a prologue that establishes the carefree mood of the departure from the ordinary world.[3] It stands in contrast to the last stage (*CW* 24:156–70), an epilogue that describes the arrival of the weary mariners in the land of the People of the Shore. This frame conveys the effects of the adventures related in the body of the tale.

The anonymous narrator, later identified as Sir Rafe, describes the commonplace departure of high-spirited Norse marauders:

> A summer cruise we went that tide
> To take of merchants toll and tax;
> Out from our tops there floated wide
> The Lion with the Golden Axe.
> . . . .
> Our holds were full of bales of goods
> Worth many a florin, so perdie
> Home we turned, counting the roods
> Of land we should buy presently.   (*CW* 24:87–88)

But "Alas!" says narrator Rafe. The journey is interrupted and redirected. The call to adventure is a dream, which provides motive and also reveals the essential character of the Wanderers, consequently projecting their failure as psychologically inevitable. Three parts of the dream are especially important: Nicholas's vision of himself as a lion with crown and ax, the appeal to Venus, and the appearance of Odin and Olaf, Norse heroes of legend and history. Each part suggests the impossible combination of mortality and immortality.

The lion is the emblem of the heroes. It appears on their banner with ax, and it is associated with their power. They are rulers of the sea, and they believe in the glory of war and sword. The mysterious and savage power of the lion is invoked in the second episode of the Prologue when the Wanderers arrive in the land of the lions, destroy the beasts, and symbolically replace them as rulers of the Land of Ladies. Although the Norse lion-men of the dream are not immortal, their relationship to the eternally "fair and young" folk of the earthly paradise intimates superior distance, a feeling broken with the transformation from lion to "man again, old, near . . . death" (*CW* 24:90). Yet these lion-men are not fierce: "blithe we seemed / And thereat nothing mazed or sad" (*CW* 24:89). Power is juxtaposed with passivity.

This contradiction is made clearer by the fact that appeal for immortality, for "rest and peace and fearless life" (*CW* 24:90), must be made to Venus, traditional lady of stone and stasis. The scene is typical of the recurrent interviews with

the goddess in the *Earthly Paradise* tales. The petitioner, growing increasingly passive—"nearer and nearer to my death . . .
with weak breath / Muttering out prayers"—is rewarded with
a brief incarnation—"soft flesh, . . . fair leg," and granted a
promise before Venus returns to her traditional form: "the
image with set smile / And colourless with gilded hair" (*CW*
24:91). The goddess in her "house of glass" introduces the
familiar equation of immortality with paralysis, explicated in
the Stony Men episode later; she also introduces the theme of
the false paradise of love, explicated in the Land of Ladies
episode. Both states require such unconsciousness as to be
inhuman and are therefore unendurable even if attainable.
They are two kinds of false idleness which *seem* curiously
incompatible with men of action. Yet as we have seen in the
Guenevere poems, Morris suggests the particular appeal of
consciousness-annihilation to active heroes. It offers peaceful
escape from activity, but it also seems the deserved prize of
conquest.

The paradox comes full circle with the introduction of Olaf
and Odin at the end of the dream. Both combine the connotations of immorality and warfare. Their appearance sanctifies
the notion that peace can be attained and that indeed it can
be *won* by forceful tenacity. St. Olaf, patron saint of Norway,
was King Olaf II (1015–1028), canonized in 1164 not only because he intoduced Christianity to the country but because of
his successful reign that freed the country from internal and
external strife. In the vision here his appearance echoes the
symbolic lion:

> of gold fine
> One wore a crown; about his head
> Shone rings of light, all armed was he
> And all his raiment was of red;
> He held a great axe handily.   (*CW* 24:91)

The other Norse hero is Odin: "One-eyed he was and held a
spear" (*CW* 24:92). The chief Norse deity, Odin is associated

with war as well as wisdom, art, and culture, and he is often identified with the Teutonic god Woden. Both heroes beckon the dreamer westward on the quest for divinity.

The symbolic chemistry that unites Norse war power, lion, and divinity is fire. It is barely suggested in the dream by Olaf's red raiment and rings of light and after the dream by Rafe's response—"hot-headed and aflame to seek new things" (*CW* 24:93). But it is known that the heroic spirit of Norse mythology was frequently embodied in fire imagery—in Eddic cosmogony in universal conception and conflagration, in cultural rituals of hearth and sacrifice, in references to the sword as "Odin's fire." [4] The importance of fire grows with the narrative. In the brutal conflict with the black savages "all the woods were red with flame" (*CW* 24:107). The men of the fierce land of lions are characterized by fire, ritual sacrifices in which "flames shot up on high" while "outlandish horns and trumpets made a strange and solemn melody," and their king's "best word was but blood and flame" (*CW* 24:117, 132). His unsuccessful siege of the Land of Ladies is trial by fire. And the tour of the Land of Ladies reveals fiery mysteries:

> The Land of Darkness too they showed,
>   The bottomless and fiery well;
> The great brass ox that ever lowed
>   Over the going down to Hell.   (*CW* 24:136)

In the city of the Stony Men the "great fire" that "burned all the while as it had done these many years" (*CW* 24:151) is like the mysterious fire in Yeats's "Byzantium," "Flames that no faggot feeds, nor steel has lit, / Nor storm disturbs, flames begotten of flame." [5] And finally there is the strange burning city that the Wanderers pass, "a sight that was full dreadful":

> A mighty city all alight,
>
> But certes with no earthly flame:
> No houses fell, no smoke arose,

> No weeping people from it came;
>   About it were no shouting foes.
>
> Upright and whole the houses stood,
>   There stood the pinnacles, blood-red;
> Marble and stone, and brick and wood
>   Were bathed in fire that nothing fed.   (*CW* 24:160)

It is clear that by this point in the narrative, the "dreadful light" of fire has assumed purgatorial significance, even while it still embodies the connotations of heroism and divinity. Both directions are implied in the initial dream in the symbolic configuration of man, lion, Odin, and Olaf.

The symbols of lion and fire are associated by Morris in an 1882 lecture. He is discussing Eastern iconography, specifically Byzantine contributions, but his remarks show interest in the mythological foundations of these particular symbols:

> There are two symbols; the one is a tree, more or less elaborately blossomed, and supported, as heralds say, by two living creatures, genii, partly or wholly man-like, or animals, sometimes of known kinds, lions or the like, sometimes invented monsters; the other symbol is an altar with a flame upon it, supported by two living creatures, sometimes man-like, sometimes beast-like. Now these two symbols are found, one or other, or both of them, in almost all periods of art; the Lion Gate at Mycenae will occur to all of you as one example. . . . The Holy Tree is common in Assyrian art, the Holy Fire is found in it. (*CW* 22:227)

Morris, anticipating Yeats here, is cautiously speculative "as to the meaning of these far-travelling symbols," but interested in their cultural sources:

> I may perhaps be allowed to say that both the fire and the tree are symbols of life and creation, and that, when the central object is obviously a fire, the supporters are either ministers of the altar or guardian spirits. As to the

monsters supporting the tree, they also, I suppose, may
be guardians. I have, however, seen a different guess at
their meaning; to wit, that they represent the opposing
powers of good and evil that form the leading idea of the
dualism that fixed itself to the ancient Zoroastrian creed,
the creed in which the Light and the Fire had become
the recognized symbol of deity by the time of the Sas-
sanian monarchs. I cannot pretend to say what founda-
tion there may be for this theory, which would fuse the
two symbols into one. (*CW* 22:228)

Here Morris's interpretation of fire echoes his use of it in the
Prologue. It is sacred, a "symbol of deity," because it is symbol
of life and creation—beyond consciousness or control. The
lions or varying manlike, beastlike supporters are guardians
or ministers, not gods, though they are closely linked in elemental character to the sacred symbol. Their relationship to
the symbol is vital but subservient. In the Prologue we see the
Wanderers, protectors of the "fire" of Norway, following out
a quest which gives them a Promethean attitude. Like Coleridge, Morris makes his characters Christian and moves the
narrative, through their consciousness, on a level that suggests
the fall of man through aspiration to godhead. This makes
their interpretation of Odin and Olaf a pagan-Christian conflict in which Odin, a satanic shape-shifter, is a false guide
toward the fires of Hell. Olaf, Norse saint, is interpreted by
the priest as an apparition created by Odin to confuse the
mariners. On a wider level, however, that level controlled by
the poet, Olaf is identified with the lion-men—their human
potential and limits. He is the divine hero of Norse power and
he embodies the Wanderers' desire to achieve glory and fame.
Their "sin" is not so much a violation of Christian precepts
as an exploitation of their longing for power.

A rapid survey of the episodes reveals the pattern of fall and
partial redemption, its movement from destructive to purgatorial fire to disillusioned peace. The first adventure with
the black savages (*CW* 24:95–113) marks the initial temptation-

fall. It is narrated in three sequences: invasion and the mysterious death of a comrade, the full-scale attack and defeat of the primitive culture, and the reverie of the Wanderers. The Wanderers' response to the dream of Olaf and Odin is mixed. Some doubt, but Nicholas and Rafe yearn for fame and fortune and escape from the land of "winter and snow" (*CW* 24:93–94). So the "sea-roving" band sails westward to conquer mortality. What they seek is the fair city of the dream—its eternity and its ideal order in which they will be crowned heroes. They are therefore rather disappointed to find beautiful but uncivilized wilderness. The mysterious death of one of their men precipitates the conclusion that the unseen inhabitants are not human but "fiends of Hell" (*CW* 24:101). The Wanderers assume themselves to be "outside the world where devils be" (*CW* 24:100; cf. also pp. 102–3). While these assumptions are based on the priest's interpretation of the dream, they lead the Wanderers to suspend the laws of man and nature, and in the second phase of this episode to unconsciously employ the destructive tactics of hell.

The black savages are hardly "great monsters" (*CW* 24:103), but they are treated as such. Their primitivism—reflected in their crude weapons, rough raiment, and pagan culture—is brutally exploited by the condescending warriors whose hearts are "joyous" and "merry" as they rush to the shore for battle:

> There in their midst ashore we leapt,
> And great and grim the slaughter was,
> In their skin coats their bodies kept,
> The great stone axes broke like glass.   (*CW* 24:105)

After leaving the savages "on the shore in heap on heap" the Wanderers press inland to destroy their town, "a poor place built of reeds and woods":

> And in the midst we saw a hall
> Wherein their filthy God they keep,

> Who had on him, for royal pall,
>   The skins of some beast like a sheep,
>
> Set round with many coloured shell.
>   So there our helmets we did off,
> And on their swine we feasted well
>   Then burnt their God with jeer and scoff.
>
> Thereafter all the place we burned,
>   Then got together some poor spoil,
> And back toward our ships returned
>   At undern.   (*CW* 24:106)

The blacks' unexpected retaliation in the night brings them another devastating attack from the Norsemen, who depart remembering "soon we should all be more than kings" (*CW* 24:107).

Essentially, the Wanderers fall to the temptation to exploit by force, and they become more bestial than their enemies. Having lost their integrity, they lose their bonds with their homeland, presented in a dream as devastated. A sin against kind has isolated the mariners from normal life, and they long for "penance" and death:

> For now have we sinned Adam's sin,
>   To make us Gods who are but men,
> To find a heaven and dwell therein
>   Whose years are but three score and ten. (*CW* 24:110)

It is clear that the temptation episode was also transitional, for now this little lost society of warriors is stranded, windless, in mid-ocean (*CW* 24:111). Then a terrible storm separates the two ships (*CW* 24:113–14), and the survivors are at the mercy of the sea. The numinous quality of the sea is suggested by their interpretation of the calm and storm as the answer to a prayer for punishment:

> I pray rather that God may stay
>   Our ship in the mid-ocean now,

> Until our flesh fall all away;
>   Or else that some great wind may blow,
>
> And drive us underneath the sea—
>   There shall [. . .] do what seemeth best
> Unto our bodies, that shall be
>   Until the Day of Doom at rest.   (*CW* 24:111)

For all their length, the two central episodes (*CW* 24:114–42
and 142–56) need little comment. They hardly provide the
penance the mariners desire, but their fabulous dreamlike
quality suggests two mirror images of death in life. The pro-
longed stay in the Land of Ladies reveals the inadequacy of
love as a permanent paradise. These fighting men are bored
without battle. They are content while defeating lions, and
then the horrible king, but the domestic life of perpetual song
and ease is in this case a version of the unearthly paradise. Toil
and suffering are eliminated, but aging and death remain; so
with memories of home and desire "to fulfil our destiny" (*CW*
24:143), the Wanderers set out again only to discover the city
of the Stony Men, where Morris superbly utilizes petrification
to symbolize the paralysis of immortality.

In a dream that balances the initial dream, the spellbound
Rafe perceives the whole folly of the quest: the palpable fear
of death, the attempt to defeat it, the momentary sensation of
eternal innocence (perhaps comparable to the arrival in the
Land of Ladies):

> Our clothes fell from us; then were we
> Naked like Adam without shame
> And fair and young as folk might be.
>
> And in a sweet green mead we were
>   With flowers all about growing
> And flowers set upon our hair,
>   And no desire for anything.
>
> And clean forgotten was the life
>   We led before, and all our friends,

> And all our foes, and all the strife
> For many unaccomplished ends.   (*CW* 24:154–55)

Even in the dream, however, this vegetable unconsciousness is temporary—"quickly was I snatched away" (*CW* 24:155) —and the dream concludes with the discovery of an eternal city (Stony Men) where unhappy people cry for death.

Ironically, it is through their own conscious will that the Wanderers break the spell and escape the "sleepless stony eyes," interpreting their dreams as sacred revelation of failure and sin:

> At last Sir Nicholas said, "Fellows,
> If ye have dreamed as I have done,
> And seen what things in sleep God shows,
> Your lust to live on earth is gone.   (*CW* 24:157)

It is in seeking a place to die, in acknowledging their mortality, that they pass the burning city. In the published Prologue it is identified as the city the Wanderers have just escaped. Here it is a mysterious sight, luring and then repulsing them with its horror. It is given ten stanzas of description that are very reminiscent of Coleridge's death ship, and its symbolic accumulation of the fire imagery of the whole narrative marks a final purgatorial separation of the Wanderers from the active life.

The city that they finally reach provides rest, but it is not eternal, nor do they wish it to be. In this final section of the poem, Morris provides a clear and extensive contrast between the appearance of a land where the "gardens might entice / The very Gods themselves to leave / The happy woods of Paradise" (*CW* 24:166) and its reality:

> O masters, here as everywhere,
> All things begin, grow old, decay;
> That groweth ugly that was fair,
> The storm blots out the summer day.

> The merry shepherd's lazy song
> Breaks off before the lion's roar;
> The bathing girls, white-limbed and long,
> Half-dead with fear splash toward the shore
>
> At rumour of the deadly shark;
> Over the corn, ripe and yellow
> The hobby stoops upon the lark,
> The kestrel eyes the shrew below.   (*CW* 24:168)

It is here in a mortal land of peaceful oppositions that the Wanderers, now isolated from their past bonds of nation and family, stay to hear "stories of the past again . . . Leeches to heal us of our pain" (*CW* 24:167), and their hosts, acting also as spiritual teachers, promise:

> Ye shall be shown how vain it is
> To strive against the Gods and Fate,
> And that no man may look for bliss
> Without an ending soon or late.   (*CW* 24:170)

Despite its "unevenness" then, the first Prologue is a charming but strong fable, a symbolic narrative of the sort that Coleridge contributed to the *Lyrical Ballads:* "the incidents and agents were to be, in part at least, supernatural; and the excellence aimed at was to consist in the interesting of the affections by the dramatic truth of such emotions, as would naturally accompany such situations, supposing them real. And real in *this* sense they have been to every human being who, from whatever source of delusion, has at any time believed himself under supernatural agency." [6] For all the Prologue's indictment of romantic quest, it shows the poet working within its traditional structure. As a result, he is deprived of authorial presence and limited to dramatic revelation. The medium is not appropriate to a framework story, which must provide contrast to the enclosed tales and offer participatory entrance to the reader. In addition, we have seen that the framework must also reflect the intention of the poet, his theme and his meditative perspective.

The changes in the final Prologue, while they understandably deactivate its narrative force, transform it from a tale to a framework. The published version engages the reader's participation, implies the contemporaneity of the medieval setting, and introduces the theme and mode of meditation. One of Morris's chief devices here is contrast. Its various uses point the reader toward the essential pastoral contrast between nature and art, between complexity and simplicity.

Morris's first task is the involvement of the reader in the fictional world in a way that delicately balances past and present, poetic and pragmatic reality. In the first Prologue we are jolted into the experience of the Wanderers without any authorial assistance. Here there are four brief stages of transition that serve this purpose. On the one hand, these transitions move the reader's perspective from external to internal space, from noise to silence, from immediately familiar existence to distant and less familiar life. At the same time, the poet is building parallels to suggest the contemporaneity of the events he will narrate. The idle singer serves as guide.

First, the "empty day" of the present is identified and apparently rejected: "Forget . . . Forget . . . Forget." Yet it is not the city locus itself that is rejected but its characteristic mechanical turbulence. The movement away from "smoke . . . steam . . . piston stroke," and "the spreading of the hideous town" is a movement from auditory distraction and chaotic space to quietness (cacophony yields to assonance) and enclosed space. While present-day London is invoked for criticism, it also invites comparison to older London, as deliberately idealized as the contemporary city is vilified. In the second "vision" of the city, the scale is reduced and controlled: "London, *small*, and white, and clean, / The clear Thames *bordered* by its gardens green." This brief view of medieval London is the poet's first blend of fictional and historical authenticity. The reference to Chaucer and the enumeration of geographical details give the picture realistic familiarity; yet the rest of the Prologue and, indeed, of Morris's writing fails to give medieval London such historic perfection. As if to underline the ideal, pastoral quality of this image of harmony, vitality, and simplicity, the narrator parallels his appeal to "forget" with the invitation to "think . . . dream . . . think," i.e., imaginatively create, the antithetical vision.

The third image "I am now fain to set before your eyes" is the locus of the framework poem. A third city, it repeats the enclosed vitality of medieval London, but it is "nameless . . . in a distant sea," and the white structures of London fade into a place "white as the changing walls of faerie." We will return to the importance of its Greek origins. At this point the poet's central implication is that the meditative locus is civilized—an "isle of bliss midmost the beating of the steely sea"—and that it partakes of natural and created worlds. It is the contemplative garden, familiar enough to be accessible but distant enough to be fictional.

The fourth stage moves us from the external order of the city, which is built around a square with fountain, temple, marketplace, and the "busy hum of men," to the "most calm" inner space of the council house. Here the meditative tableau is set for the reader, with the final contrast of the city rulers, kindly, quiet, and clad in "most fair attire" and the little band of Wanderers

> Who bear such arms as guard the English land,
> But battered, rent and rusted sore, and they
> The men themselves, are shrivelled, bent, and grey.
>   (*CW* 3:4)

The tone of the whole introductory passage is controlled by auditory suggestion and by pictorial perspective that combines narrowing vision with the invitation to contemplate contrasts. We are within and without the scene. As we literally view the tableau, the narrator reiterates the importance of pondering, gazing, and silence. With the tone established, the narrative begins.

Morris's second achievement in this Prologue is a metaphoric use of history through which he establishes the Wanderers as universal types of the hero at a moment of cultural collapse. Most critics contend that the Prologue's medieval setting and the senescence of its characters serve to remove the poem entirely from modern concerns and to emphasize the theme of human failure, especially the personal failure Morris felt in his relationship to his wife. I wish to propose instead that he utilizes history as myth to state a theme he frequently explores in his lectures—the cyclical movement of history that repeats the "blossom" and "decay" of culture. In this pattern medieval and Victorian dissolution are paralleled. As we have seen in chapters 2 and 3, Morris's comparison of medieval and modern cultures usually centers on failure of heroic ethos— "the straining life of striving well." He associates misguided heroism here with northern culture, the common background of the Wanderers and of English readers. Morris carefully identifies the backgrounds of his heroes before they begin to relate their adventures, and two important points emerge. The Wanderers represent a microcosm of western Europe at a particular point in history, and their cultural roots serve not only technically to introduce a variety of tales but thematically to emphasize the collapse of society that characterized the *Guenevere* poems.

The three primary Wanderers are Rolf, the Norwegian; Nicholas, a Breton squire; and Laurence, a Swabian priest. Each is identified with a culture that has passed its peak and is torn by warfare and dissension, and all three were already "exiles" in Norway before the motivating event, the threat of the Black Plague, caused them to flee death in search of a better life. Recent research shows that the plague was brought to Scandinavia on a wool ship which sailed from London to Norway in May, 1349.[7] The Norwegians' response was apparently slow, although the spread of the disease was rapid. We can approximate the Wanderers' departure as occurring during the 1350s. It was during this last half of the fourteenth century

that both Swabia and Britanny (Normandy) were centers of
conflict between warring powers and that Norway suffered
civil war. All three Wanderers are poor and immediately
threatened by the "bewildering care" of fatal disease, and all
recall memories of happier, more heroic days. In this role they
are sympathetic parallels to contemporary man, the readers
who experience "heavy trouble" and must "live and earn our
bread" (*CW* 3:1).

Their composite character as sea-rovers and fighting men
serves another modernizing purpose, not so sympathetic.
Their once-young trust in the power of mind and deed suggests a parallel with modern dragon-slayers, Empedocles, and
even the Philistine belief in science. All three, especially Rolf,
believe in the viability of deeds, and all three are inspired not
by dreams but by reading. Laurence, a rather domesticated
alchemist, is a research specialist. He

> knew the maladies of man and beast,
> And what things helped them; he the stone still sought
> Whereby base metal into gold is brought,
> And strove to gain the precious draught, whereby
> Men live midst mortal men, yet never die.   (*CW* 3:7)

Nicholas is familiar with "much lore of many lands" and Rolf
himself knows "the books at Micklegarth" (*CW* 3:7, 6) as well
as Norse lore. They quest for ultimate knowledge as well as
for immortality. In "The Song of the Happy Shepherd" Yeats
criticizes the modern world for infatuation with "Grey
Truth" and in pastoral disguise pleads:

> Then nowise worship dusty deeds,
> Nor seek, for this is also sooth,
> To hunger fiercely after truth,
> Lest all thy toiling only breeds
> New dreams, new dreams; there is no truth
> Saving in thine own heart. Seek then,
> No learning from the starry men,
> Who follow with the optic glass

> The whirling ways of stars that pass—
> Seek, then, for this is also sooth,
> No word of theirs—the cold star-bane
> Has cloven and rent their hearts in twain,
> And dead is all their human truth.[8]

It is conventional for the pastoral narrator to deplore the kind of abstract and mechanical logic that is a product of sophisticated civilization. He is quick to point out that "we murder to dissect." Yet to deny the will to consciousness is to make the poet an escapist. In his sympathetic evaluation of the Wanderers' risk to know and control, Morris avoids the retreat that Yeats was later to criticize in his own early pastoral poems: "it is not the poetry of insight and knowledge, but of longing and complaint—the cry of the heart against necessity." [9] When Morris as narrator finally judges his characters, he acknowledges their folly:

> Lo,
> A long life gone, *and nothing more they know,*
> Why they should live to have desire and foil,
> And toil, that overcome, brings yet more toil,
> Than that day of their vanishing youth, when first
> They saw Death clear, and deemed all life accurst
> By that cold overshadowing threat,—the End.[10]

Yet he also credits their attempt and discovery of failure as superior to the attitudes of the self-righteous readers whose false "wisdom and content" make them blind to natural human longings and whose analytic dissection of life destroys mystery: "ye whose eyes are piercing to behold / What makes the silver seas and skies and gold!" The Wanderers do ultimately discover "human truth," but its discovery is ironically the function of debility and despair. As Yeats himself was to discover in his late poetry, "bodily decrepitude is wisdom." It is only through the consciousness that deeds are limited in power that man achieves the state of "radical innocence." At this point the memory, so often the apparent curse of the hero, is rehabilitated and freed to explore the construct of life itself. For the hero, individuality is subordinated to type. The Wanderers see their lives as tales; the idle singer sees them as "hollow puppets." Through these individuals Morris also suggests the same process in culture. Speaking of the late fourteenth century, Morris says in an 1887 lecture: "However, one thing is clear to us now, the kind of thing which never is clear to most people living in such periods—namely, that whatever it was, it could not last, but must change into something else" (*CW* 23:53). In his lectures on feudal England and in his medieval setting of the poem, Morris is concentrating on a period that like his own was experiencing what Yeats would call an exchange of gyres. By use of a medieval setting he intimates the eternal recurrence of human efforts and failure, but in addition, he accentuates the mood of pastness and loss that characterizes the end of an epoch and invites meditation. Northrop Frye calls this kind of framework story the *penseroso* phase of romance: "In comedy it shows the comic society breaking up into small units or individuals; in romance it marks the end of a movement from active to contemplative adventure." [11]

The failure of heroic culture is thus evaluated through the recollected adventures of a group of symbolically medieval-modern men of action. But to avoid sheer introspective melancholy, Morris balances this story in several ways to give the "idleness" of contemplation positive aesthetic value and to convert "energy" from total failure to the subject of that contemplation. He contrasts the experience of the Wanderers with the innocence of the enclosed tales, and he then contemplates both views from the modern lyric perspective of the idle singer in the monthly interludes. But in addition, he uses the framework story itself to present his central theme of meditation. He accomplishes this both by balancing the essential character of the Wanderers and their hosts and by giving Rolf, the central framework narrator, an awareness of two heritages: one is northern, and the other is southern, the background of the listeners in the ancient Greek city.

It is through Rolf's double consciousness that Morris introduces the theme of heroic failure *and* repeats the meditative image that replaces the fire imagery of the first Prologue—the Byzantium motif. Early in his narration, Rolf tells us that his disappointing return to Norway occurred some years before the voyage, but his memories of youth are associated with the South. He was born at Micklegarth, a Scandinavian settlement in Byzantium, where his father was one of the Varangian guards who "bore the twibil valiantly" in his duties of protecting the Greek emperor. Mallet's *Northern Antiquities*, one of Morris's proposed sources, describes these "Vaering warriors":

> In the year 902 the Emperor Alexis took seven hundred of these Varaeger from Kiev in his pay, and from that period down to the fall of Constantinople the Byzantine emperors committed the care of their persons to a bodyguard chiefly, if not wholly, composed of Scandinavian adventurers, at first of Russian Varaeger, and, at a later period, of Danes, Norwegians, and Icelanders. . . . This celebrated Varangian body-guard, to use the words of Gibbon, "with their broad and double-edged battle-axes on their shoulders, attended the Greek emperor to the temple, the senate, and the hippodrome; he slept and feasted under their trusty guard; and the keys of the palace, the treasury, and the capital, were held by the firm and faithful hands of the Varangians." [12]

The tone of this passage is echoed in one of Morris's lectures where he describes the peak of Byzantine culture: "Considering how old the world is it was not too long-lived at its best. In the days when Norwegian, Dane, and Icelander stalked through the streets of Micklegarth, and hedged with their axes the throne of Kirialax the Greek king, it was alive and vigorous" (*CW* 22:159).

We have already noted Morris's interest in Byzantine iconography. His references to Byzantium are so frequent that one critic has suggested Yeats's indebtedness to the older poet for the view of Byzantium as the apex of civilization and art.[13] For Morris, like Yeats, the glory of Byzantium was its rare and perfect fusion of cultures into a people's art so historically singular that "all the world glittered with its brightness and quivered with its vigour" (*CW* 22:158). The source of its cultural and artistic dominance "in peace and war" was the clashing and blending of East and West, North and South (*CW* 22:275, 7). The structure and naturalism of the West were united with the antithetical intricacy and mystery of the East, and the result was the "rich and fruitful daughter Byzantium," the culmination of ancient art, and the birth of medieval art (*CW* 22:7, 208, 275). "Looked upon as a European city, Byzantium was for long the only great city of Europe that was really alive and dominant in peace and war; as a mistress or an enemy she dealt with all the great birth-countries of art and letters, nay, of human life." [14]

The allusions to Byzantium in the Prologue foreshadow these conclusions in the lectures. The Byzantine culture at Micklegarth is recalled six times by Rolf during his narration. For him it is a distant and happy place, the source of childhood pleasure and civilized lore, even though it represents a contrast to his Norse background. It is used as a touchstone for civilization once, and once it figures in a dream of power. For the reader, it is a summarizing image to suggest the idea of the rise and fall of civilization and to suggest a symbolic locus of meditation that enlarges the implications of the isolated Greek settlement where the story takes place. This distant city populated by "the seed of the Ionian race" provides the "chambers fair" and the "green garden[s]" for tale-sharing. Aesthetically it functions as a concrete version of the narrator's "old garden," "isle of bliss," and the "Land of Matters Unforgot." It is a racial repository of art. Its aging rulers provide companionable listeners for the Wanderers. Yet they, like their setting, are given aesthetic distance that in the beginning stages of the Prologue suggests Milton's angels, whose timeless wisdom sets them apart from the passions of ordinary experience. For Morris this Greek city is a "country for old men" only in the sense that Yeats intends Byzantium—a place of art lost in history and now symbolically set apart for meditation on the "aged man" who "is but a paltry thing." The wise "city grey-beards" of Morris's poem hardly qualify as "sages standing in God's holy fire," but they are in a very strong sense "singing-masters" of the soul, for the stories of many cultures that they invite and tell to generate memory in a "now altered world" are told in circumstances temporarily "out of nature," songs sung "of what is past, or passing, or to come." [15]

Rolf's narrative of "that strange desperate voyage o'er the sea" (*CW* 3:12) evolves slowly in four stages (*CW* 3:14–22, 22–38, 38–51, 51–80), each concluded with a response by the City Elders. These choric passages serve to structure the long story, emphasize the past time of the events, and accentuate the meditative tone of the poem. Morris structures the events as a quest, as does Rolf, but unlike the episodes of the original Prologue, the adventures of these Wanderers tend to blur as repetitions of similar situations. In every division except the first, a barbarian culture is balanced by a friendly primitive one, each equally unsatisfactory to the mariners in search of the perfect civilization. Style, structure, and tone also suggest classical balance and reflect Rolf's disillusioned tranquillity. The only note of romantic intensity is the recollection of the quest-motive, which is rapidly transformed from optimism to "that desperate cruise," "our long disastrous quest," "our foolish quest," and "that too hopeless quest" (*CW* 3:57, 77, 79, 80).

The first division marks the separation from known society. The episode, beginning with the midnight departure from Wickland, concludes:

> A little hour for evermore had reft
> The sight of Europe from my helpless eyes,
> And crowned my store of hapless memories. (*CW* 3:22)

Europe is significantly represented by Edward III, whom the mariners encounter as he crosses the channel for battle. The

symbolic association of the Wanderers with English culture
is enriched both by Nicholas' account of his family's destruction by their common French foe and by the king's claim to
royal Norse blood when he gives gifts to Nicholas and Rolf
(*CW* 3:21). The encounter with the king also summarizes and
evaluates the heroic motive of the beginning of the journey.
His reference to Odin and his speech on the meaning of conquest echo Rolf's explanation of the origin of the quest. In
those early passages (*CW* 3:6–13), Rolf identifies himself with
Norse culture, suggesting that Micklegarth (etymologically
suggesting an *earthly* paradise—"great garden") and its lore
temporarily faded before stories of northern heroism, especially the quest for Asgard or its counterparts (etymologically
suggesting an *un-earthly* paradise—"garden of the gods"). At
this early stage he is fascinated by noble tales of "Swithiod /
The Greater, Odin and his house of gold" (*CW* 3:6), by the
quest of "Leif the son of Eric," by "The Vineland voyage o'er
the unknown sea / And Swegdir's search for Godhome, when
he found / The entrance to a new world underground" (*CW*
3:13). Rolf also claims royal lineage (*CW* 3:12). The belief in
successful quest and the choice of Fighting Man as one of the
vessels derive from the first Prologue, but they also point
forward to the encounter with Edward III.

The king blesses the Wanderers but acknowledges the limitations of the life of glory:

> For you the world is wide—but not for me,
> Who once had dreams of one great victory
> Wherein that world lay vanquished by my throne,
> And now, the victor in so many an one,
> Find that in Asia Alexander died
> And will not live again; the world is wide
> For you I say, for me a narrow space
> Betwixt the four walls of a fighting place.   (*CW* 3:20)

Though he differentiates between his goal and the Wanderers',
we see their similarity of ethos, and the realistic scene with
Edward replaces the dream of the old Prologue as prophecy

of failure. Critics have noted that Morris distorts history here to underline this point. Wickert points out that the portrait of Edward III (*CW* 3:16–17) derives from a coin, also described in *News from Nowhere* (chap. 2), minted to celebrate the English victory at Sluys [16] when the king had been described by Froissart as "himself a noble knight and in the flower of youth." Actually the description, which also mentions the age of the Black Prince as thirteen, occurs in Froissart's account of the seize on Gascoyne which took place in 1346, six years after the naval battle at Sluys gave the English control of the channel for several decades. [17] Historical accuracy should concern us no more than it does Morris, however. Most important is the evidence that he deliberately ages the king to foreshadow the failure of the Wanderers and to restate the theme of cultural dissolution. In his lecture on "Feudal England" Morris refers to Edward's reign to illustrate his idea of the simultaneous blossom and decay of culture, applied elsewhere to Byzantium and Victorian England. "The Middle Ages," he says, "had by this time come to the fullest growth" (*CW* 23:53). Immediately he adds that it was also passing out of phase. The corrupt feudal system deplored by Morris was "naturally one of open war," and war was motivated by powerful self-interest:

> and such again was the great war which Edward III entered into with France. You must not suppose that there was anything in this war of a national, far less of a race, character. . . . It was the private business of a lord of the manor, claiming what he considered his legal rights of another lord who had, as he thought, usurped them; and this claim his loyal feudatories were bound to take up for him; loyalty to a feudal superior, not patriotism to a country, was the virtue which Edward III's soldiers had to offer, if they had any call to be virtuous in that respect (*CW* 23·53–54)

In the poem Morris gives the English king the age, experience, and insight to make a similar judgment on himself in order

to offset Rolf's idealism. Rolf's elegiac words, even in retro-
spect, value heroic action:

> Ah, with such an one
> Could I from town to town of France have run
> To end my life upon some glorious day
> Where stand the banners brighter than the May
> Above the deeds of men, as certainly
> This king himself has full oft wished to die. (*CW* 3:15)

King Edward sees less meaning in death. It is important that
the departing king, sea hero as he might be, has his musicians
"strike up triumphantly / Some song that told not of the
weary sea, / But rather of the mead and fair green-wood" (*CW*
3:21).

It is the "weary sea" that dominates the subsequent episodes
of the poem. "This changeless world of waters grey" is not
the romantic but the classical sea. We recall Auden's idea that
for classical writers "the great waters . . . are the symbol for
the primordial undifferentiated flux, the substance which became created nature only by having form imposed upon or
wedded to it. The sea, in fact, is that state of barbaric vague-
ness and disorder out of which civilisation has emerged and
into which, unless saved by the efforts of gods and men, it is
always liable to relapse." [18] The thirty-odd descriptive references to the sea generally emphasize its chaotic, indifferent,
or destructive qualities. Four times the Wanderers are driven
off course by a nonromantic configuration of wind and current. The result is never instructive or supernaturally puni-
tive. It is instead "baffling" (*CW* 3:23), boring, and repetitious.
At the beginning of the second division of the narrative, Rolf
recalls the story of the sailor whose agonizing "strife / With
winds and waters" only carried him back to his port of departure. Such is the pattern of the Wanderers' adventures.
Although they never return home, their "discoveries" lack
variety or interest. They merely reiterate the inevitable
similarities of unordered, uncivilized life.

The second phase (*CW* 3:22–38) of the Prologue is thus fairly representative of the two subsequent ones. It begins with separation and storm, moves to the discovery of a strange barbarian land and then of a peaceful primitive society, and it is interrupted by at least two significant meditative insights on the part of Rolf. The sea provides continuous background and frame. Eleven days out of sight of land,

> then baffling grew the wind,
> But as we still were ignorant and blind
> Nor knew our port, we sailed on helplessly
> O'er a smooth sea, beneath a lovely sky,
> And westward ever, but no signs of land
> All through these days we saw on either hand,
> Nor indeed hoped to see, because we knew
> Some watery desert we must journey through,
> That had been huge enough to keep all men
> From gaining that we sought for until then. (*CW* 3:23)

The treatment of sea as desert has no overtones of romantic trial and insight. It is an indifferent locus for mariners who in spite of their roving spirit and expert seamanship are society-oriented. The moon is also divested of romantic magic. In four associated references it reveals only human limitation and boundless space. It shows the Rose-Garland's mast as "weak and small" and reveals "the helmsman's peering face," and in "the moonlight wan" Rolf thinks:

> Then when the ocean seemed so measureless
> The very sky itself might well be less,
> When midst the changeless piping of the wind
> The intertwined slow waves, pressed on behind,
> Rolled o'er our wake and made it nought again,
> Then would it seem an ill thing and a vain
> To leave the hopeful world that we had known,
> When all was o'er, hopeless to die alone
> Within this changeless world of waters grey. (*CW* 3:24)

Hope returns only with daylight, "the talk of men, the viol's quivering strings" (*CW* 3:24)—all civilized images. The storm which immediately follows intensifies separation. Not only in Europe "reft" from Rolf's "helpless eyes" but the ships are separated as well in a tempest that stirs "the climbing sea," "the ridges of the dark grey seas," and "the ocean's weltering misery." The tenor of the stormy sea is summarized as "the waste of waves."

The first sighting of land brings anticipation of "some fresh stream to drink," "the green earth," and of course, attainment of "godless fair eternity" (*CW* 3:25, 26, 25). From the beginning of the quest, the Wanderers envision their goal as an ordered existence that completely structures human and natural life. It is essentially static in its perfection, literally an end of voyage. What is shocking about the barbarians who practice human sacrifice and disappointing about the gentle wood people, "the so simple folk and virtuous" who know "nought of iron" (*CW* 3:37), is that they represent two extremes of primitive culture insufficient to fulfill either the memory or desire of civilization as the Wanderers know it. They, like the societies of the successive episodes, are isolated cultures in process, too innocent (whether brutally or passively) of consciousness to satisfy the Wanderers' sophisticated need to know the full potential of human experience. Likewise nature on land as well as sea fails to conspire in providing order. Despite a few fascinating leopards, dragons, lizards, and many-colored birds, nature provides indifferent and confusing barriers rather than construct. It is ironic of course that such romantically idealistic heroes as these would seek perfection in external rather than internal terms. Morris criticizes the romantic quester, but he also humanizes him.

From this first pair of adventures through the following four, it is clear that these classical questers in romantic guise seek a perfected version of what they already know as the form of a kind of life that eliminates death. The desire to achieve it is a driving force that denies rest. The curse of the pursuit is not just that attainment is impossible but that its transformation of consciousness prevents either a return to known society or resignation to the impossibility of return. If Morris offers a "message" about quest, it is that it alienates man from ordinary human circumstance—the bonds of tribe, place, work, and mortality. This growing alienation is expressed early in the Wanderers' memory of home (*CW* 3:12) and increasingly in the realization that

> we, alone
> Apart from all, such desperate men were grown,
> If we should fail to win our Paradise,
> That common life we now might well despise.
>
> (*CW* 3:35)

The loss of home is manifested in the death of Kirstin (*CW* 3:42), whose youth and innocence have already suffered in the journey:

> But with the others there did Nicholas stay
> To guard the ships, with whom was Kirstin still,
> Who now seemed pining for old things, and ill,
> Spite of the sea-breeze and the lovely air.   (*CW* 3:31)

In the third phase of the voyage, Rolf says:

> So with the failing of our hoped delight
> We grew to be like devils—then I knew
> At my own cost, what each man cometh to
> When every pleasure from his life is gone,
> And hunger and desire of life alone,
> That still beget dull rage and bestial fears,
> Like gnawing serpents through the world he bears.
>
> (*CW* 3:49)

Finally, as the Wanderers are about to enter the false eternal city, comparable to the land of the Stony Men in Prologue I, they are plagued by memory and the continuing sense of commitment to the abandoned society at home:

Old faces still reproached us: "We are gone,
And ye are entering into bliss alone;
And can ye now forget? Year passes year,
And still ye live on joyous, free from fear;
But where are we? where is the memory
Of us, to whom ye once were drawn so nigh?

(CW 3:68)

It is important that The Elders of the City provide an audience for the story of the Wanderers. Its narration is exorcizing. But more to the point, they provide a civilization that combines "a peaceful and delicious land / Amongst the simple kindly country folk" (CW 3:78) with monuments of art and an ancient oral culture. The setting and its tenor of contemplation provide the Wanderers societal circumstance for translating unhappy experience into art. This situation crystallizes their growing acceptance of life—personal history—as a construct, variously called by the Wanderers a double "image" of present and past and "a tale" (CW 3:26, 38). Their story is for their listeners both "some ancient chronicle" and "our living chronicle" (CW 3:79, 80). In turn, the communal group of the Wanderers and the Elders "in their times of idleness and ease" plan to share each month "some history" (CW 3:83, 84).

The notion of history, whether personal or cultural, is necessarily temporal. In one sense, the most serious plight of the Wanderers is their painful ability to experience a sense of the past in the present. As a narrator, Morris exploits the same response in his readers, who are invited to participate in the continuous recurrence of personal and cultural flux. Such a view is not comfortable, for it acknowledges the certainty of death, of men and nations. At the same time, history structures the past and simplifies its patterns. For some, the patterns are instructive. In the framework story, the "ancient men to ancient men" speak occasionally of "grave matters of belief and polity" (CW 3:83). But Morris's primary interest is more aesthetic. The oral tradition transmitted by these "comrades" in

age provides communal pleasure and a temporary suspension
of rational complexity as the tellers and listeners release racial
memory to re-create the simplest and most basic archetypes
of their shared heritage:

> They told of poets' vain imaginings,
> And memories vague of half-forgotten things,
> Nor true nor false, but sweet to think upon. (*CW* 3:83)

Finally, as the tales begin, we see that Morris's concept of
historic or personal truth evades pragmatic categories. The
stories that follow explore the human potential to reduce experience to its essential motives, limitations, and pleasures.
They momentarily recall

> times long passed away,
> When men might cross a kingdom in a day,
> And kings remembered they should one day die,
> And all folk dwelt in great simplicity.   (*CW* 3:84)

Without the experience of the Wanderers, the innocence of the
tales would have no meaning, and without the idyllic innocence of this art of the people the frustrated energy of the
Wanderers would find no channel back into the sensuous,
communal experience that characterizes history, art, and life.

chapter five
The Four Seasons of Man and Society: the General Structure and Volume j

And nowe to shewe howe man chaungeth twelve tymes evyn as the twelve monethes do.

Kalender of Shepherdes

STRUCTURE OF THE POEM

O DESCRIBE the organization of the *Earthly Paradise* tales is inevitably to confront their similarity. In subject and style they have struck more than one reader with their repetitions, diffuseness, and display of Morris's apparently uncalculated "instinct for story-telling." [1] Easily seduced by the narrator's claim of randomness, most readers are content to assume a fairly arbitrary arrangement of the poet's favorite stories from a "now altered world."

Most often, generalizations about unity are limited to remarks about Morris's "medieval method," the term used by Mackail to describe the "architectural design of a great body of poetry." Our discussion so far has questioned the appropriateness of "romance" as a label for Morris's method, and this is clearly what Mackail has in mind when he discusses "the plan of a cycle of romantic stories connected by some common purpose or occasion." [2] Assuming the particular limitations—thematic and stylistic—of this interpretation, however, we can learn something of Morris's *kind* of unity by recalling the structural principles of the medieval narrative cycles.

Defining form and meaning in medieval romance, Eugène Vinaver distinguishes between Aristotelian structure and the "*acentric* composition" of the medieval cycles: "Whereas the Roman doctrine of *amplificatio* or *auxesis* was concerned with the art of making small things great, of 'raising acts and personal traits above their dimensions' in a kind of upward movement, the medieval variety of amplification was, on the contrary, a linear or horizontal extension, an expansion or an unrolling of a number of interlocked themes." It is the neutralizing effect of this interlocking, horizontal development that sustains continuity and accounts for the "tapestry" quality frequently cited in *The Earthly Paradise:* "And since it is always possible, and often even necessary, for several themes to be pursued simultaneously, they have to alternate like threads in a woven fabric, one theme interrupting another and again another, and yet all remaining constantly present in the author's and the reader's mind." [3] Finally, the "unity" of this kind of composition derives from its lack of center or single goal. Its expansive potential gives it its "cyclical" quality.

The unity of *The Earthly Paradise* is clearly of this sort, however much Morris departs from the philosophical assumptions of the period of romance. He values the apparently random flow of narrative achieved by the romancers; it suits what Swinburne, intending no compliment, called his "slow and spontaneous" style.[4] More important, however, are Morris's modifications of the medieval instrument. The random atmosphere is retained but its submission to the shaping effect of the double frame of the poem gives it a thematic "center." This unifying principle might be described as pastoral meditation. Simple, archetypal myths of past civilizations are repeated in a pattern and context that suggest the eternal cycle of nature, man, and culture. The suggestion of acentric composition is important to Morris's transmission of the "art of the people," but he controls its design in three major ways that are characteristic of pastoral anthologies.

First, the possibilities of infinite horizontal extension are checked by the treatment of the individual stories as idylls, with their strong sense of aesthetic closure, their balanced sequential relationships of comparison and contrast, and their characteristic pastoral themes. Second, their collection within a calendar structure transforms the generic meaning of "cycle" into the overt theme of eternal recurrence. And third, the presence of the idle singer gives the work social and personal coherence. As narrator, he links fictional and real worlds, especially in a cultural sense; as speaker in the lyric interludes, he introduces the elegiac stance of a modern pastoral poet whose goal is observation and perception of likeness or unlikeness, the kind of vision that leads to idyllic anagnorisis.[5]

The individual tales combine the traits of two related Greek forms that constitute types rather than genres—the idyll, a short descriptive piece of human or natural interest, and the epyll, a little story.[6] Both the descriptive and narrative qualities are characteristic of the pastoral poem, whether it be technically designated as idyll, eclogue, elegy, or song. In fact, even when the content of such a poem is neither pastoral nor idyllic in the sense of embodying the quality of life heretofore described, its distinguishing formal trait is its limited scale. Plot issues are simplified; the minute description of concrete natural setting assumes primary importance; and the sense of closure of the created world is insured by a comprehensive frame around the poem or tale as well as by internal descriptive frames that interrupt and deactivate the forward movement of heroic plot.[7]

Morris's tales, even when we view them as heroic myths, are inevitably submitted to these kinds of structural limitation. The framework story itself, which provides meditative continuum, also serves to interrupt, arrest, and distance heroic motion. The Wanderers speak of a "story's death" (*CW* 3:239), of the tales as "images of bygone days" (*CW* 5:396), of "stirring deeds long dead" (*CW* 6:176). Like the idle singer, they are also aware of the constructed artificiality of the "measured falling of that rhyme" and "the cadence of that ancient rhyme" (*CW* 4:125, 159). Within the tales action is frequently generated and then frozen through images of stasis and through a style that creates pictorial tableaux. Many of them are enclosed by quiet descriptive frames that suggest pastoral life. Earlier in *Jason*, Morris has the dead hero discovered by "some shepherd of the lone grey slope" and his simple friends, "vine-dressers and

their mates, who through the town / Ere then had borne their
well-filled baskets brown" (*CW* 2:296). Representative of the
pastoral frame in *The Earthly Paradise* is the setting of "The
Death of Paris," where the tale's narrator concludes:

> I cannot tell what crop may clothe the hills,
> The merry hills Troy whitened long ago—
> Belike the sheaves, wherewith the reaper fills
> His yellow wain, no whit the weaker grow
> For that past harvest-tide of wrong and woe;
> Belike the tale, wept over otherwhere,
> Of those old days, is clean forgotten there.   (*CW* 5:21)

The idyllic content of the tales is closely related to structure
in its reductive quality. Without reference to the pastoral overtones of his remarks, Walter Pater contrasts the *Earthly Paradise* stories with the mood of "delirium or illusion" in the
earlier, more romantic poetry. He calls the transition a process
of simplification, of movement from enchanted evening to
"the great primary passions under broad daylight as of the
pagan Veronese." Pater summarizes:

> Complex and subtle interest, which the mind spins for
> itself may occupy art and poetry or our own spirits for
> a time; but sooner or later they come back with a sharp
> rebound to the simple elementary passions—anger, de-
> sire, regret, pity, and fear: and what corresponds to them
> in the sensuous world—bare, abstract fire, water, air,
> tears, sleep, silence, and what De Quincey has called the
> "glory of motion."
> This reaction from dreamlight to daylight gives, as
> always happens, a strange power in dealing with morn-
> ing and the things of the morning. Not less is this Helle-
> nist of the Middle Ages master of dreams, of sleep and
> the desire of sleep—sleep in which no one walks, restorer
> of childhood to men—dreams, not like Galahad's or
> Guenevere's, but full of happy, childish wonder as in the
> earlier world.[8]

We could enumerate the distinctively pastoral touches of this simple daylight world as they emerge in sources as various as Theocritus, Virgil, Spenser, or even Wordsworth and Keats: the conflict of youth and age, the value of solitary singing, an attitude of simple fatalism, the glimpse of peaceable kingdoms, visions of love thwarted and fulfilled, the dangers of pride in possessions, and naturalistic communication between men and gods. The repetition of these tropes establishes several pastoral themes: celebration of the earth, a vision of communal society, and submission to fate.

In addition, however, the organization of the tales provides a series of comparisons and contrasts within individual volumes, and each volume in turn takes on a particular thematic coloration. The result is that while we remain acutely aware of the static discreteness of each idyll, we also begin to recognize the patterns suggested by juxtaposition and ultimately sequence: "Alternate song is what the Muses love" (Virgil III: 59).

It is impossible to deny the implication of progression in any sequential arrangement, especially when it is associated with the seasons of the year. The calendar suggests cyclical as well as linear progression, and poets have variously utilized the pattern of eternal recurrence as a pessimistic or optimistic metaphor for man. Like Tennyson in *In Memoriam*, Morris manages to do both, just as he employs the ideas of both repetition and progression. One obvious implication of the tales is the unavoidable repetition of personal and historical aspiration and failure. If their similar style dissipates interest it is because the poet challenges the possibility of unique experience. Nature has its pattern, and man his: life leads to death and finally to rebirth, but it is not for the individual man to decide how or when he will be absorbed into the great cycle. Nor is he apt to perceive the moments of transition in medias res. What continues and repeats again is not individual deed or will but the typical experience of a culture.

Man is more attuned to linear progression, to the changes

that lead toward his death. This painful recognition is the source of the concept of the ages or seasons of man, a metaphor that generalizes rather than particularizes man's fate. It functions in medieval works like the *Kalender of Shepherdes* to remind man of his end. The four volumes of *The Earthly Paradise* suggest such a structural scheme. Utilizing ancient calendar structure, Morris begins his year with spring and devotes a volume of tales to each subsequent season, concluding with winter, the traditional season of death. Both the *Kalender of Shepherdes* and Spenser's *Shepheard's Calendar* work on a similar structure, though Spenser adopts the new calendar year that begins in January. Spenser thereby achieves a particularly "northern" pastoral tone that reflects the Anglo-Saxon preoccupation with the physical hazards and emotional realism of winter. Morris achieves a similar effect, primarily through his cultural and psychological delineation of the Wanderers.

Although his division of months is different from Morris's, the Maister Shepherde of the *Kalender* offers a clear conventional statement of the seasons-of-man theme:

> It is to be vnderstonde that there be in the yere iiii. quarters that is to be callyd vere . Imnus . estas . and . autunnus. These be the foure seasons in the yere . as Prymetyme is the sprynge of the yere as Feueryere . Marche . and . Aprell. Those thre monethes. Than comethe sommer. as. May . June . and . July. and in those iii. monethes euery herbe . grayne . and tre in his kynde is in his moste strengthe and fayrnesse euene at the hygheste. Thanne cometh. Autonne . as August . September and . October . that all these fruytis waxethe rype and be gaderyde and howsyd. Than comethe . Nouember . December . and Janyuere . and these iii. monethes is the wynter. The tyme of lytell profite. We shepardis saythe that the age of a man is. lxxii. yere and that we lekene but to one holle yere . for euermore we take vi. yere for euery moneth. as Jenyuere . or Feueryere . & so forthe for as the yere chaungeth by the twelue monethes.[9]

An intricate description of each age of man follows, dividing the ages of man and the year into seasons and months. Spenser also makes his twelve eclogues "proportionable to the twelve monthes," and simultaneously stresses the four seasons of man's life. It is significant that despite Spenser's January–December arrangement Colin Clout refers in the December eclogue to the older seasonal tradition. The argument for the eclogue follows:

> This Aeglogue (even as the first beganne) is ended with a complaynte of Colin to God Pan; wherein, as weary of his former wayes, hee proportioneth his life to the foure seasons of the yeare; comparing hys youthe to the spring time, when he was fresh and free from loves follye. His manhoode to the sommer, which, he sayth, was consumed with greate heate and excessive drouth, caused throughe a Comet or blasing starre, by which hee meaneth love; which passion is commonly compared to such flames and immoderate heate. His riper yeares hee resembleth to an unseasonable harveste, wherein the fruites fall ere they be rype. His latter age to winters chyll and frostie season, now drawing neare to his last ende.[10]

The *Earthly Paradise* arrangement, while it cannot be totally "proportioned" to this pastoral design, nevertheless offers irresistible invitation to a similar reading. In addition, it is helpful to think of Morris's organization as an embodiment of the seasonal *mythoi* assigned by Northrop Frye to the major genres (a linear-symbolic pattern he also follows in describing romance alone). Briefly, spring is associated with comedy, summer with romance, autumn with tragedy, and winter with irony. Concurrently he traces the cycle of romance, the genre that Morris modifies by style and perspective into a pastoral mode, from the birth of the hero in spring to his integration into and withdrawal from society in summer, fall, and winter.[11]

Volume I, including the tales of March and April, focuses

on the birth, youth, and marriage of heroes in three of its four
stories. The youth of the hero is associated with the comic
interest in the integration of society. Age and fate are also
introduced as themes, the first primarily as a barrier to youth
and the innocent society, but emphasis is on the carefree phase
of the hero's youth, when, as Colin Clout says, "flowrd my
joyfull spring, / Like Swallow swift I wandred here and
there."

In the second volume the wandering is much more directed
(though less controlled) toward the satisfaction of love-long-
ing, "that unkindly heate" which Colin regrets. Every tale is
a quest, and almost every quester seeks immortality in the
form of love: in pastoral terms, "A comett stird up that unkindly heate, / That reigned (as men sayd) in Venus seate."
The tenor of the volume is highly idealistic: motives and
events are unusually subject to supernatural agency, and the
otherworld permeates the natural setting of the stories. It is
appropriate to both pastoral and romance tradition that the
summer volume include eight quests for immortality. For the
pastoral poet it is a season of driven desperation:

> Forth was I ledde, not as I wont afore,
> When choise I had to choose my wandring waye,
> But whether luck and loves unbridled lore
> Would leade me forth on Fancies bitte to playe:
> The bush my bedde, the bramble was my bowre,
> The Woodes can witnesse many a wofull stowre.[12]

And the myth critic reminds us that summer, the season of
romance, epitomizes the apex of the hero's life and typifies the
form of the quest.

The middle volumes, II and III, reveal a contrast even as they
mark a transition. The otherworldly idealism of II is suddenly
juxtaposed with the earthly topics of III, primarily separation
and death. Even "Acontius and Cydippe" shows young love
shadowed by the inevitability of age and death. The heroes are
driven less by supernatural force than by human error, espe-

cially in the last two stories. The Wanderer who introduces the climactic tale of Gudrun tells his listeners:

> Therefore, no marvels hath my tale to tell,
> But deals with such things as men know too well;
> All that I have herein your hearts to move,
> Is but the seed and fruit of bitter love.   (*CW* 5:250)

The "seed and fruit" figure, foreshadowed by the "harvest-tide of woe and wrong" in the first story, summarizes the concerns of the volume and sets it in the pastoral tradition of human harvest that Colin Clout describes in similar terms:

> Thus is my sommer worne away and wasted,
> Thus is my harvest hastened all to rathe;
> The eare that budded faire is burnt and blasted,
> And all my hoped gaine is turnd to scathe:
>   Of all the seede that in my youth was sowne
>   Was nought but brakes and brambles to be mowne.[13]

This third volume, the darkest of the entire work, is also Morris's closest approximation to tragedy, the *mythos* of autumn that balances fate with human weakness, especially *hybris*, in precipitating fall. In contrast to comedy and romance, tragedy tends to convey an atmosphere of mimetic reality, a quality that critics have tended to associate, correctly it seems to me, with Morris's increasing interest in the sagas that provide the primary sources for the volume.

The winter volume, IV, marks something of a departure from either of the symbolic patterns we have described. To some extent it treats age, and it does embody the meditative perspective of a winter eclogue. In the Wanderers who listen there is recognition that "Winter is come, that blowes the baleful breath, / And after Winter commeth timely death."[14] The tone of the tales, however, is closer to the irony which Frye associates with winter. The bright, cold distance of resigned perception that is strongly conveyed through the idle singer in the winter lyrics finds its counter in the tales which redefine the hero. Male or female, this hero moves into the fire of experience and out again, maintaining a balance of fidelities to man and earth. Hercules in the first tale announces the type via his strange committed distance. He is motivated less by supernatural power, intellect, or greed than earlier heroes. His "merry" spontaneity gives him the quality Yeats attributes to his mysterious but accessible Chinamen carved in lapis lazuli. The emergent hero accepts vicissitude with the assumption that "all things fall and are built again, / And those who build them again are gay." [15] Through the new hero Morris intimates that the linear movement toward death may also signal the possibility of rebirth, even if the poet as individual man can participate in this part of the great cycle only aesthetically.

The value of this kind of reading of the poem is that it accommodates Morris's dialectical approach, his simultaneous use of linear and static structures. It also expresses his "extraverted" aesthetic that fuses personal and cultural experience. The cyclical interpretation, especially popular with myth critics, has often been applied to the whole work of a writer. Dwight Culler's reading of Arnold's poetry is a fine example. He validates his pattern by reference to the thesis–antithesis–synthesis cycle of the dialectical theory of history in Herder, Goethe, Novalis, the Saint-Simonians, and Carlyle. The reading itself, however, describes the personal progress of poet (and personae) through a symbolic landscape. [16]

For all the similarity of symbol, Morris's cycle has more affinity with historical myth. Describing civilization in an early lecture, he utilizes the organic, seasonal metaphor which we have seen in the "seasons of man" pattern: "So it has been seen before: first comes the birth, and hope scarcely conscious of itself; then the flower and fruit of mastery, with hope more than conscious enough, passing into insolence, as decay follows ripeness; and then—the new birth again" (*CW* 22:11). His approach recalls Virgil's fourth eclogue; it also appears in Hesiod, the source of the Golden Age idea, and Ovid, who repeats it in the *Metamorphoses;* both were admired by Morris. In the first book of that work, Ovid announces his theme as change and fancifully relates the creation of the world. Man's appearance heralds the age of gold, an innocent phase that is free of competition, the necessity of law, or the violation of the earth. Free also of overpopulation or curiosity, it is characterized primarily by the absence of aggressive instincts. The succeeding ages of silver, bronze, and iron mark the growth of aspiration, greed, and significantly, quest. The race of bronze, remarkably similar to the world of Morris's second volume, introduces the notions of the voyage of conquest and the search for treasure. The age of iron, like Morris's volume III, is an era of "fierce strife" when all human loyalties disappear. Thus the last phase is the deluge, with which Jove punishes man and restores to the "satyrs and fauns and nymphs of hill and wood" their rightful heritage, the earth. Into this vision of completed cycle, when "earth is earth again," [17] Ovid weaves his mythologies of gods and men, always retaining the theme of metamorphosis, an idea at once literal and metaphoric.

The effect of this approach is a strange sense of perpetual motion with rhythmic interruption. Richard Wilbur describes it, with reference to Ovid, in his poem about the children's game of statues: the children fling each other

> and then hold still
> In gargoyle attitudes,—as if
> All definition were outrageous. Then
> They melt in giggles and begin again.

The unconscious children in their game "weave and then again undo / Their fickle zodiacs." [18] For their conscious adult observers, however, the game becomes an uncomfortable mirror of their own roles, their familiar and necessary myths.

Such is the effect of Ovid's narrative method, but to an even stronger degree, Morris's, with its emphasis on idyllic stasis as its aesthetic center. For the Wanderers and the Elders, for the poet and the reader, the tales of four seasons recall man's necessity for myths about himself and about history. Each volume presents one phase of this vision through the pastoral calendar metaphor. The year "That these old men from such mishap and strife, / Such springing up, and dying out of dreams / Had won at last" is finally a symbolic year, itself the subject of meditation on the cycles of nature, man, and civilization. In a sense, the meditation carries its participants beyond despair or hope into an imaginative realm that suspends conventional responses: "In the perspective of the great elemental cycles—the mystery of spring and birth, the inevitability of winter and death—the sphere of man's ambition assumes its true proportion. The pastoral becomes the vehicle for his acceptance of his human condition." [19]

VOLUME I: SPRING,
THE GOLDEN AGE OF MAN AND SOCIETY 〜〜〜

In the first tale, "Atalanta's Race," the hero seeks the help of Venus to attain "The golden age, the golden age come back!" While the Golden Age is characteristically relegated to the distant past, the establishment of a simple, harmonious society is foreshadowed at the story's end by the marriage of Milanion and Atalanta, by the marriage of Michael and Cecily in "The Man Born to Be King," and the marriage and victorious return of Perseus and Andromeda in "The Doom of King Acrisius." Although the fulfillment of love is an obvious thematic concern in most of the *Earthly Paradise* stories, it is not elsewhere so repeatedly associated with "a new society" that "crystallizes . . . around the hero and his bride." Marriage signals the "theme of the comic . . . the integration of society, which usually takes the from of incorporating a central character into it." [20] Two corollary interests of the volume give this "integration" its particular meaning and tone. One is the delineation of the heroes as young and innocent "outsiders" whose alienation is false and whose integration is preceded by or concurrent with actual birth into hostile social circumstance that must be overcome in a process of discovery or with metaphoric birth into love which releases chastity into creative innocence. The second subsidiary theme introduces and repeats the nature of the barrier to integrated society, the old order, represented by the aging king/father who seeks to deny natural process and the inevitable triumph of youth, love, and community. The figure of the tyrant occurs in each of the four stories, and in the last three it receives titular and narrative focus to an extent that makes these tales homilies against aspiration.

The comparative elements in the tales thus treat spring topics: the birth of the hero, the creative innocence of love, and the beginning of new community. The narrative pattern emphasizes integration by moving the hero (or heroine) from isolation, often in the natural world which educates him, into a city setting where he loves, marries, and blends the old order with the new. Countering this movement is the gradual defeat of the blocking agent, the doomed king, whose potential isolation grows into true alienation that balances the false alienation of the hero at the beginning of the story.

Because the first story sets the tone of the volume, it deserves a careful examination. While "Atalanta's Race" stops short of a vision of society, it traces the emergence of its agents from isolation into love. Narrative focus is on the consciousness of Milanion; yet the thematic center of the tale is Atalanta, who is rescued into love from the static chastity of Diana-worship. Because her kind of innocence makes Atalanta's character inaccessible, Milanion receives sympathetic and more extended treatment. The similarity to Keats's handling of the Porphyro-Madeline story is striking. The presence of a blocking agent, Atalanta's father, makes it clear that her destructive dedication to chastity is imposed, not natural. The conventional abandoned royal child (*CW* 3:89–90), she is figuratively yet unborn. She is described in her cruel victories over unfortunate suitors as "breathing like a little child / Amid some warlike clamour laid asleep" (*CW* 3:88). Her innocence is directly associated with her lack of natural feeling: "She seemed all earthly matters to forget; / Of all tormenting lines her face was clear" (*CW* 3:87).

Although Milanion's role is rescue, his credentials set him apart from the martial heroes of *Guenevere*. He is immediately associated with the world of natural process and given the simple sensitivity of a pastoral hero. Simultaneously his attraction to Atalanta draws him out of rustic isolation into community. The plot is handled simply and ended abruptly to isolate sharply the innocence of the lovers from the experience of the Wanderers and to suggest a happy society without really projecting it. The four stages of the plot clarify its themes.

The first introduces the worlds of nature and art and their representative characters. Milanion, who is not identified by name or lineage until much later, is a hunter who is characterized by setting, a long detailed description of "thick Arcadian woods" (*CW* 3:85), and his response to it. The "fresh spring day" reflects his youth, and the noon hour, the time of pastoral song as well as of medieval love visions, accentuates his contemplative isolation and his emotional readiness for love. There are several additional pastoral details in the introductory description. The "sun-burnt" hunter is in a woody "vale" (*CW* 3:85), and his venatical symbol, "the mighty cornel bow," is unstrung while he listens to "the echoes of his lone voice cling / About the cliffs and through the beech-trees ring" (*CW* 3:85). The human voice seems answered by the sounds of nature, presented in a balanced series:

> . . . still awhile he stood,
> And but the sweet familiar thrush could hear
> And all the day-long noises of the wood,
> And o'er the dry leaves of the vanished year
> His hounds' feet pattering as they drew anear. (*CW* 3:85)

The natural setting which Morris so carefully draws is also common to the phase of romance depicting the "innocent youth of the hero," whose locus, initially at least, is "a pastoral and Arcadian world, generally a pleasant wooded landscape, full of glades, shaded valleys, murmuring brooks, the moon, and other images closely linked with the female or maternal aspect of sexual imagery. Its heraldic colors are green and gold, traditionally the colors of vanishing youth." [21]

Drawn out of this youthful solitude by "vague sweet longing" naturally associated with the April season, Milanion moves toward civilization, which is presented in a second pastoral tableau:

> Then, turning round to see what place was won,
> With shaded eyes looked underneath the sun,
> And o'er green meads and new-turned furrows brown
> Beheld the gleaming of King Schoeneus' town.
>
> So thitherward he turned, and on each side
> The folk were busy on the teeming land,
> And man and maid from the brown furrows cried,
> Or midst the newly-blossomed vines did stand,
> And as the rustic weapon pressed the hand
> Thought of the nodding of the well-filled ear,
> Or how the knife the heavy bunch should shear.
>
> Merry it was: about him sung the birds,
> The spring flowers bloomed along the firm dry road,
> The sleek-skinned mothers of the sharp-horned herds
> Now for the barefoot milking-maidens lowed;
> While from the freshness of his blue abode,
> Glad his death-bearing arrows to forget,
> The broad sun blazed, nor scattered plagues as yet.
>   (*CW* 3:86)

In stark contrast to the apparent (and potential) harmony of this life is Milanion's discovery of the city's brutal ritual, the race which sacrifices life to Diana's cult of chastity. After the vision of the fecund earth, Atalanta is introduced as victim of cold artifice.

The second phase of the narrative presents Milanion's

dilemma. A natural man, he naturally responds to the maiden's beauty, and his determination to win her is only increased by the revelation that she is bound by parental fate to a kind of living death. Return to his lonely hunter's life is impossible (*CW* 3:91), for now isolation intensifies his longing. The pastoral, maternal world mirrors his new awareness, suggested especially through the reference to Adonis, whose love-death was mourned by nature (*CW* 3:91). It is important that Milanion defeats the boar. His natural ingenuity and heroic determination ally him with the forces of love against death, and he turns to Venus with intuitive resolve rather than desperation. In this section and the next, the interview with Venus, the story does not make love an escape from life, as it often is in the second volume, but a movement away from death. Likewise Venus is not consistently assigned the character of destructive seductress. Throughout this first volume Diana assumes that role, and Venus more frequently approximates her older role of universal mother, *natura creatrix,* "the principle of fecundity and generation" whose function is "giving all things life, constant and ineluctable, bringing order from chaos and harmony from strife." [22]

Thus the central third section of the tale, Milanion's appeal to Venus, represents his ritual arming for battle with the forces of stasis and chastity embodied in Diana. The love goddess is both "Queen" and mother, but primarily she is an immortal extension of Milanion's own natural potential for love, which he sets above power and renown (*CW* 3:96–97). In her temple framed "thick with myrtle trees," she conspires to help him "save / The cruel maiden from a loveless grave," and establish a world "blessed with Saturn's clime" (*CW* 3:95, 99, 100), a familiar reference to the Golden Age described by Hesiod and Ovid. The epiphany of Milanion, when "he staggered with his arms outspread, / Delicious unnamed odours breathed around" (*CW* 3:99), is therefore to be distinguished from the enervating experience of lovers in Volume II. Here it is a repetition of his own love-awakening in the Arcadian woods (*CW* 3:85–86, 91) and a foreshadowing of the "birth" of Atalanta during the race with the hero (*CW* 3:101–3).

The last phase of the story, the account of the race, focuses on Atalanta's self-discovery while it also incorporates Milanion into the symbolic society of marriage and the real kingdom of Schoeneus. The harmony of the occasion is underlined by the occurrence of triple images, so often associated with the integrative success of the hero. Milanion wins the third race he has observed (*CW* 3:101); the three golden apples, symbols of fertility, cause Atalanta to drop three arrows, Diana's counter-symbols (*CW* 3:103); and the triumphant epithalamion concludes by naming the three emblems of chastity which are offered up on the altar of Venus: "Her maiden zone, her arrows, and her bow" (*CW* 3:104).

The second and third stories of the volume have similar theme and structure. Each tale, one medieval and one Greek in origin, utilizes the frame of a fated old order to enclose the narrative of the birth, marriage, and political ascension of a young hero. The birth of Michael in "The Man Born to Be King" and of Perseus in "The Doom of King Acrisius" incorporates the abandoned infant motif, typical of pastoral and romance, and the flood, "the regular symbol of the beginning and end of a cycle." As Frye describes the configuration,

> The infant hero is often placed in an ark or chest floating on the sea, as in the story of Perseus; from there he drifts to land, as in the exordium to *Beowulf,* or is rescued from among reeds and bulrushes on a river bank, as in the story of Moses. A landscape of water, boat, and reeds appears at the beginning of Dante's journey up the mount of Purgatory, where there are many suggestions that the soul is in that stage a newborn infant. On dry land the infant may be rescued either from or by an animal, and many heroes are nurtured by animals in a forest during their nonage.[23]

Michael is first abandoned in a "rough box for ark and boat" into "a deep lowland stream" (*CW* 3:119, 120). He is discovered by a miller, a carle who sees

> A naked, new-born infant, laid
> In a rough ark that had been stayed
> By a thick tangled bed of weed.   (*CW* 3:125)

The story of Perseus includes a triple abandonment—of Danaë first, in the brass tower, and then of Perseus (both are put into "A little boat that had no oars or sail, / Or aught that could the mariner avail" [*CW* 3:185]), and finally of Andromeda. Likewise "The Doom of King Acrisius" expands the single blocking agent of the King in "The Man Born to Be King" into the triple villainy of Acrisius, Polydectes, and the Syrians, a repetition that also triples the narrative sequences of the story. In the tighter narrative of "The Man Born to Be King" the hero himself is thrice abandoned and discovered.

Both stories concentrate on the simultaneous preparation of the hero for ultimate victory and the discovery of the true identity of the abandoned child. The story of Perseus, handled in a conventional manner, shows Morris working closely with his sources. Several have been suggested, but he probably in this case relied primarily on Lempriere where character is subordinated to plot detail. Perseus' schooling, under the guidance of the maternal figure of Minerva (*CW* 3:189, 196–97), is decidedly in the active heroic vein. The initiatory quest for the Medusa's head carries him through minor adventures, all in the mythological otherworld, that prove his identity as the mortal child of a god and that reward him with a bride. In his rescue of Andromeda, his rescue of his mother from Polydectes, and his accidental slaying of Acrisius, he not only restores the harmony of three societies but destroys the agents who have blocked the earthly fertility associated with Danaë and Andromeda.

While he follows the traditional narrative outline of the

hero's story, Morris invents natural detail to characterize the heroines. Andromeda and Danaë function to link the themes of abandonment and natural education, which are associated with the hero himself in "The Man Born to Be King." The fundamental elements of nature, synonymous with fate in both stories, are associated in the Perseus story first with Danaë's love for nature, which persists in spite of her abandonment and bondage. When she first sees the tower, she pities its inhabitant:

> Alas, poor soul! scarce shall he see the sun,
> Or care to know when the hot day is done,
> Or ever see sweet flowers again, or grass,
> Or take much note of how the seasons pass. (CW 3:173)

Upon discovering herself the prisoner, she regrets her isolation from men less than her isolation from nature, which essentially represents fertility:

> Here every day shall have the same sad tale,
> My weary damsels with their faces pale,
> The dashing of the sea on this black rock,
> The piping wind through cranny and through lock,
> The sea-bird's cry, like mine grown hoarse and shrill,
> The far-off sound of horn upon the hill,
> The merry tune about the shepherd's home,
> And all the things whereto I ne'er may come. (CW 3:177)

Again Venus is the beneficent deity who initiates the salvation of the chaste prisoner. After Jove's assurance of his assistance, Venus returns to the sea,

> and, as she went,
> Unseen the gladness of the spring she sent
> Across the happy lands o'er which she moved,
> Until all men felt joyous and beloved.   (CW 3:179)

Thus the first abandoned child, Perseus' mother, is released into the experience of love and procreation by the gods, just as she is again rescued by her son from Polydectes' jealous lust and finally saved in a symbolic sense from her tyrannical father when Perseus kills him at the story's end.

Andromeda's abandonment is conveyed through a mock epithalamion (*CW* 3:210, 220) when the jealousy of the townspeople moves them to offer her as bride to a sea-monster. It is ironically significant that Andromeda's mother, the mad Cassiope, precipitates this living death by conspiring to grant her child eternal life (*CW* 3:219). In Perseus' rescue, the hero and his bride acknowledge the natural impermanence of love (*CW* 3:221). Thus the young and innocent display a wisdom lacking in their elders of the "fundamental elements" of nature. For young Danae and Andromeda, nature is the source of wisdom. For Perseus, it is Minerva and the experience of his initiation journey, where he encounters the Medusa. It is to her that Morris gives the story's most poignant statement of the appeal of mortality. She asks Perseus for death, for release from "perpetual anguish all alone":

> O was it not enough to take away
> The flowery meadows and the light of day?
> Or not enough to take away from me
> The once-loved faces that I used to see;
> To take away sweet sounds and melodies,
> The song of birds, the rustle of the trees;
> To make the prattle of the children cease,
> And wrap my soul in shadowy hollow peace,
> Devoid of longing? Ah, no, not for me!
> For those who die your friends this rest shall be;
> For me no rest from shame and sore distress,
> For me no moment of forgetfulness;
> For me a soul that still might love and hate,
> Shut in this fearful land and desolate,
> Changed by mine eyes to horror and to stone. (*CW* 3:204)

The stony paralysis of the Medusa's life echoes Danae's brass prison and the rocks to which Andromeda is chained. The

release of Medusa to "the rest of death" is thus the ultimate
rescue, and her head, Perseus' badge of identity, is also his
emblem of natural knowledge. It is incorporated into the
shield of Minerva as symbol of the essential wisdom which ties
the hero to "the green earth's stedfastness" (*CW* 3:210) and
enables the mortal man to establish his peaceable kingdom of
Mycenae:

> Peaceful grew the land
> The while the ivory rod was in his hand,
> For robbers fled, and good men still waxed strong,
> And in no house was any sound of wrong,
> Until the Golden Age seemed there to be,
> So steeped the land was in felicity.   (*CW* 3:238)

In "The Man Born to Be King" Morris draws on four
sources,[24] but he edits and blends to achieve a thematic emphasis clearly his own. The theme of fate in the source tales
changes to the broader theme of discovery. The king discovers
the identity of the hero and the reader discovers their antithetical characters and the implications of the contrast. In
both cases, pastoral nature is the setting and the medium of
characterization. Extensive natural description recurs in the
moments of discovery to reinforce the theme. That Morris
intended to give the narrative this pastoral atmosphere is
borne out by its comparison to his literal translation of one
of the sources, "The Tale of the Emperor Coustans," first
printed in 1894.[25]

The significance of the natural world is suggested by the
appearance of the shepherd-seer, by the king's alienation in
the wilderness, by the simplicity of the original and foster
homes of Michael, by his own response to natural beauty, and
by the setting of his love-encounter with Princess Cecily. This
sequence of "natural history" is initiated by the king's misinterpretation of the shepherd sage's advice and his subsequent
attempt to abandon the child to the very elements that will
foster it best.

The mysterious prophet of the sources is identified here with natural solitude. When the king, apparently fond of astrologers, asks him for chronicles of old wars, knowledge of "change of stars . . . and transmuting stone," or resurrection (*CW* 3:108), the old man answers:

> And now, for all the years I gave
> To know all things that man can learn,
> A few months' learned life I earn,
> Nor feel much liker to a God
> Than when beside my sheep I trod
> Upon the thymy, wind-swept down.   (*CW* 3:109)

He significantly refuses to offer solutions or judgments; with the king in the "close, / Shaded with grey-leaved olive-trees" (*CW* 3:110), he only reveals what he perceives as human truth: the king will be succeeded by an unknown common man "no better born than I" (*CW* 3:109), and he urges the king to acquiesce to fate, a pattern of natural order:

> "Rightly thou namest my weak lore,"
> The Sage said, "therefore to the end
> Be wise, and what the fates may send
> Take thou, nor struggle in the net
> Wherein thine helpless feet are set!"   (*CW* 3:110)

Forgetting both the prophecy and advice, the king discovers his fate in "the forest wild," where he is lost, lonely, and unrecognized by the common woodsman who has sired the future king. The folly of the king is suggested by his unfamiliarity with the world of nature and his contempt for simple life (*CW* 3:112). The king's lack of harmony with simple nature and people is contrasted with Michael's keen awareness of both. The three attempts to destroy Michael simultaneously show the natural alienation of the king and the natural simplicity of the hero, and move the plot toward the natural society implied in these visions of pastoral life.

The "wretched home" of the woodsman and Michael is detailed to show the poor but earth-bound life of its inhabitants. Likewise, the home of the miller who rescues Michael from the stream is given extensive pastoral description. As the king approaches it to discover his enemy a second time he sees

> A mill upon the river's brim,
> That seemed a goodly place to him,
> For o'er the oily smooth millhead
> There hung the apples growing red,
> And many an ancient apple-tree
> Within the orchard could he see,
> While the smooth mill walls white and black
> Shook to the great wheel's measured clack,
> And grumble of the gear within;
> While o'er the roof that dulled that din
> The doves sat crooning half the day,
> And round the half-cut stack of hay
> The sparrows fluttered twittering.   (*CW* 3:122)

The miller approaches,

> bringing there
> Such as he could of country fare,
> Green yellowing plums from off his wall,
> Wasp-bitten pears, the first to fall
> From off the wavering spire-like tree,
> Junkets, and cream and fresh honey.   (*CW* 3:123)

Shaken then by his confrontation with young Michael, identified by the ark, the king leaves and sends Samuel his seneschal to carry out his orders, death under the guise of adoption. Samuel, as the king's counterpart, shows the king's contempt for the miller by purchasing the boy with gold. And he mocks Michael's "churl's breeding" (*CW* 3:130) when the boy offers his credentials for the anticipated new life. His awareness of homely detail is in fact the evidence of the pastoral education that will make him a good ruler:

> Sir, please you to look up and down
> The weedy reaches of our stream,
> And note the bubbles of the bream,
> And see the great chub take the fly
> And watch the long pike basking lie
> Outside the shadow of the weed.
> Withal there come unto our need
> Woodcock and snipe when swallows go;
> And now the water-hen flies low
> With feet that well-nigh touch the reeds,
> And plovers cry about the meads,
> And the stares chatter; certes, sir,
> It is a fair place all the year.   (*CW* 3:130)

This is the hero's only speech of any length, but it reflects the acuteness of observation and the sensitivity elsewhere conveyed by Michael's thoughts as

> He saw the sunny country-side
> Spread out before him far and wide,
> Golden amidst its waning green,
> Joyous with varied life unseen.   (*CW* 3:133)

The second attempt to kill Michael, Samuel's ghastly wound, is again thwarted by rustic intervention. Monks in an abbey in the wood save and educate him, although they admit that despite his facility with Latin he "hath no will / To turn into religion still" (*CW* 3:144).

It is in his third attempt to defeat fate that the king is himself finally defeated and that fate is clearly allied to natural process. The king plans to have Michael lured to the castle and beheaded in the place where his only offspring, Princess Cecily, awaits her bridegroom. The approach to the Castle of the Rose, a traditional love-pleasance, is again presented as a pastoral frame that symbolically surrounds the virgin's castle with varied promises of life, natural and human (*CW* 3:147, 153). Several exemplary passages show Michael's harmony with nature and prophesy Cecily's love-release:

Now the road turned to his left hand
And led him through a table-land,
Windy and barren of all grain;
But where a hollow specked the plain
The yew-trees hugged the sides of it,
And mid them did the woodlark flit
Or sang well sheltered from the wind.
And all about the sheep did find
Sweet grass, the while the shepherd's song
Rang clear as Michael sped along.   (*CW* 3:148)

Reaching the hill-top, Michael gazes into the valley below:

For, hedged with many a flowery close,
There lay the Castle of the Rose,
His hurried journey's aim and end.   (*CW* 3:149)

To reach the castle he must pass among the "unseen folk," the reapers, who gradually become visible, resting with their sickles and eating

Slices of white cheese, specked with green,
And green-striped onions and ryebread,
And summer apples faintly red
Even beneath the crimson skin,
And yellow grapes, well ripe and thin,
Plucked from the cottage gable-end.   (*CW* 3:149)

The suggestion of the descriptive frame is that the Castle of the Rose, and hence Cecily, is set apart from the external world but is in potential harmony with it. Two worlds exist without, the martial world of the king and the pastoral world of Michael. It is the harmonious pastoral life which he recalls in vivid sequence (*CW* 3:150) as he enters the castle. That the king's world will fall is suggested by the refrain Michael hears as he crosses the drawbridge: "*The Kaiser lieth on his bier,*" later "*The King lieth on his bier*" (*CW* 3:151, 152). The song, a reference to Frederic Barbarossa, functions within the story to point up the ironic reversal of the king's expectations, but it also recalls the fall-of-heroes theme of the Prologue, where Swabian Laurence remembers "tales of the Kaiser Redbeard" (*CW* 3:8). Cecily's world too, will fall with her cloistered innocence; yet the result will be a union like that of Madeline and Porphyro, "as the rose / Blendeth its odour with the violet." Michael's entrance through what "seem like the gates of Paradise" (*CW* 3:152) heralds the mutual discovery of the lovers and the fusion of the new earthly paradise with the old unearthly one. The events in "that garden green," "that pleasance sweet" (*CW* 3:153), are descriptively rich and balanced. Both lovers sleep near the "fountain in the midst" (*CW* 3:154) and wake to new life. The hearty peasant meal that precedes the encounter is balanced by the Keatsian feast spread by Lady Agnes to revive Cecily, "faint, weak and white / Within that fair bower of delight" (*CW* 3:159), and the returning king, his orders changed by his daughter, finds the anticipated death scene replaced by marriage festivity.

The epithalamion which climaxes the story is the most extensive and most pastoral of such passages in the volume.[26] It combines the classical tropes of royalty with pastoral references to simple nature and life. The king

> saw the crowd before him part,
> And down the long melodious lane,
> Hand locked in hand, there passed the twain,
> As fair as any earth has found,
> Clad as kings' children are and crowned. (*CW* 3:164)

Then he acquiesces and blesses the couple:

> So mid sweet song and tabouring,
> And shouts amid the apple-grove,
> And soft caressing of his love,
> Began the new King Michael's reign. (*CW* 3:167)

It is begun with the insight provided by his pastoral education:

From point to point my life is brought
Through wonders till it comes to this;
And trouble cometh after bliss,
And I will bear all as I may,
And ever as day passeth day,
My life will hammer from the twain,
Forging a long enduring chain.　　　　(*CW* 3:161)

The story is one of Morris's most idyllic creations in both its form and content. Maurer comments: "His selection of incident is directed toward the characteristic effect in Morris's narrative verse, a series of framed tableaux which has often provoked the comparison of Morris's work in this *genre* to the weaving of tapestry." [27] It is true that this descriptive method serves to engage the reader on a visual sensuous level and that the sequence of idylls within an idyll very clearly embodies Morris's simple aesthetic. In this tale, however, it also reflects the epistemology of the hero, whose simplicity defeats the rational machinations of the king. Morris's method in this volume suggests that unconscious natural spontaneity is part of the necessary myth of the spring of man and the world. The Wanderers who listen, however, experience painful distance from the tales of the Golden Age. The last tale therefore creates a bridge between the innocence of the tales and experience of the listeners as it repeats the motifs of the earlier tales, especially the fallacies of the old order, the necessity of rebirth, and the educational value of nature.

Morris takes the tale of "The Proud King" from the *Gesta Romanorum*, where the story of Jovinian is treated in the bare moralizing style of the exemplum. The theme of both source and adaptation is loss of identity through pride, a subject Morris treats again in *A King's Lesson* (1886), a fable of the period of *John Ball* and *News from Nowhere*. Even at this early period, he transforms the focus from "notable humiliation" [28] to something of a sermon on self-discovery through proletarian simplicity. Elements added by Morris make the story an appropriate conclusion to the volume. The king's loss of clothes—and consequently identity—occurs on a May morning and in deep woods. Like the ruler of the second story, he is isolated to discover separation from humanity and natural process. Finding that "his rich attire" has been stolen, he curses and threatens:

> But little help his fury was to him,
> So lustily he 'gan to shout and cry;
> None answered: still the lazy chub did swim
> By inches 'gainst the stream; away did fly
> The small pied bird, but nathless stayed anigh,
> And o'er the stream still plied his fluttering trade,
> Of such a helpless man not much afraid.   (*CW* 3:244)

Again Morris expands the source and has his king make repeated attempts to regain recognition, employing the image of the roadside to emphasize Jovinian's quest, metaphorically an inner journey back to native simplicity. The king calls himself "Thomas the Pilgrim" (*CW* 3:252). His nakedness is compared to Adam's and the image of Noah's flood (*CW* 3:247, 248) suggests that his imminent fall can be averted only by return to his real sources of power. Unrecognized by his own men and his queen, he is given assistance by two "borel folk." Christopher a-Green gives him "milk from out a beechen cup" and a ride in his wagon (*CW* 3:252). Humbled by all lack of recognition, Jovinian seeks penance, but Morris changes the confessor of the source to a "hermit wise and old" who lives in "a lowly clay-build hovel" (*CW* 3:258). The king, clad finally in "rough gown and cord" and fed "scant food" (*CW* 3:261), is put on the hermit's ass to re-enter his kingdom with new humility. The discovery of his limitations is a spring rebirth, and the story is concluded by the recurrence of a "sweet May morning" thirty years later when Jovinian records his king's lesson, making of his own experience a tale to be repeated after his death.

The story of Jovinian admits the subjects of age and failure, but it does not change the tone of the spring tales. The volume seems the most purely pastoral of the entire work; yet its harmony is too simple, its innocence too unconscious to give it the resonance of mature pastoral vision. Its reception by the Wanderers reveals its limitations. They feel intensified "weight" of heart and separation from "the light of common day":

> For as a child's unmeasured joy brings pain
> Unto a grown man holding grief at bay,
> So the old fervent story of that day
> Brought pain half-sweet to these.   (*CW* 3:105)

The world of the stories presents a mythical phase of individual and cultural life that cannot be recovered. So limited that it excludes all conflict, this version of pastoral is close to the innocence of *Guenevere*, irrevocably divorced from experience. Yet the movement toward wiser innocence depends on the appeal and impossibility of this beginning.

chapter six
The Burning Days of Midsummer Suns: Volume ij

Than cōeth June & thā is the sōne hyest
ī his meridyornall he may assende no
hyeer in his stacyone his glemerrynge
goldene beames rypenethe the corne and
than . . . man . . . may assende no more
for than hathe nature gyven hym beauty
and strength at the full.

Kalendar of Shepherdes

NTRODUCING "The Love of Alcestis," an elder describes the tale as sad:

> Sad, though the life I tell you of passed by,
> Unstained by sordid strife or misery;
> Sad, because though a glorious end it tells,
> Yet on the glorious end of life it dwells,
> *And striving through all things to reach the best*
> *Upon no midway happiness will rest.*   (*CW* 4:88)

Striving for immortal perfection is the theme of summer, the phase of man's and civilization's cycle that is "the flower and fruit of mastery, with hope more than conscious enough." Moving away from the spring themes of the Golden Age, the "birth" when "hope [is] scarcely conscious of itself," [1] the second volume of tales, more than any other, utilizes the *mythos* of romance. The hero typically engages in the quest for an ideal state, aided by the gods and the frequent suspension of natural law. "Translated into dream terms," says Frye, "the quest-romance is the search of the libido or desiring self for a fulfilment that will deliver it from the anxieties of reality but will still retain that reality." [2]

In the romance the motive toward wish-fulfillment is released without check, asserting "mastery" of the impossible without critical acknowledgment of the mode's essential paradoxes: that the presence of heroic conflict and struggle, the *agon* of romance, contradicts the hero's dependence on exter-

nal forces; that the full realization of conscious will is countered by desire for its annihilation; that the assumed "return"
to society is prevented by experience in an otherworld,
whether it in fact destroys consciousness or unbearably
heightens it. While he treats his summer legends as romances,
Morris characteristically qualifies their idealistic attitudes
through a more realistic pastoral vein that gives him critical
access to their contradictions.

First, the dialectical form central to romance is modified
from heroic conflict between the hero and his enemy into a
format resembling pastoral debate, the use of the eclogue "as
an instrument for the clash of conflicting ideas, demonstrating
the weakness of one of them." [3] It is probably in the tradition
of medieval *débat*, influenced by Virgil, that Spenser uses his
summer eclogues to explore disparate points of view about
love, society, and responsibility. For example, his criticism of
"proude and ambitious Pastours" occurs in the July debate
between Thomalin and Morrell. Morris's transformation of
active quest into meditative dialectic is less conventional, although he again uses pastoral frames to distance, interrupt,
and criticize the heroic narrative. There is also a clear pattern
of "alternate song" in the pairing of complementary stories
for each month of summer.

A second concern of both romance and pastoral is the nature
and effects of love. While the romance is apt to make wooing
peripheral to dragon-slaying or a reward for heroic conquest,
Morris and the pastoralists make it central. In the pastoral
world, summer brings the heat of the sun and of love. The
wiser shepherds seek shelter for themselves and their sheep
"under midsummer suns. The burning days are coming in and
the buds already swelling on the tender shoots of the vine." [4]
But the love-sick shepherd, driven by passion beyond his control, wanders abroad to sing of his plight. As Gallus says,
"Omnia vincit Amor: et nos cedamus Amori" (Virgil x:69).
Several love-motifs of the pastoral illustrate some incipient
dangers only suggested in the romances.

The ardor is often attributed to external agents, especially Venus and Cupid, and it becomes an irrational force that drives its victim to restless despair, madness, or destruction. In many cases, though not all, the doomed quality of love results from the passion of a mortal shepherd for a god, goddess, or at least a person of different degree. The story of Hylas, related in Theocritus XIII and incorporated by Morris into the story of *Jason*, reverses the pattern to show the attraction of the immortal Nymphs to the young Argive, a tale prefaced by the poet's sober reminder: "From what God soever sprung, Nicias, Love was not, as we seem to think, born for us alone; nor first unto us of mortal flesh that cannot see the morrow, look things of beauty beautiful." [5] The story of Polyphemus, alluded to in Theocritus VI and developed in XI, combines the elements of external compulsion and the fateful passion for a person of differing degree. The love typically grows in proportion to rejection. Wounded by "the shaft of the great Cyprian," the old Cyclops yearns for fair Galatea. "His love was no matter of apples, neither, nor of rosebuds nor locks of hair, but a flat frenzy which recked nought of all else" (XI:10–11).

The result of frenzy is sometimes appeal to the gods for assistance, as in the case of Simanthea, the rejected heroine of Theocritus II (cf. Virgil VIII), who casts spells under moonlight to punish the lover who has abandoned her after capturing her heart. Recalling a previous tryst she says,

And no sooner was I ware of the light fall o's foot across my threshold,—
List, good Moon, where I learnt my loving—than I went cold as ice my body over, and the sweat dripped like dewdrops from my brow; aye, and for speaking I could not so much as the whimper of a child that calls on's mother in his sleep; for my fair flesh was gone all stiff and stark like a puppet's.
List, good Moon, where I learnt my loving. (II:103–10)

It is to counteract the burning effect of Venus and Cupid (ll. 130–34) that Simanthea invokes the paralyzing power of the moon, Diana's emblem, to lead her lover to a death (l. 162) which echoes her symbolic one. More typically, however, unrequited pastoral love effects alienation or death in the lover himself. It first separates him from nature and his fellow shepherds. Of Polyphemus the narrator says: "Time and again his sheep would leave the fresh green pasturage and come back unbidden to fold, while their master must peak and pine alone upon the wrack-strown shore a-singing all day long of Galatea, sick at heart" (Theocritus XI:12–14). Corydon, of Virgil's second eclogue, acknowledges his restless alienation: "This is the hour when even cattle seek the coolness of the shade; when even the green lizard lies hidden in the thorny brake; when Thestylis brews a fragrant soup of pounded garlic and wild-thyme for the reapers wearied by the scorching heat. Yet I am wandering in the paths that you [the beautiful Alexis] have trod, under the burning sun, while the orchards echo to the harsh cicadas' notes and mine" (II:8–13). Turning away to "hard life in the forest, where the wild beasts have their caves" (Virgil X:52–53), Gallus rejects his pastoral surroundings: "No; all is over. Tree-nymphs and poetry itself have ceased to please. Even you have failed, woodlands; away with you!" (X:62–63).

Its separating effects make love a disease (Theocritus XI:1–18; Virgil X:60–61). The medicine is music, which soothes Polyphemus who "got more comfort thereout than he could have had for any gold" (Theocritus XI:80–81), but song is also apt to intensify the sickness. If the singer has a modifying audience, introspective isolation is averted: Colin's emotionally complex despair in Spenser's sixth eclogue is balanced by Hobbinol's mundane simplicity. Without a human listener, the singing lover frequently exhibits extreme solipsism that produces the pastoral of the self. This lover, like Gallus, carves his love on trees for others to read. Or like Daphnis (Virgil V:43–44), he carves his own epitaph:

Countrymen, Daphnis is my name:
The very stars have heard my fame.
Here in the woods I lived and lie—
My flock was lovely: lovelier I.

The association of death, self-celebration, and carved images carries the cycle of alienation to completion, echoing the static imagery of Simanthea's spells and climaxing the implications of disease. The configuration also gives a poet like Morris a way of criticizing some of the central attitudes and symbols of romance.

A third interest of romance that is countered by pastoral criticism is wealth, especially the descent to an underworld and the discovery of buried treasure. The subject synthesizes the themes of love, self-interest, paralysis, and death. In the quest buried treasure is associated explicitly with material wealth and symbolically with power, wisdom, sexual fulfillment, and even immortality. After its discovery, a display of ingenuity, it must be wrested from its hiding place and its dragon guardian, a forceful act of an energetic hero. Such aggression is praised by the romancer, but it is condemned by the pastoral writer. Following Ruskin, Morris sees this kind of exploitation as the antithesis of natural earthly process; thus he describes it variously as vicious plundering or as death, the ultimate stasis. Morris's underworld is a Cave of Mammon whose seeker is motivated by greed or narcissism; or it is Hell, the unearthly Garden of Persephone. This pastoral evaluation of wealth is expanded in the stories of summer as Morris associates it, especially gold, with the paralysis of doomed love or the unnatural quest for immortality. In each case wealth is associated with carved images, gold, statues, or other static images.

If quest in Volume II can be reduced to a single theme, it is the paradox unconsciously implied by romance and explicated by the pastoral: the desperate attempt to avoid death and unhappiness, or to find love, immortality, or worldly wealth leads to an inversion of the romantic assumption of apotheosis. When the desiring self is unsuccessful, the anxieties of remembered reality are magnified while the reality itself is impossible to reattain. When the quest is successful, the teller, listener, or reader is blocked from the experience of the characters in a way that collapses the reality of the tale. The controlling imagery contrasts motion and stasis, attributing motion to pastoral, earthly process and stasis to the otherworld of romance.

"The Story of Cupid and Psyche" at first appears to be a spring tale revealing an innocent heroine whose quest for love is completed in marriage, "a wonderful new birth." But the marriage announces no human society; it is a union between mortal and immortal characters. Instead of reflecting the themes of the preceding volume, it points toward the otherworld of the summer volume, which concludes with a similar union in "Ogier the Dane." Both characters literally vanish from sight as they achieve the apotheosis of fictional experience. Besides introducing the thematic frame of the volume, the story initiates its dialectical format by developing the first complementary motifs of the summer tales—the fabulous terrain of romance, specifically the descent into the underworld, and the earthly landscape of the pastoral. Psyche is in addition Morris's first fully developed type of the radically innocent, earthly heroine, repeated in this volume in Alcestis and in subsequent volumes in Aslaug and Philonöe. The story thus curiously blends assertion and rejection of romance, achieving unity through the characterization of Psyche.

The external force typical of romance is apparent in the tale, especially its love quest. Psyche's exile is initiated by Venus; her love is the work of Cupid; and in her desperate quest she is both deterred and assisted by principal and minor deities as well as by nature. Yet she is consistently characterized as passive, earthly, and self-delighting, with "divine fresh singleness of heart" (*CW* 4:29). Viewed always in contrast to hostile society, her jealous sisters, her weak father, and vindictive Venus, she embodies the principles assigned to Michael in "The Man Born to Be King." Her innocence and passivity are virtues which tie her to earthly process, which protect her from the artificiality of the gardens of Venus and Persephone, and which reward her with unsought immortality. Informed of her imminent sacrifice at the beginning of the story, she is sad but resigned to "the woe the gods have dowered me" (*CW* 4:7). Discovered by Cupid, she converts his indifference by her beauty mirrored by nature—a harmonious configuration of sleeping girl, splashing fountain, and "all sweet sounds and scents" in "a fair green close, / Hedged round about with woodbine and red rose, / Within the flicker of a white-thorn shade" (*CW* 4:14). Rescued to his palace, she responds simply to its intricate otherworldly detail, a process conveyed by a series of sense verbs—*feel, smelt, touched* (*CW* 4:19). She wanders, "still noting everything" (*CW* 4:22), eats, bathes, and sleeps in mortal curiosity and weariness.[6]

Although Psyche is in many ways a pastoral heroine, the pastoral idea cannot be sustained within the powerful linear movement of quest-romance. The alternatives of the poet are detached pastoral contrast or synthesis. In this initial story of the solstice season, he chooses the latter, indulging the fantasy of "a fulfilment that will deliver [the desiring self] from the anxieties of reality but will still retain that reality."[7] Before the withdrawing narrator finally denies the reader access to the union, he allows its evolution, transforming pastoral mortality into romantic immortality. Love is idealized as the alchemy that alters mutability and material flux even while it depends upon them. The plot subjects Psyche to quest and temptation to measure and purify her love of mortal weakness and to heighten its strength; simultaneously, it reveals the feeling of the god who cannot weep. Since Cupid, already immortal and omniscient, cannot essentially change, it is Psyche who must. Her discoveries must reveal to her and to the gods that it is possible to retain *self* at the same time it is offered, selflessly, in "deathless love" to another. In short, Psyche must embody both her earthly vitality and Cupid's otherworldly immutability.

The various garden paradises of the story—Cupid's, Venus's, Persephone's—reveal and test potential in Psyche's
character. As a result, her quest unfolds a series of balances
that are resolved only momentarily at the tale's conclusion.
Cupid's garden appropriately represents a mean between the
other two, which lack its ambiguity. His palace garden, "like
a paradise" (*CW* 4:18), is associated with artifice. It is "void of
mankind," and "all amidst the trees / Were strange-wrought
founts and wondrous images" (*CW* 4:18). Yet the garden also
suggests process. Nature is useful as well as decorative; there
are images of harmony to balance those of isolation and stasis:

> And all about were dotted leafy trees,
> The elm for shade, the linden for the bees,
> The noble oak, long ready for the steel
> Which in that place it had no fear to feel;
> The pomegranate, the apple, and the pear,
> That fruit and flowers at once made shift to bear,
> Not yet decayed therefor; and in them hung
> Bright birds that elsewhere sing not, but here sung
> As sweetly as the small brown nightingales
> Within the wooded, deep Laconian vales.   (*CW* 4:17)

The garden's ambiguity thus reflects the antithetical characters of Psyche and Cupid, natural and immortal, and suggests
their potential harmony. Inside Cupid's palace, we are also
aware of the potential barriers to its realization. The "wonders
of the place" include "silver mirrors" that reflect the lonely
mortal figure and

> a chamber cool
> Paved cunningly in manner of a pool,
> Where red fish seemed to swim through floating weed.
> (*CW* 4:19)

Again the mirror image occurs when "the glassy floor" gives
back Psyche's face. Artifice, illusion, and stasis are here linked
to suggest the possibility of narcissism. In Psyche its form is

not self-celebration but self-destruction, a temptation developed in her three suicide attempts after her expulsion from the garden. It stems from separation from kind within the garden and separation from Cupid without.

The decisive dream which Venus induces appeals to Psyche's love for kind, her aging father; but its results, the arrival and temptation of her greedy sisters, are directly related to the deadly stasis represented by Venus herself and by the acquisitive motive Cupid has warned against:

> And thou—beware—for, fresh and good and true,
> Thou knowest not what worldly hearts may do,
> Or what a curse gold is unto the earth.   (*CW* 4:26)

These lines recall Cupid's description of ideal love as antithetical to greed, associated with static images:

> Come then, beloved one, for such as thee
> Love loveth, and their hearts he knoweth well,
> Who hoard their moments of felicity,
> As misers hoard the medals that they tell,
> Lest on the earth but paupers they should dwell:
> "We hide our love to bless another day;
> The world is hard, youth passes quick," they say.
> (*CW* 4:21–22)

Thus stasis is linked variously with the positive immutability of love (Cupid and Cupid's palace) and the negative qualities of greed and death. Psyche's quest must deny the negative impulses and affirm the positive. She must prove her faith in things unseen while she preserves her vital mortality.

The Venus garden is chanced upon when Psyche "her back upon the world [has] turned" (*CW* 4:42). Thus it represents a temptation to self-annihilation, already once countered by nature when the "kind river" denies her attempt to die and casts her ashore near "Shepherd Pan," who reprimands her "hurrying to the feeble Shade" (*CW* 4:41). Seeking "deathless love" she is oblivious to human types—the huntsman, shepherd, and soldier (*CW* 4:42–43)—and even to familiar natural detail (*CW* 4:40–41, 45). Her plea for help rejected by Ceres, she arrives "wearily" (*CW* 4:48) in Venus's garden where she is attracted to its peace and the goddess's apparent kindness but where "her heart" recovers strength to warn her through consciousness of "small flowers as red as blood," "restless sparrows," and all the paralyzing artifice of the place (*CW* 4:48). Again the garden is evaluated through Psyche's response: her senses are confused and dulled, her fear is killed, she seems to lose memory of good or evil; her vision is "dizzied," and she feels "half-dead" (*CW* 4:48–49). The garden's illusion, a kind of living death, is penetrated by Psyche, but she lacks strength to prevail even though she can endure.

The tests which follow are designed to sustain Psyche's misery and to tempt her to self-destruction. Yet she is saved by ants, "the kingless folk" (*CW* 4:55); by a friendly reed, "soother of the loving hearts that bleed" (*CW* 4:57); an eagle (*CW* 4:59); and by the ghost of a dead queen (*CW* 4:62–64).[8] The descent to the underworld, the climactic task, reveals a setting that repeats the deadly implications of the Venus garden. Because her first longing for death called for "whatsoever dark place dwell the dead" (*CW* 4:41), the world of Persephone is the ultimate test of her will to live and pursue mortal vitality. The dark "changeless place" (*CW* 4:64) intensifies many of the images of stasis heretofore introduced. Death is of course prominent, linked with royalty and wealth in this kingdom where "on a throne, the Queen of all the dead" sits "with gold-embracèd head, / in royal raiment, beautiful, and pale" (*CW* 4:67). In addition there are negative mirrors, "still pools" whose "dull surface cast no image back" (*CW* 4:64), and the prevailing notion of sleep, significantly enclosed in the golden casket which Psyche brings to be filled. Psyche saves herself by isolation, refusing to touch all the artifice "strange of shape and of strange-blended hues." She refuses underworld cuisine and eats "the food that mortals eat" (*CW* 4:67). When she leaves with the casket, she at last submits to mortal weariness, curiosity, and death-wish; but she opens the casket full of "deadly sleep" having proven herself to both Venus and Cupid, who rescues her and wins her immortality. The darker side of immortality is shadowed for a moment in the static imagery of her sleep (*CW* 4:69). It is a concept developed in succeeding stories. Here, however, the deus ex machina conclusion reveals a brighter glimpse of "fate" and the mysterious world beyond: self-delighting mortality seems simply to be granted continuation, appropriately at the moment when selfhood is paradoxically fulfilled and sacrificed.

While the apotheosis of quest-romance structurally displaces the unresolved tendency of idyll, the story does generate distinctly pastoral feeling, partly through its descriptive style but primarily through a quest that is essentially nonaggressive. Psyche's quest, much like Endymion's, shows a passive character, of properly established natural sympathies, responding to the proper agents of the otherworld and rejecting the others. Morris, bound more to his sources, fails to complete Keats's circle which finally locates the ideal in the natural. Part of the reason, of course, is that Morris consistently withholds personal vision from the stories, preferring to entertain the limiting and fragmenting perspective of second-hand narration. Futhermore, no single story of the collection is allowed to resolve the tensions of its particular context. In this case the tensions themselves are characteristically a result of organizational hindsight, since the Psyche story, one of Morris's first compositions for the *Earthly Paradise*, assumed its initial position in Volume II after the composition of other tales, including "The Writing on the Image." The published arrangement reveals the appropriateness of their juxtaposition.

Following the elaborate narrative of Psyche, "The Writing on the Image" is a powerful footnote. The oldest version of the tale as Morris might have known it was in William of Malmesbury's *De Gestis Regum Anglorum*, where an erring Pope, accompanied by a servant, uses magic to open the ground and explore a mysterious golden palace. In this early version the servant shoots the carbuncle and plunges the cavern in darkness, but with the aid of a lantern both master and servant escape, "their boundless avarice unsatiated." [9] Morris, however, seems more directly guided by the treatment of the tale in Brunet's *Gesta Romanorum*, where the moral is retained but the plot simplified to relate the death of a lone clerk in the underground setting.

The tale's stark force is preserved in its recounting by Laurence the Swabian priest, whose four assigned tales [10] reflect his ironic preoccupation with man's darker side, especially his pride and failure. Maurer, who emphasizes Morris's mutability theme, says: "The allegory . . . of the *Gesta* is gone. There is no punishment here of the cardinal sin of avarice, but rather the melancholy example of the shortness of life, the vanity of human wishes and the mockery of fate." [11] While it is undeniable that Morris expands the thematic center of the tale, it is also true that he retains its suggestion of avarice, employing static imagery in a way that comments on the themes of Psyche and succeeding stories.

The dialectical contrasts with "Psyche" arise from negative echoes of character and setting. The innocent, passive character of Psyche is countered by the aggressive drive of the unnamed scholar of "much strange lore" (*CW* 4:77). She seeks the fellowship of love and harmony with earthly process. He delves beneath the earth for knowledge, wealth, and immortality which will give him singular power. Because Psyche's primary resources are internal and self-delighting, she wins the sympathies of the gods; the scholar, whose limited bookish wisdom forces him to seek external power, ultimately defies fate and precipitates self-destruction. In some ways the two tales contrast innocence and analytic experience, criticizing the cold pursuit of rational control in a romantic fashion. The use of similar settings, however, multiplies possibilities of meaning.

Following the classical treatment of the palace of Persephone, the underworld cavern recalls its suggestions, but it introduces nonclassical ones as well. When the tale is told, the listeners respond variously to this second descent into the earth. First, the hero is associated with other

> treasure-seekers balked,
> And shame and loss for men insatiate stored,
> Nitocris' tomb, the Niblungs' fatal hoard,
> The serpent-guarded treasures of the dead.   (*CW* 4:85)

The Christian condemnation of avarice is thus expanded into the Germanic fear of buried treasure and its implication that wealth is sacred to the memory of its first and only rightful owners. The mysterious symbol, most familiar in *Beowulf*, is therefore elegiac in recalling dead heroes and the brevity of fame as well as life. This second consideration leads to a third meditative topic, the sacredness of the earth itself as man's appropriate setting and as object of stewardship, not exploitation:

> Strange hopes and fears for what shall be but nought
> To dead men! better it would be to give
> What things they may, while on the earth they live,
> Unto the earth, and from the bounteous earth
> To take their pay of sorrow or of mirth,
> Hatred or love, and get them on their way;
> And let the teeming earth fresh troubles make
> For other men, and ever for their sake
> Use what they left, when they are gone from it.
> (*CW* 4:85–86)

The acquisitive theme is the basis for the others. It is associated with the simple desire for wealth but more prominently with belief in the magical power of human consciousness to convert wish into reality. The desires are linked in the Prologue's reference to the search for "the stone . . . whereby base metal into gold is brought" (*CW* 3:7). It is thus possible to see the underworld journey as a descent into self, an idea already suggested by Psyche's quest for complete identity.

Identity here is first associated with the scholar's sorcery—an unnatural art, the narrator implies. It draws him away from society, at midnight, to delve with pickaxe and shovel for a goal he cannot initially describe. The first discovery, "some metal thing. . . a brazen ring" (CW 4:78), crystallizes his longings, which are as essentially static as the series of images that follow. Everything is "wrought all curiously" (CW 4:78) to suggest both value and artifice. He now anticipates "the treasures of a king to see" or the creation of "some sweet paradise" as enervating as a Venus garden:

> And if my soul I may not save
> In heaven, yet here in all men's eyes
> Will I make some sweet paradise,
> With marble cloisters, and with trees
> And bubbling wells and fantasies,
> And things all men deem strange and rare,
> And crowds of women kind and fair,
> That I may see, if so I please,
> Laid on the flowers, or mid the trees
> With half-clad bodies wandering.
> There, dwelling happier than the King,
> What lovely days may yet be mine!   (CW 4:79)

The function of illusion, a sorcerer's art, is distinguished from vision of the sort that literally keeps Psyche awake to reality. Seeing for the scholar is voyeurism, an act that converts life into object. It is therefore ironically significant that his final discovery of the inner chamber, "the goodly hall hung round with gold," presents a static tableau mocking and revealing his aspirations:

> He raised the cloth and entered in
> In hope that happy life to win,
> And drawing higher did behold
> That these were bodies dead and cold
> Attired in full royal guise,
> And wrought by art in such a wise

> That living they all seemed to be,
> Whose very eyes he well could see,
> That now beheld not foul or fair,
> Shining as though alive they were.   (*CW* 4:80–81)

A terrible echo of Persephone's hall, the scene fuses wealth, artifice, and death—three forms of stasis that in both stories have causal links.

Fear coexists with the desire "to know / What all these marvellous matters meant" (*CW* 4:82). It is greed that eases the scholar's fear, and Morris makes it even clearer than the *Gesta* that greed also precipitates death. Morris has the mysterious archer shoot the carbuncle as the scholar reaches for an especially "wonderful green stone" (*CW* 4:83). It is at once the magic stone of the Prologue and "that fatal stone" (*CW* 4:84) that grants knowledge of death's mysteries.

Full knowledge or self-discovery is thus equated with darkness and the ironic metamorphosis of the scholar into the ultimate stasis he has coveted. Psyche's transformation among a heavenly company was accompanied by dazzling light and birth of new feeling. Imprisoned in darkness with the royal dead, the scholar experiences a brief flash of memory before consciousness is annihilated: "And midst the marvels of that hall / This Scholar found the end of all" (*CW* 4:84).

The brief tale provides a good example of the prismatic effects of archetypal story, choice of narrator, structural location, and audience response. The listeners' reactions clearly depends on the other elements even as it reflects their own preoccupation with death. The tale is wisely given to Laurence, whose cynicism seems channeled through the short tetrameter lines and simple syntax, a contrast to the slow enumerative style of Psyche. His consciousness also dominates the frame, which focuses the listeners' attention on the wooden image that gives the tale its title. Recognized and respected by the simple folk as a guidepost to forbidden mysteries, it is left to endure the natural elements, "the hot sun and summer air, / The snow-drift and the driving rain" (*CW* 4:92), the same forces that set it back in place after the scholar's violation. Granted, the folk are superstitious enough to replace the wood with a statue of Jove, but they escape Laurence's sarcastic criticism of "some Lord or other" who "being in need, / Took every ounce of gold away" (*CW* 4:103). Finally, the brevity of life is an important topic, but it is undeniable that Laurence—and likely the poet—is pleased to correlate inevitable death with inevitable avarice, two versions of stasis that do not affect nature's eternal recurrences.

The June and July tales are two pairs of idylls that repeat the quest theme while they control its romantic fulfillment. Instead of excluding the reader from the vision of immortality (as Psyche does), they suggest its alienating force. In almost every case, the sought immortality is some form of love, which is increasingly revealed to be an ironic fulfillment of Cupid's promise to Psyche of "The glory and the joy unspeakable / Wherein the Treasure of the World shall dwell" (*CW* 4:24). Treasure, stone and stasis, already associated with death and greed, are now overtly linked with love. Separation is of course experienced between lovers, but it is also universalized as cultural alienation because three of the four heroes are kings.

The June tales, "The Love of Alcestis" and "The Lady of the Land," link love with rescue, contrasting Alcestis' selfless rescue of Admetus from death with the selfish failure of an Italian mariner to save the Lady of the Land from immortality. Both tales again posit the value of mortal process through female characters and associate weakness with heroes whose fear of death is akin to desire for wealth. Several elements, besides character contrast, link the two tales. Most important perhaps to the four tales of mid-summer is the characteristic use of a descriptive frame to establish the earthly norm from which the heroes wander in search of immortality. In the more complex Alcestis, however, Morris introduces a mysterious external agent—Apollo—who invites comparison with the

seer of "The Man Born to be King" (Vol. i), Guest the Wise
in "Gudrun" (Vol. iii), Nereus in "The Golden Apples" (Vol.
iv), and even Cupid in this volume. Two of these figures are
mortal and three are immortal, but all share a prophetic role
and a philosophical distance that give them narrative overview
even though none of the stories are shaped from their perspectives. The agent becomes a pastoral mediator whose insight
is divorced from judgment. In the cases of Cupid, Nereus, and
Apollo, this quality of nondirective insight is a function of
immortality, a state which dissociates vision from mortal limitations and actions. It is familiar even in the mortal character
of Sophocles' Teiresias, who perceives Apollo's oracle but
leaves others to act on his revelations. In the play, as here,
Apollo is associated with total insight that transcends individual human suffering or pleasure. His eyes cannot weep
(*CW* 4:112). Cupid, though a lesser and more limited deity,
shares this immortal quality.

In "Alcestis" a pastoral role is also suggested by Apollo's
disguise as a shepherd. While his homespun coat and herds-
man's staff and horn serve to hide his identity as a god, they
also direct our attention to revelations that are particularly
pastoral. First, the immortal disengagement of the god is channeled through the familiar detachment of the *fortunate senex*
(Virgil i) whose simple visions emerge in music. With his bow
and lyre, Apollo is something of an idle singer who leaves
evaluation to his audience (*CW* 4:114). He arrives at Admetus'
prime to offer choice without the limitation of advice. Second,
the choices are directly related to the conflict of aspiration and
mortal acquiescence. The one song shared with the reader
foreshadows Admetus' conflict. A shepherd's song with a
god's perspective, it is apologetically "translated" by the tale's
narrator, whose own description of the harmonious setting
must imply what he cannot perfectly repeat. The "new herds-
man" lay

> Close by the white sands of a little bay
> The teeming ripple of Boebeis lapped;

There he in cloak of white-wooled sheepskin wrapped
Against the cold dew, free from trouble sang,
The while the heifers' bells about him rang
And mingled with the sweet soft-throated birds
And bright fresh ripple: listen then, these words
Will tell the tale of his felicity,
Halting and void of music though they be.

Song

O dwellers on the lovely earth,
Why will ye break your rest and mirth
To weary us with fruitless prayer;
Why will ye toil and take such care
For children's children yet unborn,
And garner store of strife and scorn
To gain a scarce-remembered name,
Cumbered with lies and soiled with shame?
And if the Gods care not for you,
What is this folly ye must do
To win some mortal's feeble heart?
O fools! when each man plays his part,
And heeds his fellow little more
Than these blue waves that kiss the shore
Take heed of how the daisies grow.
O fools! and if ye could but know
How fair a world to you is given.   (*CW* 4:94–95)

This song, Morris's invention, gives direction to the long first
half of the story—Admetus' quest, for Morris's own "translation" of Alcestis' sacrifice requires a context that points up its
depth. A gift of love through self-annihilation, it comprises a
separate idyll within the story of her husband's search for
self-fulfillment. Ultimately, the story of Alcestis is dialectical
commentary on the central story of Admetus. In this light,
Apollo's song states the antithesis of character. It also repeats
the suggestions of Morris's pastoral frame which asserts at
beginning and end the bounty, harmony, and peace of the
kingdom of Thessaly—enough, the poet implies, to satisfy and
engage any man. Admetus, a king of the "old simple days,"

rules in a pastoral setting, "Midst sunny grass-clad meads that
slop adown / To lake Boebeis" (*CW* 4:89):

> this King Admetus sat
> Among his people, wearied in such wise
> By hopeful toil as makes a paradise
> Of the rich earth; for light and far away
> Seemed all the labour of the coming day,
> And no man wished for more than then he had,
> Nor with another's mourning was made glad.
> (*CW* 4:89–90)

Admetus' quest begins when he returns, a victim of love,
from Iolchus. He wanders "in the fresh and blossom-scented
air" at dawn:

> Yet by his troubled face set little store
> By all the songs of birds and scent of flowers;
> Yea, rather unto him the fragrant hours
> Were grown but dull and empty of delight.   (*CW* 4:94)

The cause of this alienation is revealed in his interpretation
of the events in Iolchus. He describes love at first sight, but
his rhetoric betrays his early identification of love with immortality and of Alcestis herself with a paradisal prize. His
picture of Alcestis employs the negative hyperbole of paradise
descriptions [12] and metaphors of wealth (*CW* 4:96–97). His own
response of "Kindness, and hot desire, and rage, and bliss, /
None first a moment" he interprets as love, but he notes that
he felt "now half a God" and "as God-possessed" (*CW* 4:97)
as he claimed the power to free Alcestis from Diana's curse.
    Apollo's assistance, though freely granted, should not be
interpreted as intervention. It merely extends the possibilities
of Admetus' own choice, albeit without his full realization of
its irreversible direction. The ivory chariot and mysterious
beasts are a fitting symbol for Admetus' aspiration. Taking his
bride away he anticipates "at least one godlike hour" (*CW*
4:103); and all mortal process seems held in aesthetic stasis:

Grief seemed a play forgot, a pageant vain,
A picture painted, who knows where or when,
With soulless images of restless men;
For every thought but love was now gone by,
And they forgot that they should ever die.   (*CW* 4:106)

Although the chariot must be returned to Apollo, its supernatural power has produced lingering effects in Admetus.
Having secured his bride and prize, he ignores the larger patterns of necessity and tries to claim her before proper settlement with Artemis. The goddess's emanation as a serpent,
while on one level associated with sexual tabu and thus with
female character, is also an interesting reflection of the darker
side of Admetus' quest. The "dreadful coil," which recurs in
many of the stories, guards the treasure that Admetus unconsciously equates with his bride. The serpent's appearance is
also directly effected by Admetus, momentarily unaware that
his impetuosity endangers Alcestis, who wishes *him* away:

O get thee hence; alas, I cannot flee!
They coil about me now, my lips to kiss.
O love, why hast thou brought me unto this?

The force of this single scene of horror is its glimpse of the
mysteries of the unseen immortal world that attracts Admetus. Like Milton's hell or the wilderness of *Beowulf*, the
world just beyond the frontiers of imagination reveals multiple chaos from a human perspective. In the pastoral romance,
it can mirror human potential as well. Consciousness is capable of ordering and simplifying it; aspiration releases it. Love,
as it is represented by Alcestis, is an ordering relationship.
Admetus confuses love with possession of ultimate knowledge
and transforms its ordering potential into a barrier between
the two lovers, one isolated in unselfish simplicity and the
other isolated in irreversible longing for total experience.

The momentary association of Admetus and the serpent
foreshadows the conclusion of the story, where again Alcestis

must be "sacrificed" to fulfill Admetus' will. This final phase
of the tale is set within a second frame reiterating Admetus'
earthly bounty. Apollo has revealed himself and departed,
leaving the shafts to offer final choice. With his revelation, the
god offers advice for the only time:

> And now my servitude with thee is done,
> And I shall leave thee toiling on thine earth,
> This handful, that within its little girth
> Holds that which moves you so, O men that die;
> Behold, to-day thou hast felicity,
> But the times change, and I can see a day
> When all thine happiness shall fade away;
> And yet be merry, strive not with the end,
> Thou canst not change it.   (*CW* 4:112–13)

The idyllic frame of the second part of the story offers
extensive evidence of Admetus' felicity. His marriage to Alcestis seems an emblem of a good society. The narrator extols the
king's virtues and blessings: a happy man, he does not search
for fame; he saves the earth from war, spoil, corruption, and
idleness. "Honour and love, plénty and peace, he had" (*CW*
4:116). The narrator summarizes:

> In all things grew his wisdom and his wealth,
> And folk beholding the fair state and health
> Wherein his land was, said that now at last
> A fragment of the Golden Age was cast
> Over the place, for there was no debate,
> And men forgot the very name of hate. (*CW* 4:115–16)

The tale then distinguishes between ordinary and ultimate
aspiration. Admetus, certainly in many ways a sympathetic
character, lacks the petty desire of the scholar in the "Image."
His deep desire is to conquer death, to gain entrance to Apollo's world. He neither dreads death nor forgets it; "Rather
before him did a vague hope gleam" (*CW* 4:116) with the memory of Apollo's intimation of final assistance. Literally facing

death, all fades but his loneliness. He feels separated from
Alcestis and bound to the old longing for eternal life: "O Thou
who madest me, / The only thing on earth alike to thee, / Why
must I be unlike to thee in this?" (*CW* 4:118). The final appearance of Apollo, again in shepherd's attire, is before the joint
audience of Admetus and Alcestis, who both hear the decree
that life requires life—or put another way, that one life requires another death. Alcestis' decision shows her willingness
to face alone what Admetus cannot; but close to bitterness, she
also states what the story has implied about her position in
Admetus' life—a form of treasure:

> Alcestis! O Alcestis, hadst thou known
> That thou one day shouldst thus be left alone,
> How hadst thou borne a living soul to love!
> Hadst thou not rather lifted hands to Jove,
> To turn thine heart to stone, thy front to brass,
> That through this wondrous world thy soul might pass,
> Well pleased and careless, as Diana goes
> Through the thick woods.   (*CW* 4:122)

Her literal metamorphosis into cold stasis parallels Admetus'
more terrifying change into an eternal mortal (*CW* 4:123). He
has now attained the state of the gods who cannot weep even
though he experiences traces of human feeling.

The tale might well have taken the shape of romance, celebrating as "Psyche" does the victory of the hero over the
limitations of the flesh. Admetus' stewardship of the earth
stands him in good stead for reward in an unearthly paradise.
Yet the story operates to qualify his success. Alcestis, in narrative emphasis little more than an instrument of contrast, receives the final sympathy of the narrator, who fuses her life-
principles with the idyllic frame that defines natural and
human reality. She finally becomes the symbol of the *earthly*
paradise of Thessaly, where immortal Admetus is forgotten
as the world grows old and men

> gather unseen harm and discontent,
> Along with all the alien merchandise
> That rich folk need, too restless to be wise.   (*CW* 4:89)

Human memory, however, preserves the story of Alcestis, whatever men "are dwelling now on that green spot." Her "fame / Grew greater . . . / Lived, in the hearts of far-off men enshrined" (*CW* 4:124). Apollo's role is also recalled by the frame. His capacity of vision identifies fate with total insight. The narrator's more limited vision identifies human insight with temporal and aesthetic distance. The construct of tale is finally associated with the projected overview of its supernatural agents. The shaping power is memory: "The gods at least remember what is done."

"The Lady of the Land," based on a single episode, seems at first to expand its counterpart in "Alcestis," the scene on the wedding night where Diana's emanation takes similar form and Admetus must perform rituals to release his bride. In this sense, Admetus and the Italian knight-mariner are parallel examples of successful and unsuccessful quest. The mariner's failure is related to acquisitive instincts that intensify Admetus' weaknesses. An adventurer by nature, he is drawn to the isolated spot

> with a heart that burned
> To know the most of what might there be learned,
> And hoping somewhat too, amid his fear,
> To light on such things as all men hold dear. (*CW* 4:128)

The underground palace, also a version of the two preceding underworld settings, offers the illusion of life to veil its death:

> It seemed that time had passed on otherwhere,
> Nor laid a finger on this hidden place,
> Rich with the wealth of some forgotten race. (*CW* 4:130)

Its perfect stasis, which produces "in his heart a longing for some bliss, / Whereof the hard and changing world knows

nought," is linked in his consciousness with the incredible
wealth on every hand, "the glory of great heaps of gold" (*CW*
4:131). When the Lady of the Land is finally discovered and
presented through his perspective in a lengthy tableau, she
embodies both the wealth and stasis which dominate his im-
pressions. Surrounded by precious stones, she appears to be
a statue with golden hair. For a long time motionless, she
seems to be asleep.

The treatment of the Lady herself, however, shifts the dialectical relationship of the two tales. Her situation extends the
implications of the immortal state Admetus attained and reveals the dark, heretofore hidden side of eternal life in death.
Desiring rescue into mortality, she requires a "saviour" (*CW*
4:134) like Alcestis, whose simple love and courage can effect
"natural magic" to restore natural form. Ultimately then, the
Lady is compared to Admetus and the mariner to Alcestis.

The Lady is the lone survivor of another age, spellbound
for four hundred years (*CW* 4:138). Her account of her doom
gains sympathy and authenticity from that fact and from her
own interpretation of her fate. That she is the victim of a tabu
is less important here than her original motives that precipitated the curse—human longing for love—and her desire now
for release from the static isolation of immortality:

> Ah! with what joy then shall I see again
> The sunlight on the green grass and the trees,
> And hear the clatter of the summer rain,
> And see the joyous folk beyond the seas.
> Ah, me! to hold my child upon my knees
> After the weeping of unkindly tears
> And all the wrongs of these four hundred years.
>
> (*CW* 4:138)

It is not her story of fate that frightens the mariner, who
is in fact compelled by its mystery, challenge, and promise of
a "prize" (*CW* 4:137). It is the purely physical horror of viewing the Lady's imposed form that changes him to a trembling

man who "Ran swiftly, with a white and ghastly face" (*CW* 4:141). Finally he dies, the effect of internal turbulence the narrator can only guess to be shame and nightmare of the supernatural metamorphosis he has witnessed (*CW* 4:141). Buried at Byzantium, "between two blossoming pomegranate trees," he ironically and unhappily achieves what he has failed to give the Lady of the Land. It is clear that being "maddened with love" (*CW* 4:137) is not enough to effect rescue, which requires more fortitude and less narcissism.

We might note several directions of the volume to this point. First, there is the obvious concern with human mastery or self-assertion. Certainly it is compatible with the linear drive of romance and its heroes. Within the work as a whole, the poet acknowledges action as human necessity. It is the concept of goal that poses the dilemma. Romance not only locates the ideal in an otherworld but grants the hero mastery by quest. Romance, especially the nineteenth-century variety, also recognizes human consciousness as the means of mastery. Equating "romance" and "romantic" in this sense, we might recall T. E. Hulme's distinction between romanticism and classicism: "Put shortly, these are the two views, then. One, that man is intrinsically good, spoilt by circumstance; and the other that he is intrinsically limited, but disciplined by order and tradition to something fairly decent. To the one party man's nature is like a well, to the other a bucket. The view which regards man as a well, a reservoir full of possibilities, I call the romantic; the one which regards him as a very finite and fixed creature, I call the classical." [13] Morris's proximity to the latter notion is especially clear in this volume. He seems to contrast ultimate control or mastery with order—in the sense of recognition of bounds. The characters who exceed the bounds find immortality to be a form of paralysis. Part of the implication is that "mastery" is often a kind of possession or an attempt to separate oneself from society. Put more strongly, man appears to be incapable of asserting mastery in more ideal terms. While he feels that he lives on two levels, only the earthly, mortal one is accessible to his order. Man's finest hour is earthly order of the sort that Admetus achieves in Thessaly. It is clearly pastoral in the sense of contained vitality. The kingdom is simultaneously organic, temporal, and structured. In the romance, if love is the goal, it too appears to be either drive or object, two forms of external meaning that prevent its incorporation into mortal and temporal kinesis. It either remains inaccessible or becomes overwhelming to consciousness. Thus all the forms of the "ideal" are associated with stasis, a state of being which separates or is separate from the hero. Pastoral stasis is a containing order; eternal stasis, or its counterpart, chaos, is an absolute.

Second, there is the matter of perspective in the volume. Bush has remarked that even in the most supernatural stories, Morris "changes some of [the otherworld's] more naive manifestations." [14] He always acknowledges man's interest in the unseen, in the larger patterns of "fate," but he also recognizes the cloudiness of the otherworld, sometimes suggesting that it is imaginary. He is interested in human response, and all the stories of this volume—in fact of all four volumes—approach the otherworld, immortality, or the ideal from the limited perspective of mortal vision. Thus vision itself becomes a way of ordering experience, whether it involves distance or immersion. The Alcestis story even suggests that what we call fate is what we might also imagine to be total vision.

Finally, some of the structural rhythms derive from the rhythms of perspective. "The Lady of the Land," a medieval tale from the *Voyage and Travel* of Mandeville, confirms a fairly consistent pattern in the larger work: that the nonclassical tales offer a darker and often closer view of life than their classical counterparts. "Ogier" is an exception in this volume, but the pattern becomes overtly thematic in the final volumes. Although the style is fancifully decorative, the tale of the Lady operates on a realistic level that tempers supernatural actions with a human perspective. Both temporal and spatial setting are vague but accessible. We are given to feel that the time of the story is closer to the medieval present of the framework than some of the others. There is an initial suggestion of "modern" corruption, a suggestion of other stories as well, and the castle itself is a ruined and vandalized paradise of another age. The effect of this painterly shift of perspective is both spatial and temporal, producing varying degrees of aesthetic participation and recalling the idea of historical change, especially the movement toward complexity and economic corruption. The framing structure of each story works similarly within the individual tale.

The tales of July, "The Son of Croesus" and "The Watching of the Falcon," do little to alter or elaborate the concerns of the volume; rather they reiterate the topics already introduced: fear of death, pursuit of immortality, desperate love, and avarice. Two attempts to avert death through love make the tales complementary versions of quest as escape.

King Croesus tries to save his son by isolation when he dreams that he is to be killed by an iron weapon. The son, unafraid, is eager for earthly play, heroic deeds, and natural life. It is finally in a boar hunt deep in the woods that he is accidentally slain by his closest friend, Adrastus, who sacrifices his own life as a token of fidelity. The story's focus, however, is Croesus. Characterized by his wealth, he hoards his "great heaps of gold" and his son's life alike. In his "golden hall" he seeks to buy protection for Atys from the gods (*CW* 4:147); and ironically, the young Adrastus, the potential slayer he befriends, is grandson of Midas, "rich enow / In corn and cattle, golden cup and ring" (*CW* 4:148). The story is given a typically medieval interpretation by the listeners as a tale of fortune, of the fall of great men; but they also give its theme of wealth an interesting assessment:

> Purblind are most of folk,
> The happy are the masters of the earth
> Which ever give small heed to hapless worth;
> So goes the world, and this we needs must bear
> Like eld and death: yet there were some men there

> Who drank in silence to the memory
> Of those who failed on earth great men to be,
> Though better than the men who won the crown.
>
> (*CW* 4:159)

"The Watching of the Falcon" is a deeper exploration of consciousness by the Swabian Laurence, who links the questing king's "wilfulness and sin" with the tradition of "searchers for fine stones and gold" (*CW* 4:160). He also frames the king's encounter with the fairy lady with another outspoken introduction. It is a vision of the land that the king abandons in his quest:

> For it is fair as any land:
> There hath the reaper a full hand,
> While in the orchard hangs aloft
> The purple fig, a-growing soft;
> And fair the trellised vine-bunches
> Are swung across the high elm-trees;
> And in the rivers great fish play,
> While over them pass day by day
> The laden barges to their place.
> There maids are straight and fair of face,
> And men are stout for husbandry,
> And all is well as it can be
> Upon this earth where all has end.

Laurence interprets death as a blessing because it interrupts human weakness as well as life:

> That envy, hatred and hot love,
> Knowledge with hunger by his side,
> And avarice and deadly pride,
> There may have end like everything
> Both to the shepherd and the king:
> Lest this green earth become but hell
> If folk for ever there should dwell.   (*CW* 4:161–62)

The Swabian's point, which he does not hesitate to state, is that this land appreciates the blessings of neither life nor death. People teem with restlessness; the king is their representative type. Supernatural temptation is represented by the immortal lady. She links the themes of immortality and love, impossible alchemy, through her total vision and permanence which make her incapable of experiencing love, capable only of inducing it. Her effect on the king, who attempts to return to society, renders him incapable of continuing temporal happiness or success. The unearthly paradise (*CW* 4:166–67), the promise of mastery and bliss (*CW* 4:168), the lady's cold and golden perfection (*CW* 4:172), and her Blakean warning of the destructive quality of illusion (*CW* 4:174) all summarize the tropes of the volume and prophesy the king's shameful and tormented death. It is a pattern summarized first through the lady:

> Better it were that men should live
> As beasts and take what earth can give,
> The air, the warm sun and the grass,
> Until unto the earth they pass,
> And gain perchance nought worse than rest,
> Than that not knowing what is best
> For sons of men, they needs must thirst
> For what shall make their lives accurst.   (*CW* 4:173)

Then it is summarized by Laurence as he concludes:

> And at this day all things are so
> As first I said; a land it is
> Where men may dwell in rest and bliss
> If so they will—Who yet will not,
> Because their hasty hearts are hot
> With foolish hate and longing vain,
> The sire and dam of grief and pain.   (*CW* 4:185)

For all their apparent similarity, these two voices express two extreme views of man's condition. One reduces him to an animal; the other criticizes his aspiration. Both are cynical, and neither presents a synthetic view of the dilemma of the story. As curious an example of the form as it is, the tale is a typical idyll that presents unresolved tensions.

The volume concludes with a pair of quests which echo Psyche's success and combine with the opening tale to seal off the volume from ordinary reality. All three narrators withdraw apologetically, like a pastoral poet from his idyll, subtly bringing down night with "dim moon" and "fleecy cloud" (*CW* 4:207) or overtly blocking their readers' perceptions:

> O for me! that I,
> Who late have told her woe and misery,
> Must leave untold the joy unspeakable
> That on her tender wounded spirit fell!
> Alas! I try to think of it in vain,
> My lyre is but attuned to tears and pain,
> How shall I sing the never-ending day?
> ("Psyche," *CW* 4:72)

The assertion which must be checked in all three stories is their fulfillment of the summer ethos, expressed by Rolf, the narrator of "Ogier":

> Hope is our life, when first our life grows clear,
> Hope and delight, scarce crossed by lines of fear;
> Yet as the day comes when fain we would not hope.
> But forasmuch as we with life must cope,
> Struggling with this and that, who knoweth why,
> Hope will not give us up to certainty,
> But still must bide with us.   (*CW* 4:215)

Each of the three enclosing stories achieves the "certainty" that the cycle of man culminates without decay at its full blossom, or as all three stories express it, its "new birth." The withdrawal of the narrator denies perception of the certainty, but it cannot quite dispel the dream of metamorphosis.

Laurence introduced "The Writing on the Image" with a "shudder" at his own young belief

> in many a mystery
> I thought divine, that now I think, forsooth,
> Men's own fears made, to fill the place of truth
> Within their foolish hearts.   (*CW* 4:75)

He also once believed in "the stone . . . whereby base metal into gold is wrought" (*CW* 3:7). The magic stone, the romantic symbol for knowledge and power, is also introduced in *The Prelude* with its antithetical symbol, the shell, representing natural truth. In the poet's apocalyptic dream in Book V, the mysterious Arab "wandering upon [his] quest" [15] holds both symbols and calls them "books":

> The one that held acquaintance with the stars,
> And wedded soul to soul in purest bond
> Of reason, undisturbed by space or time;
> The other that was a god, yea many gods,
> Had voices more than all the winds, with power
> To exhilarate the spirit, and to soothe,
> Through every clime, the heart of human kind. (ll. 103–9)

The stone the Bedouin calls "Euclid's Elements," but the shell he says,

> "Is something of more worth;" and at the word
> Stretched forth the shell, so beautiful in shape,
> In colour so resplendent, with command
> That I should hold it to my ear. I did so,
> And heard that instant in an unknown tongue,
> Which yet I understood, articulate sounds,
> A loud prophetic blast of harmony;
> An Ode, in passion uttered, which foretold
> Destruction to the children of the earth
> By deluge, now at hand.   (ll. 89–98)

Although Morris considerably alters this romantic view, reducing the shell's scope and expanding the stone's, he gives the stone—with its various associations of power and immortality—a similar evaluation in this volume. Yet the summer ethos of romance insists on releasing its power to transform mutability into permanence. Surrounding the more negative middle tales, the framing stories achieve the impossible. Forsaking earthly passion, Pygmalion, "loving the form of immortality" (*CW* 4:195), pursues and accomplishes incarnation of his marble sculpture. Driven by "vain desire, / the ever-burning, unconsuming fire" (*CW* 4:194) and assisted by Venus, he transforms the statue, "motionless and white and cold" (*CW* 4:193), into a lover and wife who enraptures him with her mechanical recitation about "my new-made soul" (*CW* 4:203). The pursuit divorces him from nature, a separation described in almost exactly the same terms as Psyche's (*CW* 4:192 and 45), but no matter: in the same way that Psyche contains her own potential wishes and Cupid's, Pygmalion's image embodies the dreams of her creator.[16]

Ogier, a more sympathetic character, likewise profits from alchemy. Wrecked on the loadstone rock (*CW* 4:216ff.), he is transformed into the eternal lover of Morgan le Fay, who obliterates his memories and doubts. She triumphs through a paradisal setting that induces regressive sleep (*CW* 4:226–30) and witchcraft that reduces him to passivity (*CW* 4:233). When he returns to France for battle, he is compared to an effigy (*CW* 4:236), his eyes are calm (*CW* 4:237, 239), and he sleeps frequently. With the reappearance of Morgan, the "noises . . . of wakening folk" and "the changing rush of the swift stream / Against the bridge-piers" (*CW* 4:253–54) all turn into "dream," and he goes with the immortal lady to Avalon.

The volume criticizes the stone, even while it triumphs, but it remains the task of the subsequent volumes to tell of the shell and to acknowledge the end of human life, "destruction to the children of the earth," by the recurring figure of "the deluge," the eternal sea of flux.

chapter seven
Earth's Voices As They Are Indeed: Volumes iij and iv

. . . and than is harvest daye
And fro that tyme wynter entreth alway. . . .
Kalender of Shepherdes

All things fall and are built again,
And those who build them again are gay.
Yeats, "Lapis Lazuli"

HE descending themes of the concluding volumes, like the arrangement of the spring and summer tales, seem at first to be felicitous accident. Volumes III and IV emerged indirectly from Morris's introduction to Eirikr Magnússon and the Icelandic sagas, appropriately an autumn event which Mackail assigns to October, 1868.[1] Prior to the study of Old Norse language and literature, Morris planned to complete the entire body of tales in two volumes (March–August and September–February). The result of the winter, however, was two translations in collaboration with Magnússon and "The Lovers of Gudrun," finished in June.[2] The length of "Gudrun," which he wanted to include in *The Earthly Paradise*, necessitated revision of the original format. He then composed "The Death of Paris" and "Acontius and Cydippe" and rewrote portions of "The Land East of the Sun and West of the Moon."[3] With addition of new work and rearrangement of old, Morris created two new volumes, both dated 1870.

The result, while it profits little from "Acontius and Cydippe," effects a pattern and tone that are hardly arbitrary, in spite of appearance. We might note initially that Morris's original plan of one summer and one winter volume suggests the contrapuntal theme of all northern pastorals. Spenser's similar emphasis of the stark contrasts of climate and of external and internal closure revealed his instinctive identification with English literary tradition. According to one medieval scholar, only two seasons were emphasized in "northerly climes" from *Beowulf* to the *Shepherd's Calendar.* Only the season-words *summer* and *winter* are to be found in all the Germanic languages: "Anglo-Saxon heroic poetry was strongly preoccupied with winter; apparently the year was divided into two main seasons, a grim season that furnished poets with much excellent material, and a pleasant season whose delights were not as a rule thought worthy of poetic treatment." [4]

Although Morris maintains his alternate arrangement of classical and northern tales, the concluding volumes derive their tonality from the sagas and their preoccupation with "the grim season," just as the first two volumes of more "pleasant season" expand the motifs of southerly climes. We have seen the effects of division and expansion in the early volumes. They are similar in the final ones.

First, the expansion of winter stories into two volumes facilitates an internal movement of tragic descent and emergence that provides two themes while it preserves the controlling atmosphere of human limitation. The harvest of human choice and error, appropriate to autumn, is balanced by acquiescence to natural process, the theme of winter. Autumn introduces the irreversible processes of natural decay of individual happiness and the correlative dissolution of the tribe. The separation of the hero from his kind, the direction of summer romance, is culminated in Volume III, although attention is directed toward its internal rather than external causes. Winter restores order, suggesting return to society while enlarging the vision of society from the innocent spring concept to a cosmic vision of man, nature, and destiny.

Second, both notions belong to a northern vision which would crystallize for Morris with his journey to Iceland in the summer of 1871 and his ensuing translation of the Volsunga Saga (1875–1876). Always attentive to landscape and its revelations of human experience, Morris was stunned by Iceland's stark singularity. Of a similar pilgrimage, Auden said, "Europe is absent" in "the fabulous / Country impartially far." [5] Morris, already familiar with the literature, also found his presuppositions confirmed by new spatial and temporal insights. The combination would yield his closest approximation to objective correlative for the paradoxical relationship of man and nature.

The land, seen and experienced, suggested a lonely order that simultaneously had independent existence and supported a tribal community of toil and heroic activity. It seemed to provide pleasure less than labor, a vital harmony hard for man to achieve in more indolent natural circumstance. The classical (contra romantic) view of nature was toughened rather than destroyed by his observations, for he discovered a new construct of natural tensions. The landscape, particularized in his journals, combined desolate waste and stark mountains with green meadows:

> Most strange and awful the country looked to me we passed through, in spite of all my anticipations: a doleful land at first with its great rubbish heaps of sand, striped scantily with grass sometimes; varied though by a bank of sweet grass here and there full of flowers, and little willowy grey-leaved plants I can't name: till at last we come to our first river that runs through a soft grassy plain into a bight of the firth; it is wonderfully clear and its flowery green lips seemed quite beautiful to me in the sunny evening, though I think at any time I should have liked the place, with the grass and the sea and river all meeting, and the great black mountain (Esja) on the other side of the firth. (*CW* 8:28)

It is as if this new landscape sharpened the poet's perceptions and perhaps his preferences too for the pastoral enclosures typical of all his other descriptions, real or imaginary. His journals note the strange combination of natural forms, wastes and flowers, with a rhythmic accuracy that produces the same stylistic gestalt Symonds had sensed in Greek pastoral landscape. An example is his description of Midfirth valley, the birthplace of Grettir:

> Thence we are soon down into the flat of the valley, which turns out to be much better than it looked from farther off, and has a great deal of character: there are flat, well-grassed meadows all along the river, which runs in a well-defined bed, sometimes bounded by steep dark-grey banks, that break off sometimes and leave it bare amidst the meadows: the valley is very narrow, and looking toward its landward end one can see the grey banks aforesaid rising high and pinching the river very close, and winding round beyond till they get blue in the distance and seem to stop it. (*CW* 8:98)

The spatial rhythms of landscape were related to the temporal rhythm of history, an orderly combination of permanence and change. The place evoked an elegiac sense of human and historical heroism, failure, and endurance. Morris called the visit to Bathstead, Gudrun's home, "one of the best and most memorable days we had" (*CW* 8:114); yet what struck him most in his journey was "how every place and name marks the death of its short-lived eagerness and glory; and withal so little is the life changed in some ways" (*CW* 8:108). Herdholt, Kiartan's home, typifies this "mournful place—Iceland I mean" (*CW* 8:108). The relationship of time, man, and landscape is expressed in one of Morris's best lyrics, "Iceland First Seen," which concludes:

> Or rather, O land, if a marvel
> it seemeth that men ever sought
> Thy wastes for a field and a garden
> fulfilled of all wonder and doubt,
> And feasted amidst of the winter
> when the fight of the year had been fought,
> Whose plunder all gathered together
> was little to babble about;
> Cry aloud from thy wastes, O thou land,
> 'Not for this nor for that was I wrought
> Amid waning of realms and of riches
> and death of things worshipped and sure,

> I abide here the spouse of a God,
> and I made and I make and endure.'   (*CW* 9:126)

Finally, it follows that saga literature had an effect on the style of the final volumes. Mackail says, "The treatment of the Bellerophon legend clearly shows the epic manner rising beside and partially overmastering the romantic." [6] The meaning of epic manner is illuminated by Douglas Bush, who concedes that some of the final poems avoid the "usual idealization" he deplores. Of "The Death of Paris" Bush says, "This poem has more dramatic edge and vitality than most of the collection"; he admires the treatment of the Bellerophon stories, which he places in an "epic group" with "The Lovers of Gudrun." [7]

To extend Bush's observations, we can say that epic manner describes the emphasis, scope, and style of the dominant tales of III and IV. Morris dignifies human deeds, dwelling on the themes of "Love, strife, sickness" as the sources of both destruction and hope. In the stories of Gudrun, Hercules, and Bellerophon he also utilizes ordinary messengers to report incidents of valor or violence, a device that emphasizes the human limitation of vision and provides a common chorus for significant events. In addition, however, Morris reasserts a cosmic context, especially in the concluding volume. As Bush notes, it is not an otherworld that intervenes but rather the suggestion of an unseen order with which the heroes, particularly Hercules and Bellerophon, experience temporary harmony. Both the focus on human activity and the sense of cosmos contribute to the creation of the new self-accepting heroes of the final volume, of whom even the lesser Walter ("The Hill of Venus") is an example:

> No ignorance, no wonder, and no hope
> Was in his heart as his firm feet passed o'er
> The shallow's pebbles, and the flowery slope,
> And reached the black-mouthed cavern, the dark door
> Unto the fate now his for evermore.   (*CW* 6:323)

The descriptive style, still decorative in places, tends to convey a stronger sense of natural and historical realism. In Volume III we will examine the framing stories, for they control the theme of the "harvest of human woe." "Acontius and Cydippe" is obviously an unsuccessful filler, a story that Morris himself did not feel "sanguine" about.[8] It belongs elsewhere, if anywhere, although its conclusion foreshadows failure of human relationship. Two of the tales, "The Land East of the Sun and West of the Moon" and "The Man Who Never Laughed Again," also seem to be quest romances, but there is an important difference. In their narratives of mortal-immortal union, both include a medial separation and final return to the otherworld, suggesting the importance of human choice in both events.

TALES OF AUTUMN

Morris's treatment of Paris, the shepherd become Trojan hero, is an appropriate announcement of autumn themes—human error, bitter love, separation, and death. When Tennyson explored the same material in 1832, he focused on Oenone and her longing for death. In contrast, Morris not only concentrates on Paris but on the Trojan collapse foreshadowed by his initial choice and symbolized by his death. Morris again unites pastoral and cultural themes and utilizes the story as a vehicle of both criticism and sympathy. The attitude resembles that of the Renaissance. Commenting on the sixteenth-century popularity of Paris as pastoral hero, Hallett Smith says, "Paris, the son of Priam, King of Troy, was the most famous of all classical shepherds because from his actions sprang the whole epic narrative of the Siege of Troy." Besides providing an interesting plot, says Smith, the story had symbolic appeal in its emphasis on the shepherd's choice. Although Elizabethans generally condemned Paris's choice, it did represent for them rejection of the aspiring mind for pastoral content:

The simplicity of the shepherd's conditions makes for an invulnerability to appeals in the name of wealth or chivalry. It is only beauty, of the three ideals represented by the goddesses, which has any significant power in pastoral life.

Paris is the judge precisely because the conditions of the pastoral life provide the greatest independence, the greatest security. The shepherd is not motivated by ambition or by greed. Free from these two common human passions, he enjoys "content" or the good life.[9]

Morris, always attracted to the Trojan narrative, similarly criticizes the weary bickering of the "last month of Troy's beleaguerment," the indirect result of Paris' rejection of pastoral life for the love of Helen (*CW* 5:4). But he sets the poem in a pastoral clearing on Mount Ida where, free of martial chaos, both Paris and Oenone can contemplate past and present, where both can make a final choice. There is no languidness about the encounter, which replaces the introspection of Tennyson's version with bitter dialogue and revelation of the eternal separation of the lovers. In the familiar setting of past love and pastoral duty, under "the light / Of the clear western sky, cold now, but bright" (*CW* 5:9), neither Paris nor Oenone is able to reverse circumstance to "harvest" their love. His failure is expressed through Paris' consciousness as "Thoughts half thought out, and words half said, and deeds / Half done, unfruitful, like o'er-shadowed weeds" (*CW* 5:11).

Driven by the demands of her own integrity, Oenone refuses aid, and Paris makes his final choice—Helen. He dies amid the nature that fostered him and that continues unalterably:

> —yet the sky
> Changed not above his cast-back golden head,
> And merry was the world though he was dead. (*CW* 5:21)

His progress toward final decision and death is marked by the three soundings of his shepherd's horn "Wherewith he erst was wont his herd to wake" (*CW* 5:9). While the horn on the one hand suggests Paris's alienation from his former life, it also implies his human strength to exercise choice even if it is wrong—a quality, we recall, of Sir Peter Harpdon, who drew moral strength from Paris's example. Paris's first two attempts, to summon Oenone, are weak, but the final "wild and shattering blast" that announces his fidelity to Helen is reminiscent of Childe Roland's last action, an act of will that Morris admired. The gesture, which Bush calls "romantic," [10] suggests that in death Paris achieves a synthesis of character which earlier heroes could not achieve, the natural and heroic man.

"The Death of Paris" briefly evokes the theme of history to suggest the autumn realism of art. "The Lovers of Gudrun," "this history / Of a few freemen of the farthrest north" (*CW* 5:250), is a fuller exploration of the relationship of life and art. Like the Prologue, it is a "history" and a "tale." History, associated with the harvest metaphor, has several implications. It is a pattern of causation, and it is "real." Both qualities originate in the idea of human action. In addition, causation is temporal, a fact which tends to give the histories in this work a pessimistic cast. We might recall, for instance, that this is the effect of the Wanderers' personal chronicle and the first story that is called a history, "The Writing on the Image." Tale, on the other hand, suggests the element of perspective, the apprehension of past events by the narrator, audience, or even the characters. The distance afforded by fictional construct converts mutability into stasis, at least to a tempering degree, and accentuates vision rather than action. The interest in "tale" is thus related again to the theme of visual perception as order.

The story is introduced as a history. It is told by a Wanderer who claims Icelandic ancestry, who speaks of the characters' lives as "the fruit of deeds recorded," and who says:

> . . . know withal that we
> Have ever deemed this tale as true to be,

> As though those very Dwellers in Laxdale
> Risen from the dead had told us their own tale.
> (CW 5:250)

Historical realism is conveyed within the story by the strong sense of particular location, by treatment of the reign of King Olaf Tryggivson who Christianized Iceland, by the temporal structure provided by Northern Yule feasts, and even by passing reference to simultaneous cultures, e.g., the Byzantine culture at Micklegarth.

The sense of the story as tale is provided by this same narrator. His editorial interruptions—"the story says" (CW 5:278); "men say" (CW 5:286); or "though says not certainly my tale" (CW 5:274)—remove the present intensity of events and locate them in the elegiac past, which itself becomes a subject of meditation. It is the same sense of the past that gives the Beowulf poet his elegiac tone and reminds his listeners that the poem-song of the scop transforms history into myth.

Both levels of the story are conveyed by a simple, descriptive style that is primarily evocative rather than instructive or otherwise prescriptive. Naming and seeing, the respective principles of history and visionary tale, serve to produce realism, the quality of history, and perceptive order, the purpose of the tale. The causal sequence of human action immerses us in character, in this case psychologically turbulent. The submission of "plot" to scene-sequence invites a participation equally sensuous but more aesthetically distanced. Its tenor is simplicity. Ultimately the latter mode dominates. As the narrator concludes the story, he substitutes scene for summary, showing Gudrun alone, aged, and blind:

> This one more picture gives the ancient book
> On which I pray you for a while to look,
> If for your tears you may.   (CW 5:393)

This consistent method in the story is like that of Spenser's February eclogue:

It specially conteyneth a discourse of old age, in the persone of Thenot, an olde Shepheard, who for his crookednesse and unlustinesse is scorned of Cuddie, an unhappy Heardmans boye. The matter very well accordeth with the season of the moneth, the yeare now drouping, and as it were drawing to his last age. For as in this time of yeare, so then in our bodies, there is a dry and withering cold, which congealeth the crudled blood, and frieseth the wetherbeaten flesh with stormes of Furtune, and hoare frosts of Care. To which purpose the olde man telleth a tale . . . so lively, and so feelingly, *as, if the thing were set forth in some Picture before our eyes, more plainly could not appeare.*[11]

It is a technique that repeats the situation of the Wanderers, resting within a meditative closure and looking out into the temporal flux of nature and culture. It works especially well here to illustrate the shared associations of audience, seasonal setting, and tale—a configuration both realistic and aesthetically distanced. The November link introducing the tale describes the "ruggedness" of autumn and its human occupations. Seated within the house around the fire, "the ancient folk" look out to see a horseman, a shepherd, a ferryman, and a goodwife as well as the emblems of harvest labor: "a climbing row of corn-ricks," a "smouldering weed-heap," and a "plough beside the field-gate" (*CW* 5:249). The Wanderers, nearing death, view a scene of natural conclusions and human tenacity. Its realism is apparent but distanced as a tableau. It is an appropriate backdrop for meditation on the story, "that bitter harvesting, / That from the seed of lust and lies did spring" (*CW* 5:390).

The relationship of action and vision is introduced in the story's frame and its first section, "The Prophecy of Guest the Wise." One function of the introductory frame is genealogical, providing the heroine's background. More important, however, is its initial submission of history to scene. It is a vision of tribal harmony, the good society that is to be destroyed by the human error of the story's events. Herdholt and Bathstead are named and described. Both acts are ordering.

> Herdholt my tale names for the stead, where erst
> Olaf the Peacock dwelt, nowise the worst
> Among the great men of a noble day:
> Upon a knoll amidst a vale it lay,
> Nigh where Laxriver meets the western sea,
> And in that day it nourished plenteously
> Great wealth of sheep and cattle.   (*CW* 5:251)

Then the family is named. A similar process locates Bathstead and its inhabitants, who, we are shortly to learn, also experience a pastoral existence:

> Upon a day, amid the maids that spun
> Within the bower at Bathstead, sat Gudrun:
> Her father in the firth a-fishing was,
> The while her mother through the meads did pass
> About some homely work.   (*CW* 5:252)

The assumption here and throughout the story is that individual conflict precipitates tribal dissolution, viewed briefly at the end of the tale in the complementary summary of the "harvest's" effect on Herdholt and Bathstead: tribal heads are dead, tribal bonds are violated, weaker offspring wage war. Concern for the tribe provides temporal and thematic structure: the Yule feasts, symbols of fellowship and the exchange of gifts become occasions of revelation of discord.

The framing section of the story extends into the account of Guest's visit. It is significant that we first see the characters through the dispassionately perceptive eyes of this "seer." The central characters of each household are presented in almost still-life tableaux, Gudrun first at Bathstead and then Olaf's family at Herdholt, which Guest sees first as a pastoral construct: he and his guide

> Rode slowly by the borders of the bay
> Upon that fresh and sunny afternoon,

> Noting the sea-bird's cry and surf's soft tune,
> Until at last into the dale they came,
> And saw the gilt roof-ridge of Herdholt flame
> In the bright sunlight over the fresh grass,
> O'er which the restless white-woolled lambs did pass,
> And querulous grey ewes; and wide around,
> Near and far up the dale, they heard the sound
> Of lowing kine, and the blithe neat-herd's voice,
> For in those days did all things there rejoice. (*CW* 5:262)

Likewise, the sons of Olaf present a single impression of harmony:

> Then Guest looked, and afar
> Beheld the tide play on the sandy bar
> About the stream's mouth, as the sea waves rushed
> In over it and back the land-stream pushed;
> But in the dark wide pool mid foam-flecks white,
> Beneath the slanting afternoon sunlight,
> He saw white bodies sporting, and the air
> Light from the south-west up the slopes did bear
> Sound of their joyous cries as there they played.
> (*CW* 5:265)

Then as Olaf describes his sons, Guest perceives the distinctness of Kiartan and Bodli, another framed perception (*CW* 5:267). In each description there is some telling detail—the superiority of Kiartan's swimming, Kiartan and Bodli's sword, or the vaguer suggestion of pensive pride in Gudrun. But it is not the details that give the descriptive method its importance; rather it is the thematic contrast of these scenes with the revelations that compose the rest of this first section. Guest's vision encompasses the clear perception of simple innocence and insight into the turbulence of experience. The latter, apocalyptic vision, begins in the conversation with Gudrun.

> At last, amid their speech,
> The old man stayed his hand as it did reach

> Out to the beaker, and his grey eyes stared
> As though unseen things to his soul were bared.
>   (*CW* 5:254–55)

He inquires about her dreaming, which she later describes as
a visual process:

> I . . . lay back in my bed and shut my eyes,
> To see what pictures to my heart would rise,
> And slept, but dreamed no more.   (*CW* 5:257)

Gudrun is interested in her dream-pictures but perceives no
pattern. Guest does: "'Speak quick,' he said, 'before / This
glimmer of a sight I have is o'er'" (*CW* 5:255). His "glimmer
of a sight" interprets the dreams as a chronological projection
of Gudrun's life, a harvest of deeds. But he acknowledges the
limitation of vision, which cannot alter act or temper its existential reality:

> So is thy dream areded; but these things
> Shall hang above thee, as on unheard wings
> The kestrel hangs above the mouse; nor more
> As erst I said shalt thou gain by my lore
> Than at the end of life, perchance, a smile
> That fate with sight and blindness did beguile
> Thine eyes in such sort—that thou knew'st the end,
> But not the day whereon thy feet did wend
> On any day amid the many years.   (*CW* 5:260)

This becomes a thematic summary of the story and the whole
work: vision, a static ordering of past and future, coexists with
the inevitability of action. Both involve sorrow as well as
happiness.

The cosmic significance of this paradox is confirmed with
Guest's experience at Herdholt. He arrives with Olaf Peacock
at the great hall:

> . . . then in they went and Guest
> Gazed through the cool dusk, till his eyes did rest

Upon the noble stories, painted fair
On the high panelling and roof-boards there. (*CW* 5:263)

The painted history of the gods is a familiar descriptive detail
in Morris, but here its northern variation supports Guest's
sadness. The splendid tableau reverses the summer fantasy of
man as a god to show the gods as men.[12] Odin, for example,
is depicted not as fiery warrior but in his less familiar contemplative emanation:

. . . and last of all
Was Odin's sorrow wrought upon the wall,
As slow-paced, weary-faced, he went along,
Anxious with all the tales of woe and wrong
His ravens, Thought and Memory, bring to him.
(*CW* 5:263)

We are told that "Guest looked on these until his eyes grew
dim," for what he perceives in the pictures of supernatural
deeds is "Death even amid the Gods" (*CW* 5:264). This version
of *Et in Arcadia ego* combines with Guest's insight into Gudrun's dreams and Herdholt's future to comment on the pastoral tableaux we have noted. Herdholt and Bathstead are threatened pastoral paradises, in effect the only way a paradise can
have meaning. The illusion of peace before the deluge is
heightened by the sense of impending doom. Through Guest's
"eyes / Distraught and sad, and face made over wise / With
many a hard vain struggle" (*CW* 5:260), pastoral "life" is
clearly defined as pastoral "vision"—one imaginary pole of the
temporal and spatial rhythm of existence. Its perception is a
function of wisdom or radical innocence, experience returned
to a higher plane of simplicity. An outsider, Guest can already
see the pattern of the tale. Yet for the characters who will
effect and be affected, he acknowledges the pain of consciousness. For these participants, blindness seems a happier state,
and Gudrun's "end" is an ironic fulfillment of Guest's
prophecy. The lone survivor of personal and cultural destruc-

tion, she attains retrospective insight even as "her bodily sight failed too, / And now no more the dark from day she knew" (*CW* 5:393).

Gudrun's perceptive isolation is indeed the final harvest of the story in which family, friendship, marriage, and life are destroyed by a concatenation of human misunderstanding. The harvest metaphor, implied or stated ten times in the narrative, is most frequently associated with the effect of lies in the triangular relationship of Gudrun, Kiartan, and Bodli. Yet lies have various meanings in the story. Only at the turning point of the tale, when Kiartan returns to find Gudrun wed to Bodli, is his anguish fed by the outright deceit of Oswif's sons, "fierce hearted fools" (*CW* 5:337), who exploit the opportunity for strife with Olaf's house:

> So cunningly they turned them to the game
> As such men will, and scattered wide the seeds,
> Lies, and words half-true, of the bitterest deeds.
>
> (*CW* 5:337)

More characteristic are the subtler lies of being, some more consciously imposed than others. They reveal discrepancy between appearance and reality. First there is the lie that withholds self and projects partial truth. Both Gudrun and Kiartan are proud and self-contained, literally a golden pair of willful lovers who shape their own lives to an extent that each hurts the other. They experience the cold isolation given by Lawrence to the doomed alliance of Gudrun Brangwen and Gerald Crich. Kiartan's self-determined destiny, foretold by his excellence in swimming, is to win fame "beyond the sea" (*CW* 5:280, 281). He never foresees the alienating potential of his adventures until they have sown the seeds of eternal separation from Gudrun. Then he silently harbors his anguish until he reaps hate. Concurrently, Gudrun facilitates his blindness by withholding her loneliness. She indulges in unspoken "half-rebuke" (*CW* 5:281). Accustomed to loss, she urges Kiartan away:

Go forth, my love, and be thou not beguiled
By woman's tears, I spake but as a fool,
We of the north wrap not our men in wool,
Lest they should die at last; nay, be not moved,
To think that thou a faint-heart fool hast loved!

(*CW* 5:285)

As her doubts grow and her heart hardens, she maintains a calm exterior while acknowledging the effect of brooding (*CW* 5:304). Gudrun never expresses her longing for Kiartan on his return. Kiartan withholds his purgative anger toward Bodli and Gudrun; yet his marriage to Refna complicates the unspoken tensions between all four people.

For Bodli, unconsciously caught between two powerful personalities, an innate lack of control precipitates his form of lying: revealing too much at critically inappropriate times, most clearly illustrated when his "honest" disclosure of Kiartan's various conquests in Norway solidifies Gudrun's doubts into hatred. The ensuing marriage between Gudrun and Bodli thus becomes a living lie in which Gudrun's hatred is turned upon Kiartan, Bodli, and herself. Both Gudrun and Kiartan (*CW* 5:333) accuse Bodli of being "A follower on the footsteps of great men, / To reap where they have sowed" (*CW* 5:306), but the "evil crop by evil sown" (*CW* 5:313) has deeper causes and wider effects.

Within this "history" we see more clearly than elsewhere in the work the destructive complexity of human consciousness. It is this quality of the story that gives it epic magnitude in Morris's version. His interest in this particular facet of character may seem a departure from "the authentic Norse atmosphere" of the original,[13] but it is consistent with the themes of *The Earthly Paradise*. In this story the "deluge now at hand" is brought about by heroic pride.

In the three main characters heroic energy is characteristically converted into a destructive turbulence that originates in incipient narcissism and results in cultural collapse. While

Yule festivals come and go with their illusion of order, Gudrun feels "consuming anguish" (*CW* 5:308), "pain," and "passion" (*CW* 5:310); Bodli feels "black despair" and "agony" (*CW* 5:309); and Kiartan experiences a "flood of bitterest gall" (*CW* 5:338). The final effect is fierce hatred between houses, a separating emotion that becomes concrete in the death of Kiartan. Yet here as before, circumstance is dictated by the choices of the combatants: Kiartan faces death alone; Bodli, torn by guilt, fear, and passion, chooses the compromising combination of single combat and the supporting forces of his deceitful in-laws. The dissolution of both houses follows.

The bitterest irony of the theme of heroic consciousness is that its agents confuse its limited insights with visionary truth. On hearing of Gudrun's marriage to Bodli, Kiartan

> turned and staggered wildly from the place,
> Crying aloud, "O blind, O blind, O blind!
> Where is the world I used to deem so kind,
> So loving to me?"   (*CW* 5:320)

He refers to his own former blindness to Gudrun's betrayal, but the words convey ironic ambiguity. He assumes he now knows a truth heretofore concealed. In fact the real blindness for all three characters is a compulsive adherence to destructive isolation, increasing withdrawal from the community into self. The human-natural contrast now a convention of *The Earthly Paradise* conveys his narcissism:

> he turned about,
> And far away he heard the shipmen's shout
> And beat of the sea, and from the down there came
> The bleat of ewes; and all these, and his name,
> And the sights too, the green down 'neath the sun,
> The white strand and the far-off hillsides dun,
> And white birds wheeling, well-known things did seem,
> But pictures now or figures in a dream,
> With all their meaning lost.   (*CW* 5:321)

Gudrun likewise responds to Kiartan's wedding with theatrical introspection that employs visual imagery:

> Deaf, dumb, and blind, long hours she went about
> Her father's house, till folk began to doubt
> If she would ever speak a word again;
> Nay, scarce yet could she think about her pain,
> Or e'en know what it was, but seemed to face
> Some huge blank wall within a lonely place. (*CW* 5:342)

After Kiartan's death, Bodli rationalizes his action as the necessity of love and says that now Kiartan's eyes "made clear" by death can surely see his passion for Gudrun (*CW* 5:381). It is the language of perception that records the illusions of the love-competition so close to self-celebration. The same imagery conveys the story's final visual irony. For Gudrun, the primary seed of this harvest, evaluative perception comes finally when "her sightless eyes" comprehend: "I did the worst to him I loved the most" (*CW* 5:395).

The conclusion recalls Guest's "prophecy" at the beginning of the story:

> "Since thou thus hast told
> Thy dreams," he said, "scarce may I now withhold
> The tale of what mine eyes have seen therein;
> Yet little from my foresight shalt thou win,
> Since both the blind, and they who see full well,
> Go the same road, and leave a tale to tell
> Of interwoven miseries, lest they
> Who after them a while on earth must stay,
> Should have no pleasure in the winter night,
> When this man's pain is made that man's delight."
> (*CW* 5:258)

While dream is distinguished from the "blind" activity of personal history, the difference is important only to the participants. For others the function of tales, dreams, and histories is aesthetic. This is a notion also explored in "The Land East

of the Sun and West of the Moon." Although it comes early
in the volume, it offers final commentary on the relationship
of real and aesthetic experience. The quest story, a version of
the Swan-maiden group of folk-tales, is set within a frame of
Morris's invention. In the frame he gives the story an internal
narrator whose setting, "Norway in King Magnus' days," and
identity, "Gregory the Star-gazer," set up the tension between
history and fantasy, reality and dream. It is a contrast prepared by the narrating Wanderer:

> A dream it is, friends, and no history
> Of men who ever lived; so blame me nought
> If wondrous things together there are brought,
> Strange to our waking world—yet as in dreams
> Of known things still we dream, whatever gleams
> Of unknown light may make them strange, so here
> Our dreamland holdeth such things dear
> And such things loathed, as we do; else, indeed,
> Were all its marvels nought to help our need. (*CW* 5:23)

This introduction—comparable to Guest's words, "Only foreshadowing of outward things . . . dream-lore brings" (*CW*
5:258)—expresses the dilemma made concrete in Gregory,
both a "real" character experiencing the dream-reality conflict
and a "created" character presenting the same conflict of the
Wanderer-narrator.

In the story surrounding a story, Gregory, a pleasant man
who "served withal / The Marshal Biorn in field and hall"
(*CW* 5:24), is sent by King Magnus to command a fishing expe-
dition. At the end of a successful day his sleep is interrupted
by a dream in which a stranger tells a tale at Magnus' Yuletide
feast. In the four sections of the frame, which also serve to
structure the dream-story into initiation-separation-return,
Gregory experiences increasing identification with and withdrawal from the dreamworld. First he is observer, then tale-
teller, then character, and finally himself again. The pattern
is a negative parallel to the story, in which young John discov-

ers and yields to otherworldly love, returns to his earthly
home, and finally searches out his mysterious love for permanent union in the otherworld.

Both the frame and the Wanderer's introduction suggest
that the dreamworld is a translation of reality. On the one
hand, the dream rearranges reality elements within a construct that is aesthetically pleasing to the dreamer. This perfect roundedness prompts the narrator to say, "Woe's me! an
idle dream it is!" (CW 5:120). Yet this is a partial interpretation.
Remarkably close to Freudian theory, it necessarily gives the
dream surrogate value and reduces its symbols to symptoms.
It is not a particularly humane view of the ordering principle.
The other implication, more compatible with Morris's work,
is that dreams intensify life and carry experience into un-
charted regions—at once familiar and new. Here the symbol
is not to be regarded as sign or symptom of conscious reality
but in Jung's words, "the expression of an intuitive perception
which can as yet, neither be apprehended better, nor expressed differently." These "genuine symbols" are "bridges
thrown out towards an invisible shore." [14] Here the dream
becomes a journey, not necessarily into self but into racially
shared consciousness. Its process is palpably concrete and expansive rather than reductive. Its medium is extremely sensuous, and the connection between dream and real worlds is
primarily visual.

Gregory's transitional experience is described in terms of
sight. In the first part of the frame the concrete world of
nature merges with the dream-scene in the hall, where the
king gazed on the stranger and where Gregory

> dreamed he turned his head
> Unto the stranger, and their eyes
> Met therewith, and a great surprise
> Shot through his heart, because indeed
> That strange man in the royal weed
> Seemed as his other self to be
> As he began this history.   (CW 5:27)

When the dream breaks for the first time, the intensity of his experience separates Gregory from "The sturdy sleepers, all unseen / Of sleep-bound eyes" (*CW* 5:50). As he falls again into dream-sleep, the "stranger-guest" disappears and he "Himself, Star-gazing Gregory, / Sat by King Magnus, clad in gold, / And in such wise the sequel told" (*CW* 5:50). When the dream breaks a second time, the imagery of sight and journey are blended:

> then, e'en as one
> Who through a marvellous land hath gone
> In sleep, and knowing nought thereof
> To tell, yet knows strange things did move
> About his sightless journeying,
> So felt he; and yet seemed to bring,
> Now and again, some things anigh
> Unto the wavering boundary
> 'Twixt sight and blindness.   (*CW* 5:84)

As sleep closes his eyes for the final phase of the dream, his own life seems to be "A new and marvellous history" or an intense fusion of dream and reality that provides solace on a level heretofore unattained:

> Adown the stream of fate he moved
> As the carle's son, the well-beloved,
> The fool of longing; in such wise
> He dealt with his own miseries.   (*CW* 5:85)

The concluding frame marks the "return" to reality: "O'er Gregory's eyes the pain of morn / Flashed suddenly" (*CW* 5:119). His alternative responses are presented—retreat from the ordinary world or recognition of its tenuous relationship with the dreamworld. Tempted by the first (*CW* 5:119), Gregory chooses the second and thereby gives the "idle" dream new meaning:

> And when they landed at high-noon,
> From all men would he go apart

> In woods and meads, and deal by art
> With his returning memory;
> And, some things gained, and some slipped by,
> His weary heart a while to soothe,
> He wove all into verses smooth,
> As tells the tale.   (*CW* 5:120)

Although this tale is clearly of a different sort than "Gudrun," it speaks to similar antinomies that are united through aesthetic alchemy. Whether the stories of autumn relate "innocent" dream or "experienced" history, they deal with the past or inner world of man in the same way. The pleasure or pain that is subjected to spatial or temporal distance of aesthetic construct serves "to help our need" or as Guest puts it, produces "a tale to tell / Of interwoven miseries . . . When this man's pain is made that man's delight" (*CW* 5:258).

TALES OF WINTER

The tales of the winter volume re-establish the simplicity of subject and tone that characterized the stories of Volume I: the hero, his society, and the earth are re-examined now, with the distinction that mere youthful innocence is transformed into "radical innocence," an attitude that respects the uncontrollable forces of nature and human destiny without passive despair. Elements from other volumes are similarly repeated and modified: the otherworld, quest, and love-temptation of Volume II and the heroic choice and deed of Volume III. The tonal effect is qualified optimism about the possibilities of life within the context of inevitable mutability. The delicate balance of death and rebirth is facilitated by the aesthetic distance of both heroes and the framework audience.

The framework, reflecting the concern of the season, emphasizes imminent death for the Wanderers. This movement, begun in III, is almost complete now. Morris makes it clear that death, the central truth of "earth's bitter lore" (*CW* 6:326), is the subject of winter. One of its symbols is the sea, the element of flux. As sea imagery enters the framework again, it is likewise asserted in the tales. The sea journey, a motif begun in Volume III with the conclusion of "Rhodope" and suggested again in "Gudrun," provides the structure for "The Golden Apples," "The Fostering of Aslaug," and the two Bellerophon stories. It also appears in the otherworld setting of "The Ring Given to Venus." While it is still the locus of adventure, the sea is clearly associated with separation, mystery, and death. The voyage over "the troublous sea" is related to pilgrimage, the image which appeared in the last story of Volume I and which recurs in the final story of the work when Walter, preparing for infamous death, joins and leaves the Christian pilgrims on their way to the Holy City.

The corresponding symbol of death is darkness. The framework setting of the winter tales is generally late day, night, or the transitional period "Midmost the time 'twixt noon and dusk" (*CW* 6:66) when "shone the westering sun / Through frosty haze of the day nearly done" (*CW* 6:20). Here again, death threatens heroes as well as common men. The concluding morning scene in "The Fostering of Aslaug" is quickly undercut by the reminder that "death made end of all at last" (*CW* 6:64), and "Bellerophon in Lycia" is an account "of bliss and praise / That erst befell Bellerophon the bright, / Ere all except his name sank into night" (*CW* 6:176). The Venus stories both conclude with a death; in the final one it is the certain death of the hero behind the "dark door" of the Hill of Venus where "dull dark closed betwixt him and the earth" (*CW* 6:323).

In this atmosphere of flux and darkness, the prevailing tone of "brave clearnesse" derives from the familiar element of perspective in the handling of framework and tales. The Wanderers, so close to death, find a new response to its threat. It is both more realistically direct and more distant. The framework has of course conveyed their meditative separation from active experience; it has been an enforced withdrawal which encourages the mingled emotions of hope and fear, especially in dealing with their own past failure. Now in the last months of the dying year this blend of pleasure and pain is retained but its components are sharpened. The process is again delineated by the imagery of darkness and light.

The "frosty haze" of winter vision has equivalents in preceding volumes that identify the refraction of light with partial vision. It resembles the romantic idealization effected by "accidents of light and shade," by the "modifying colors of imagination." [15] In spring the "quivering noontide haze" which Michael sees is echoed in the moonlight setting of the tale's conclusion (*CW* 3:168); and the sun half hidden by "the purple hills" provides background for "Acrisius," which casts a "painted veil" around the Wanderers' softened hearts (*CW* 3:239). In summer they imagine "a new golden light" (*CW* 4:74) at the end of "Psyche"; and under the "lime-tree's shade" they "Began to feel immortal and divine" (*CW* 4:88). In summer, as they match the tales' illusions with their own, they are shaded by chambers and trellises (*CW* 4:144, 160). They wander "From sun to shade, and shade to sun again" as "shadows longer grew." As a result, "The grass seemed greener and the flowers more sweet / Unto the elders as they stood around" (*CW* 4:126). Finally in autumn, as the year decays, they view reality through an "autumn haze" (*CW* 5:121). As distortions of light, these perceptions are a kind of darkness, a state that literally controls the settings of winter.

The immersion in winter's night brings recognition of the dark, unknown side of nature and releases the honest fear of death. Three times in the volume's framework an apostrophe to nature expresses this palpable dread (*CW* 6:64, 174, 278–79). The last, the address of the "Many-peopled earth!" acknowledges the pain of loneliness in facing death. It also accepts nature's duality, the "storm and sunshine of the changing year."

The light which balances the darkness is in part an effect of the inner dialectic of the Wanderers, whose descent produces its opposite, a calm acceptance of change. We are aware of the "bright eyes" (*CW* 6:20) of a Wanderer, or the "wrinkles bright" of men "less pensive now" (*CW* 6:176). The cold, clear winter realism is especially well captured in "the old Swabian's glittering eyes" (*CW* 6:135); he compares himself to an old forester he remembers: "his deep-set eyes, / Bright mid his wrinkles, made him seem right wise" (*CW* 6:280).

A more important source of light, however, is the tales, where the light associated with the heroes [16] returns us to the old quest tradition of *Beowulf.* While the stories acknowledge the conventional classical meanings of the sea and of darkness, they provide glimpses of a hero committed to society. With "gaiety transfiguring all that dread" he establishes temporary order against the forces of chaos before he disappears. Lest this distinctly northern vision of the cosmos seem mere nostalgia for the heroic past, Morris distills its universal meaning in a lecture on "Early England":

> to live is good and to die is good if you are valiant and faithful and if you reckon great deeds and the fair fame that comes of them of more account than a few more short years of a trembler's life upon the earth. . . . In later times it has become a commonplace and is no longer believed, therefore except for moments of spasmodic excitement life is dull shapeless, so that some in their foolish despair will ask, is it worth the living? Clearly it is not unless we can live fearlessly and confident of our immortality not as individuals but as part of the great corporation of humanity; and that I say was the faith of our forefathers.[17]

There is equal emphasis here on heroic tenacity and on society as vehicle for human tradition. In the stories of this last volume, the relationship of these two elements determines the tenor of the work.

Although the tales continue to explore the consciousness of the main characters, they are presented from the limited viewpoint of the ordinary society that will transmit the memory of the heroes when they are dead. The story of Hercules is related entirely from the perspective of the sailors of Tyre, an anonymous group who cooperate, spy, marvel, and return to their homes, "Teaching their tale to whomso'er would learn" (*CW* 6:19). In "Aslaug" the union of the heroine and Ragnar, itself the subject of many "ancient stories" (*CW* 6:63), is a result of the reports of the hero's stammering mariners (*CW* 6:44). Most notably, the climactic events of the Bellerophon stories, the suicide of Queen Sthenoboea (*CW* 6:128–33) and Bellerophon's victory over the three-formed monster in Lycia (*CW* 6:246–58), are reported by conventional messengers, a fisherman and a common soldier. This indirection, initiated with the churl who witnessed the mortal conflict of Kiartan and Bodli in "Gudrun," enhances the mystery of the heroes. Its primary effect, however, is to confirm "the people's voice" (*CW* 6:132) as emblem of the society the hero serves.

"The Golden Apples" presents a clear profile of the hero and the supporting society. The latter is identified as pastoral, peaceful, and "midmost" the reign of King Eurystheus in "fair Mycenae" (*CW* 6:3). The frame recalls others in its temporal distance ("As many as the leaves fall from the tree, / From the world's life the years are fallen away") and spatial simplicity:

> Fresh was the summer morn, a soft wind stole
> Down from the sheep-browsed slopes
>   the cliffs that crowned,
> And ruffled lightly the long gleaming roll
> Of the peaceful sea, and bore along the sound
> Of shepherd-folk and sheep and questing hound;
> For in the first dip of the hillside there
> Lay bosomed 'midst its trees a homestead fair.
>   (*CW* 6:3)

Yet the setting suggests a lost paradise less than ordinary reality. It is dominated by commonplace activity of the most basic sort, the agrarian past suggesting the temporal and spatial limitations of all ordinary life. The pace of this world is interrupted by the delayed entrance of the hero. Like Bellerophon in subsequent tales, Hercules brings mystery with his anonymity and his characterizing trait of disinterested gaiety. Before he speaks, "A smile gleamed" (*CW* 6:4). He speaks "merrily"; his eyes "gleam with joy," "blaze," and burn with "A wild light" (*CW* 6:4, 5, 9); he faces his task "with a happy smile" (*CW* 6:13); and his laughter and "joyous cry" reveal "his hardy heart" (*CW* 6:11). His manner and appearance—"a man huge of limb, / Grey-eyed, with crisp-curled hair 'twixt black and brown" (*CW* 6:4)—look forward to the description of Dick Hammond in *News from Nowhere:* "He was a handsome young fellow, with a peculiarly pleasant and friendly look about the eyes,—an expression which was quite new to me then, though I soon became familiar with it. For the rest, he was dark-haired and berry-brown of skin, well-knit and strong, and obviously used to exercising his muscles, but with nothing rough or coarse about him, and clean as might be" (*CW* 16:7). Yet Hercules is not quite so unreflective as Hammond. Although he performs his task with economy of word and action, he is speculative to a degree that bothers some critics. This dimension of character is Morris's way of humanizing the "Strong Man" and explaining his merriness as existential necessity rather than complacency. The subject of his overheard meditation in the Garden of the Hesperides is Fate. Like Beowulf before battle, he faces his destiny with courage but realizes his lack of foresight:

> "So be it," he said, "the Fates that drive me on
> Shall slay me or shall save; blessing or curse
> That followeth after when the thing is won
> Shall make my work no better now nor worse." (*CW* 6:12)

These words, before the "violation" of the garden, are echoed in his final words to the daughters of Hesperus:

> O sweet, O fair, and shall this day
> A curse upon my life henceforward lay—
> This day alone? Methinks of coming life
> Somewhat I know, with all its loss and strife.

> But this I know, at least: the world shall wend
> Upon its way, and, gathering joy and grief
> And deeds done, bear them with it to the end;
> So shall it, though I lie as last year's leaf
> Lies 'neath a summer tree, at least receive
> My life gone by, and store it, with the gain
> That men alive call striving, wrong, and pain. (*CW* 6:13)

The figure of "last year's leaf," a repetition of the first lines of the story, acknowledges the reality of change. Hercules sees his life, like nature's, as process. It is a series of deeds, each task one of many. Saved by detachment from heroic solipsism, he comes and goes, risking loneliness. It is interesting in this respect that the role of Nereus is de-emphasized in Morris's version of the tale. The Shepherd of the Shore, or Old Man of the Sea, is undoubtedly the "great figure of the guide, the teacher, the ferryman," and as such he represents "the benign, protecting power of destiny." [18] Yet Morris's account of the combat between hero and helper suggests that assistance must be wrested from the guide and that its effects are temporary.

The locus of adventure clarifies these traits of the hero. The Garden of the Hesperides has no particular symbolic suggestion as it does in Tennyson, where the apples are associated with "the wisdom of the West." Instead it repeats the archetypal qualities of all the paradise gardens of the work. Distant, enclosed, and unnaturally beautiful, the "guarded place" (*CW* 6:10) is static; and its protective spirits, the daughters of Hesperus, tempt Hercules with the conventional arguments of paradise dwellers: because life within is immutable, return to known reality will be unbearable. It is an appeal to the desire for peace and the fear of life as it has been experienced. Hercules, immune to these narcissistic appeals, not only escapes but restores the balance between the garden and the world. With a mighty shout, he shatters the "great door" of the garden, "And into the guarded place bright poured the day" (*CW* 6:10). The light of day recalls both Hercules' own realistic spirit and the ordinary world of the frame, where light is joined with motion and sound to produce the earthly paradise

of pastoral existence. By bringing the earthly world into the
unearthly, Hercules in a sense brings process into the static
garden. He tells the nymphs:

> "And now, behold! in memory of all this
> Take ye this girdle that shall waste and fade
> As fadeth not your fairness and your bliss." (*CW* 6:14)

The social significance of the adventure, like the meaning
of the garden, is in its symbolic action rather than the specific
value of the apples. When Hercules speaks to the sailors of
"The world made better by me" (*CW* 6:18), he refers to the
broad implications of his adventure. First, it is a testimony to
the temporary union of seen and unseen worlds—the activity
of Hercules and the assistance of Nereus, the earthly and
unearthly worlds of the hero and the garden. The sailors are
witnesses. Second, they are also helpers: "Nought ill have ye
done / In helping me to find what I did seek" (*CW* 6:18). In
both roles they provide the continuous action of the story,
returning with new faith to repeat the tale. The distinction
between hero and society does suggest a hierarchy of potential,
but sympathy is with the common man, who "turned toward
the bright day's end / On the last ness, round which the wild
goats wend" (*CW* 6:19). The contrast is like that between the
higher and lesser arts of the lectures. The higher arts bloom
individually and temporarily, but the lesser arts, the arts of
the people, provide continuing tradition.[19]

"The Golden Apples" seems simple fare indeed when compared with the Bellerophon stories. Morris might well have
been thinking of these tales when he wrote Swinburne that
"they are all too long and flabby, damn it!"[20] However, "Bellerophon at Argos" and "Bellerophon at Lycia" do one aesthetic service simply by repeating the implications of the first
story of the volume. The hero and his society are thereby
developed by extension. Two additional points emerge: the
hero's "light" is connected with wisdom as well as detach-

ment, and the forces which assail society from without and within require constant battle for temporary restraint. The first story, which shows the hero's emergence, is an elaboration of the subject of Volume I; yet the defeat of the old order, represented by Queen Sthenoboea (who rules weak King Proteus), cannot be effected by "mere" innocence. Her guile can be countered only by the perceptive innocence that penetrates appearance and consciously shuns its temptations. The extended contrast between Sthenoboea and Bellerophon is thus an effective variation on several themes: the Venus garden and the earthly garden, the motives of self-serving and sacrifice, and rule through power and through service. The description of the queen's "close of love" (*CW* 6:84) dominates the tale. The setting offers yet another hero escape from the world in a bower of bliss. The queen with "strange desires," "cruel visage," and "false voice" (*CW* 6:86, 84, 87), seeks possession of Bellerophon, "As round his soul her net she strove to cast" (*CW* 6:88). Her failure is a function of her self-adulation (*CW* 6:94, 108) and of Bellerophon's wisdom in recognizing the reality beneath appearance: he is "A wary walker on the road of life; E'en as a man who in a garden, rife / With flowers, has gone unarmed, and found that there / Are evil things amid the blossoms fair" (*CW* 6:91). Therefore

> yet indeed from wise Bellerophon
> Right little by Queen Venus' wiles was won:
> Joyous he was, but nowise would forget
> That long and changing might his life be yet,
> Nor deemed he had to do with such things now,
> So let all pass, e'en as a painted show.   (*CW* 6:104)

The political implications of the narrow view and the wide make Sthenoboea hated by the people Bellerophon champions. He is kind

> To man and maid, and all men's hearts did bind
> With bonds of love, for mid the struggling folk,

The forgers and the bearers of the yoke,
Weary with wronging and with wrongs, he seemed
As one on whom a light from heaven had beamed,
That changed him to a god yet being alive. (*CW* 6:92)

It is true that Bellerophon's escape from Argos is assisted
by Proteus and that the hero is "innocent" of factual knowledge of the plot; but the real enabling agent is his combination
of *sapientia et fortitudo* (his wisdom and his hardihead—*CW*
6:100) and his desire to serve the world. His bright light of
detached dedication bears him inevitably into the sea of flux:

Now go I forth alone
To do what in my life must needs be done,
And in my own hands lies my fate, I think,
And I shall mix the cup that I must drink:
So be it; thus the world is merrier,
And I shall be a better man than here.   (*CW* 6:122)

"Bellerophon in Lycia" portends his marriage and ascension to the throne, but we are more aware of the perpetual
necessity of battle. Never sure of the plot against him, he never
interprets his feats as tests. His satisfaction is to bring light,
to defeat death when it is possible and to affirm life: "Life or
death, / But never death in life for me, O King!" (*CW* 6:238)
That life is for society is revealed by the nature of his enemies,
especially the three-formed monster who destroys the pastoral
balance of peasant life. The destruction of the harvest (*CW*
6:224–29) is reported by "a country carle" (*CW* 6:223), "a poor
and toiling man" (*CW* 6:224) who concludes:

This thing is true,
Though thou believe it not—that I was glad
Within the hour that yet my life I had,
Though this I saw—the garth made waste and bare,
Burnt as with fire, and for the homestead fair
The last flames dying o'er an ash-heap grey—
Gone was the mill, the freed stream took its way
In unchecked shallows o'er a sandy bed.   (*CW* 6:229)

When the monster's destruction is likewise reported by an ordinary survivor, the hero's motive and effect are given final statement: Bellerophon has wakened the soldier with "a kindly word: 'Be of good cheer! the earth is earth again' " (*CW* 6:252).

The Bellerophon stories are treated, like "The Golden Apples," with a distance that echoes the distinguishing trait of the heroes. All three present selected episodes and produce an effect

> Like to the middle of some pleasant dream,
> Which, waked from, leaves upon the troubled mind
> A sense of something ill that lurked behind,
> If morn had given due time to dream it out. (*CW* 6:19)

The narrator of "Bellerophon at Argos" is aware that "no third tale there is, of what befell / His fated life, when he had won his place" (*CW* 6:66). This treatment accentuates the theme of flux. Its sobering atmosphere dominates the Venus tales, the concluding statement of the work. Yet even here where death is permitted rather than distanced, we see the contrapuntal reassertion of hope. The renewal of the earth, the hero's goal in preceding stories, robs death of finality.

The Venusburg stories seem to predate other compositions for the volume, for they revert to the fantasies of summer.[21] The fantasies, however, are now subjected to the realistic alchemy of Laurence the Swabian, who again assumes his role as cynical priest (*CW* 6:280). His tendency to scoff at magic has served before to discredit the world of his tales, to invert even their internal qualifications. Here his skepticism is directed also toward his comrades. His tales of ordinary heroes "may perchance be of much less worth / Than tales of deeds that reddened the green earth" (*CW* 6:135). This deference to the more elevated stories of the volume appears to deflate their narrative motive; yet we have seen how these tales reject the egotism Laurence deplores. Likewise, he deliberately returns to the theme of death. Here again, he merely explicates the implications of the volume. Finally, his stories reject the illusion of immortality still tempting to the Wanderers; he associates it with Christianity and replaces the unpalatable asceticism of this "civilized" sorcery with pagan trust in "the green earth." Ultimately then, smiling Laurence "so old and grey" makes the cold bright light of winter palpable.

The Venusburg heroes are both weak men. They do not attain gaiety because the dread is too overwhelming. Their distinction is dogged perseverence and celebration of the world of the senses. Both journey to the otherworld of Venus. One returns to ordinary life, and the other returns to the Hill of Venus. Yet their fidelities to "earth" are similar; it is the symbol of the otherworld which shifts.

For Laurence in "The Ring Given to Venus" marriage to the otherworld queen would represent the same false spirituality attributed to the Christian Pope in "The Hill of Venus," where Walter chooses marriage to Venus as a more honest expression of mortal emotion. Laurence is the product of an "ancient" society which finds death frightening and life boring. In an attempt to deny both aspects of mortality, it turns to "wicked sorcery" (*CW* 6:137). While the Swabian describes this "ill" as worship of "Gods of old" (*CW* 6:137), he identifies its most ardent practitioners as Christian priests. Dan Palumbus, like Keats's beadsman, is typical. In this way the antagonistic worlds of Christianity and Venus-worship conspire to offer immortality as escape. Laurence's affinity for ordinary life with his mortal bride is strengthened by his journey to recover his wedding ring. The otherworld near the sea reveals immortality to be changeless change, a limbo where fallen civilizations linger, love dies, and the dead wander restlessly. Although "Laurence strove with tears in vain, / And his flesh trembled" (*CW* 6:168), he proceeds with determination to secure the ring and return to the simple pleasures of earth. His return is marked by his joyful response to a pastoral setting (*CW* 6:172–73). Dan Palumbus likewise receives just reward of his hypocrisy, death in which "tossed about / His soul might be in dread and doubt" (*CW* 6:174).

"The Hill of Venus" utilizes a conventional otherworld, but spiritual immortality is criticized through the "earnest pilgrim train" that seeks forgiveness of the flesh in Rome (*CW* 6:313). Before this concluding sequence of the tale, Walter has willfully entered the Hill of Venus, experienced its delights and pain, and chosen return to familiar life. Struggling now between the desire to return to Venus and fear of final judgment, he joins the pilgrims in search of peace. They babble of the millennium, and "time and again did seem / As though a cold and hopeless tune he heard, / Sung by grey mouths amidst a dull-eyes dream" (*CW* 6:313). Their dream, more insubstantial than Walter's, lacks the dimension of "the pain of fierce desire" because it denies all that is earthly: "Cloud-like the very earth grew 'neath men's feet," and the pilgrims were proud "that they / Had lived to see the firm earth melt away" (*CW* 6:313). The Pope, seeking Walter's confession, urges him to

> be forgiven—these things are of earth:
> The fire of God shall burn them up apace,
> And leave thee calm in thy pure second birth. (*CW* 6:320)

Walter's dramatic choice of the Hill of Venus—a conscious choice to prolong conscious pain—is precipitated by this interview, but before he renounces the Pope's asceticism, he rebukes the myopia of Christian doctrine by creating a vision of the natural harmony of man, earth, and the gods in pagan religion:

> Hast thou not heard about the gods, who erst
> Held rule here where thou dwellest? dost thou think
> That people 'neath their rule were so accurst
> That they forgot in joy to eat and drink,
> That they slept not, and loved not, and must shrink
> From the world's glory?—how if they loved these
> Thou callest devils and their images?
>
> And did God hate the world, then, for their sake,
> When fair the sun rose up on every day,
> And blade and bloom

> through the brown earth did break,
> And children were as glad as now?—nay, nay,
> Time for thy wrath yet—what if these held sway
> Even now in some wise, father?   (*CW* 6:322)

The natural potential of this other "heaven"—an earthly
paradise—is realized in the story's postscript, a scene in which
melodrama is controlled only by the Swabian's understatement. Walter has disappeared, pursuing his chosen fate with
"firm feet" (*CW* 6:323). It is a quiet afternoon, the day after
the Pope has dismissed Walter to hell, his view of the Venusburg: "Yea, dwell there ever more!" / He cried: "just so much
hope I have of thee / As on this dry staff fruit and flowers to
see!" (*CW* 6:323) The ironic conclusion of course provides just
that:

> With a great cry he sprang up; in his hand
> He held against the sky a wondrous thing,
> That might have been the bright archangel's wand,
> Who brought to Mary that fair summoning;
> For lo, in God's unfaltering timeless spring,
> Summer, and autumn, had that dry rod been,
> And from its barrenness the leaves sprang green,
>
> And on its barrenness grew wondrous flowers,
> That earth knew not; and on its barrenness
> Hung the ripe fruit of heaven's unmeasured hours;
> And with strange scent the soft dusk did it bless,
> And glowed with fair light as earth's light grew less,—
> Yea, and its gleam the old man's face did reach,
> Too glad for smiles, or tears, or any speech. (*CW* 6:325)

The blossoming rod converts pilgrim staff to pagan symbol,
but it also reasserts the mysteries of the earth in the moment
of death. If the metamorphosis seems magical in its references
to heavenly and unearthly occurrence, it is because intense
natural magic is required to offset orthodox spirituality. The
miracle is of the sort Yeats referred to when he contrasted

Morris's magic with the Christians': "The early Christians were of the kin of the Wilderness and of the Dry Tree, and they saw an unearthly Paradise, but he was of the kin of the Well and of the Green Tree and he saw an Earthly Paradise." [22] The Swabian's tale thus at last converts stone to shell to affirm natural truth, the theme announced in "The Golden Apples" when Hercules brought the earthly unto the realm of the unearthly. At that point his magnanimity issued in blessing:

> So for my part I rather bless than curse,
> And bless this fateful land; good be with it;
> Nor for this deadly thing's death is it worse,
> Nor for the lack of gold; still shall ye sit
> Watching the swallow o'er the daisies flit;
> Still shall your wandering limbs ere day is done
> Make dawn desired by the sinking sun. (*CW* 6:14)

The context of the tale works in a similar way. After the long nights of winter, there is a promise of spring as the story begins. As it ends, there is bright daylight, and the "old men learned in earth's bitter lore" leave their meditative closure. Their response to the natural world is both distant and sensuous. It is their closest approximation to the radical innocence of the tales. They

> wandered forth into the noonday sun,
> To watch the blossoms budding on the wall,
> And hear the rooks among the elm-trees call,
> And note the happy voices on the breeze,
> And see the lithe forms; making out of these
> No tangled story, but regarding them
> As hidden elves upon the forest's hem
> Gaze on the dancers through the May-night green,
> Not knowing aught what troubled looks may mean.
> (*CW* 6:326)

There is qualified intimation that the "plenteous feast" of tales has given the Wanderers perspective to "light / The sons of men to that unfailing night, / That death they needs must look on face to face" (*CW* 3:82).

chapter eight
The Poet and the Poem

Ceasse now, my song, my woe now wasted is;
O joyfull verse!
Spenser, *Shepheard's Calendar*

THE cycle of *The Earthly Paradise* ultimately returns to the narrator, Morris's most complex creation in the poem. The work affords two views of the "idle singer"—in the Apology, Epilogue, and framework, where we see him as poet, and in the monthly interludes, where we see him as individual man. It is to this composite narrative persona that we turn for guidance in inferring Morris's attitude toward the relationship of man, art, nature, and society at the conclusion of his early period of poetry. Again, we find that our own vision is sharpened by context, especially by the narrative perspective of *News from Nowhere*, where the subject and style of vision yield Morris's final version of pastoral.

The use of a narrator in Morris's work is rather unusual. There is first-person narration in some of the early tales, e.g., "The Story of the Unknown Church" and "The Hollow Land"; but only the two late political romances, *A Dream of John Ball* and *News from Nowhere*, utilize the kind of narrator we see first in *The Earthly Paradise*. He is a persona for the poet; he stands outside the narrative, or more precisely, between the narrative and the real worlds, for he seems to feel at home in neither. In all three works the real, contemporary world is characterized as industrial and complex; the fictional world, distant in time (though not in space, in the later works), is agrarian or simple.

On one level, the narrator is the conventional traveler-observer, a device frequently employed in utopian literature for introducing the ideal society through the eyes of an ordinary and acceptable contemporary. The convention is obviously at work in *A Dream of John Ball* and *News from Nowhere*, supported by the journey structure, especially in *Nowhere*,

where the plot is formed around a journey up the Thames. In *The Earthly Paradise* the traveler-observer convention operates on two levels. Within the framework story, the Wanderers are weary travelers whose sole activity is to recite and hear, i.e., to observe, the happier life and adventures of past heroes in a simpler world. On this level they are the narrators of the poem, reduced from heroic to ordinary human proportions by their fatigue and failure, and granted the narrator's necessary anonymity by their characterization as "hollow puppets." On another level, however, we are aware of the narrative persona of the poet, the "idle singer," whose travel experience presents both parallels and contrasts to that of the Wanderers. As we have noted, he alludes initially to his visit "awhile ago within a flowery land" (*CW* 3:81) and treats the opening lines of his Prologue as an invitation to the reader to travel into the world of the poem. That travel is a metaphor for aesthetic experience is strongly reiterated in the "Envoi" where the image is applied to the poem itself; the narrator bids the book in "pilgrim's weed" to "speed / Upon thy perilous journey" to the world (*CW* 6:330). To the extent that the narrator is poet, his attitudes and functions are in a relationship of contrast with the Wanderers: he has created them and their world, and his chief function is to link their world to that of the readers. Yet we have seen how he makes their situation a contemporary parallel. The similarities are also emphasized in the lyric interludes. Although the speaker, by virtue of age and quality of experience, is deprived of hope by potentially reversible circumstance, his frustration and temporal consciousness resemble that of his characters. In short, to emphasize the cultural recurrence of hope and despair Morris creates, as it were, double narrators to distance the innocent core of the poem.

The most significant effect of this technique is to shift the meaning of travel from active to visionary adventure, or from energy to idleness. Where there is motion, it is vertical rather than horizontal. The movement is apt to be a gradual descent into distant time and inner space, a process we observed in the

beginning of the Prologue. Another common vehicle of vertical movement in Morris is the dream-vision, used in *A Dream
of John Ball, News from Nowhere,* and many of the *Earthly Paradise* stories. Here the descent is sudden and stunning, rather
like Alice's fall into Wonderland. Although we have acknowledged the psychological interest of both patterns, their most
important element is the tension of double vision that is
created by the narrator's simultaneous awareness of two
worlds. While disparities automatically appear through juxtaposition of different worlds, especially the simple and complex, the implications are heightened by the presence of a
conscious viewer.

Morris's narrators embody this consciousness and the sense
of alienation it produces. Perceiving the two worlds, the narrator feels at home in neither, and his double vision intensifies
the character of each. On the one hand, modern civilization
repels him: the "smoke, . . . the snorting steam and piston
stroke" (*CW* 3:3) of industrialized England, the "sooty and
muddy" roads of London (*CW* 16:287), the dirty Thames, or
the dehumanized workers that are typified in *News from Nowhere* when the narrator's jolting return to reality echoes Gul-
liver's:

> as I turned round the corner which led to the remains
> of the village cross, I came upon a figure strangely
> contrasting with the joyous, beautiful people I had left
> behind. . . . It was a man who looked old, but whom I
> knew from habit, now half-forgotten, was really not
> much more than fifty. His face was rugged, and grimed
> rather than dirty; his eyes dull and bleared; his body
> bent, his calves thin and spindly, his feet dragging and
> limping. His clothing was a mixture of dirt and rags long
> over-familiar to me. As I passed him he touched his hat
> with some real good-will and courtesy, and much ser-
> vility. (*CW* 16:209–10)

The horror of return to contemporary England is like seeing
a "black cloud rolling along to meet me, like a nightmare of

my childish days." On the other hand, the narrator is not at home in his dreamworld either. In *A Dream of John Ball* and *News from Nowhere* he is welcomed, entertained, and even consulted, but his narrative is interrupted by comments that remind us of his presence, his sense of alienation, of his awareness of disparities. The source of his alienation is consciousness itself. He is keenly aware of his age, his sense of personal and cultural time, his cynicism, doubt, and sadness. Above all, he is conscious of being conscious. Like Keats after the nightingale, he tries to perceive the meaning of his experience in the land of Nowhere; he tries to distinguish between dream (in this case, impossible wish) and vision (which seems to mean insight into real potential). He chooses the latter on the basis of his acute double perception:

> I lay in my bed in my house at dingy Hammersmith thinking about it all; and trying to consider if I was overwhelmed with despair at finding I had been dreaming a dream; and strange to say, I found that I was not so despairing.
> Or indeed *was* it a dream? If so, why was I so conscious all along that I was really seeing all that new life from the outside, still wrapped up in the prejudices, the anxieties, the distrust of this time of doubt and struggle? (*CW* 16:210)

In traditional terms, the narrator is fallen man; he has acquired knowledge, and he looks through tainted eyes at Eden before its beauty, joy, and simple harmony have been spoiled by the cumulative actions of centuries of "civilization." That the utopia is placed in the future does not substantially change the metaphor. Just before the narrative experience breaks off, the narrator stands outside the building where a harvest feast will culminate the natural cycle of the earth and the communal joys of man within that cycle. The building, now a community hall, was once a church. The lonely observer cannot cross the threshold; he is denied access to the "sacred" mysteries.

His prototype is Satan, the weary traveler whose first view of Eden intensifies his consciousness of his own isolation, alteration, and capacity for destruction. Certainly Morris's narratives have Edenic overtones, especially the despair of existence in this "now altered world." But like Milton, Blake, and Yeats —all architects of the myth of innocence and experience— Morris seems less interested in regaining a state of prelapsarian innocence than in defining and, ultimately, celebrating experience as a state of mind that creates both paradise and chaos, needs both simplicity and complexity, craves both idleness and energy. Milton was to bring the antithetical poles of human potential together in the *felix culpa* and "a Paradise within." Morris, professedly "pagan," was to move closer to building Blake's New Jerusalem "In England's green and pleasant land" and to affirming with Yeats that

> all hatred driven hence,
> The soul recovers radical innocence
> And learns at last that it is self-delighting,
> Self-appeasing, self-affrighting. . . .[1]

News from Nowhere embodies the "radical innocence" of Arcadian utopia. Although the writer of 1890 places in the future the vision he had located in the mythical past in *The Earthly Paradise*, both visions are the culmination of temporal cycle, a similarity more significant than the contrast. Although Morris was unable in 1870 to foresee the shape of his utopian society, he knew that it would have to evolve through "more complete civilization." Its fulfillment in Nowhere is called a "second childhood of the world," but it is a world "grown old and wiser" (*CW* 16:136, 144). Explaining the society of Nowhere, Old Hammond alludes to the cyclical pattern Morris frequently describes in organic terms:

> This is how we stand. England was once a country of clearings amongst the woods and wastes, with a few towns interspersed, which were fortresses for the feudal

army, markets for the folk, gathering places for the craftsmen. It then became a country of huge and foul workshops and fouler gambling-dens, surrounded by an ill-kept, poverty-stricken farm, pillaged by the masters of the workshops. It is now a garden, where nothing is wasted and nothing is spoilt, with the necessary dwellings, sheds, and workshops scattered up and down the country, all trim and neat and pretty. (*CW* 16:72)

The garden society of Nowhere is explicitly pastoral—ordered kinesis. While it excludes neither seasonal change, age, death, nor the vicissitudes of love (acknowledged as including perversity and self-will (*CW* 16:35), it does exclude the false and complicating drives of capitalism—competition, abstraction, and the acquisitive instinct. Instead, its primary motive is a sensuous love of the earth, what Ellen calls "The earth and the growth of it and the life of it!" (*CW* 16:202). Old Hammond says: "the world was being brought to its second birth; how could that take place without a tragedy? Moreover, think of it. The spirit of the new days, of our days, was to be delight in the life of the world; intense and overweening love of the very skin and surface of the earth on which man dwells, such as a lover has in the fair flesh of the woman he loves; this, I say, was to be the new spirit of the time" (*CW* 16:132). The effect of this anti-doctrine in Nowhere is an acknowledgment of death but a lust for life. As Ellen puts it simply, "I love life better than death" (*CW* 16:158). *News from Nowhere* thus concretizes the hope of *The Earthly Paradise* and reverses the emphasis of the great antinomies, life and death. This shift, like the exchange of past and future location, is a result of the poet's growing optimism. The same optimism synthesizes into single vision the glimpses of "radical innocence" in the tales and in the atmosphere of Volume IV, where the phase of rebirth is still distanced as myth.

Two essential elements of the later work are present in *The Earthly Paradise*, however. One is the double vision we have noted. It is of critical importance, for it is as distinctly pastoral as the quality of life it contains. The world of Nowhere, like the dream of Gregory the Star-gazer, the kingdom of Admetus, the vision of the "wizard to a northern king," or the idle singer's medieval London, is a vision. It is viable only as it reveals its antithesis in the contemporary world of the narrator. It is created through the poet's "idleness" as an expression of present despair and future hope, the components of experienced innocence. Never are the people of utopia as compelling as the narrator, and never are we allowed to forget him. The work derives its utopian and pastoral qualities from the simultaneous distance and immersion of a narrator who says, "I was using my eyes with all my might" (*CW* 16:31).

The other element foreshadowed in *The Earthly Paradise* is the "return," the essential characteristic of successful quest journey and pastoral vision. It is of course suggested in the cyclical movement of the tales, but its primary statement is in the aesthetic activity of the narrator as man and poet—first in the lyric interludes and finally in the framework.

The lyrics are the most personal expression of the poem. Striking for their first-person, present-tense intensity, they hark back to the "poetry of experience" of *Guenevere*. With the summer volume, the similarity is increased by the inclusion of an auditor, usually assumed to be Jane Morris, poetically significant as a person separated from the speaker both as loved one and as an individual whose unhappy innocence complicates the meditation of the more experienced narrator.

The theme of the lyrics is cognitive, and the controlling imagery is visual. Like the Wanderers of the framework and many of the characters of the tales, the speaker struggles toward synthesis—of man and nature, man and woman, change and permanence. The movement toward synthesis characterizes the individual lyrics as well as their corporate body. Yet two antiromantic elements are readily apparent: (1) The unimpeded flow of lyric expression is checked by structure, style, and perspective, an acknowledgment of limitation that foreshadows the final vision. (2) This vision, though clear, is not ultimately synthetic. Rather, it is a recognition of irreconcilable disparities. Thus the traditional movement from light to darkness to light dispels illusion to discover that reality is rather stark. This is pastoral vision in one of its oldest forms, an elegiac recognition of the cycle of experience. The visionary journeys of the narrator as man and poet look meditatively at loss without gaining or granting control. The effect is similar to that which one critic finds in *Lycidas:* "Innocence is exchanged for bleak experience, in turn to be replaced by a wiser innocence." [2]

The structure of the lyric journey is provided by the imagery of darkness and light and by the medieval calendar. Both metaphors suggest man's relationship with nature, but the first, because epistemological, expresses individual insight; the second depersonalizes and universalizes that experience. The combination is another testimony to the poet's determination to transform subjective retreat into communal experience. Light imagery is related to "the elegiac mode" which Abbie Potts defines as the poetry of *anagnorisis:*

> The usual symbol of such poetry is light out of darkness. Moreover, whereas drama and epic are primarily concerned with action and didactic poetry with dogma, elegy is the poetry of skeptical and revelatory vision for its own sake, satisfying the hunger of man to see, to know, to understand. Whether the reader be purged or indoctrinated, he must be enlightened. In its latest as in its earliest guise elegy labors toward human truth as its end in view.[3]

Such is the process of the lyric interludes. They never reveal the speaker's union with kind in the manner of *In Memoriam* or *The Prelude,* but even more than the Apology, Epilogue, and framework, they establish rapport with the reader, providing an intimate channel for empathy with the discoveries of the poet.

The spring lyrics suggest the character of illusion, although they, like succeeding lyrics, entertain it within a limiting con-

text. The result is a feeling of separation between man and
nature. The spring vision of nature is abstract and idealized.
"March" and "April" personify the months and invest them
with a paradisal quality of perfect, independent loveliness. For
example, the rhetoric of the first stanza of "April" perfects
nature through apostrophe, line and sound balance, and the
negative syntax of conventional paradise descriptions:

> O fair midspring, besung so oft and oft,
> How can I praise thy loveliness enow?
> The sun that burns not, and thy breezes soft
> That o'er the blossoms of the orchard blow,
> The thousand things that 'neath the young leaves grow,
> The hopes and chances of the growing year,
> Winter forgotten long, and summer near.   (*CW* 3:169)

In the first two lyrics paradise is associated with nature's unconsciousness ("unmindful brown birds"), the illusion of temporal suspension (medial stasis between winter and summer),
and the defeat of death by cycle ("thou diest not"). The
speaker's separation is implied by the lack of these possibilities
in himself.

The two poems focus on nature, and the narrator's presence
is weakly felt and initially undefined. The narrative "I," given
subordinate entrance in the second stanza of "March," serves
primarily to qualify the ideal vision with which the speaker
fails to find unity. We note understatement close to litotes
("March," ll. 3–4), negating juxtapositions ("March," l. 8, and
"April," ll. 8–9), and interrogative syntax. These elements produce a sense of shadowed loveliness.[4] The shadow is caused
by the narrator's consciousness of the illusionary quality of the
ideal vision he wishes to entertain. It is immediately established that consciousness inhibits and saddens the speaker; yet
the poetic process is an exercise of consciousness that insists
on separation of experiential elements ("April," l. 18: "Striving my pleasure from my pain to sift"), on submission of ideal
to what consciousness acknowledges as real. Syntactic negation is one indication of this process, a constant undercutting

of assertion. It is most clearly conveyed, however, by structure. Morris uses the rime royal stanza to control emotion but also to analyze it in the meditative tradition. The technique assumes thematic clarity in the later lyrics, but here we see it already in the stanzaic reversals of the spring lyrics. However qualified the vision of the first two stanzas may be, it remains temptingly viable until checked by the final stanzas: "Ah! . . . Ah! . . . Alas!" In each case the stanza recognizes death, change, or personal loss as that which creates the ideal vision. Twice in these first two lyrics Morris employs the word *striving* to suggest the meditative energy of the speaker. It intimates both his hope and his process of bringing to consciousness the very elements which necessarily frustrate it.

The "May" lyric shares stylistic features with the other spring poems, but its introduction of an auditor, however vague, marks progress toward a more corporate vision. Throughout the remaining poems the societal element of elegy is distilled into the relationship between the speaker and listener. It is primarily a relationship of separation which intensifies the already suggested separation from nature. Union of either sort is at best temporary. Of special interest is the interrogative form of the first stanza. It compares the perceptions of speaker and listener, although the succeeding stanzas imply the rhetorical nature of the questions.

In this first instance of visual experience, the dual vision of the Lord of Love and of Eld and Death is prompted by the implied situation between narrator and auditor. The ideal relationship of speaker and listener is transformed into the vision of the Lord of Love, "Ringed round with maids, and youths, and minstrelsy"; the ideal is shadowed by the impermanence of reality, translated into Eld and Death. Despite its vague language, the poem has dramatic force. The speaker seems to doubt his perceptions, wishing human confirmation of his ideal vision. Lack of response induces the real one, a vision of double isolation from natural and human harmony. There is emphatic identification of light with reality: "Didst thou *see* aught? . . . For then *methought* the Lord of Love went by. . . . And the *light* gathered; then I held my breath, / And shuddered at the *sight* of Eld and Death. . . . On these twain *shone out the golden sun*" (*CW* 4:1). No natural or human being perceives Eld and Death; they are the solitary vision of the narrator. Loneliness is increased by an unresponsive audience.

Like the tales of summer, the lyrics of June, July, and August reassert "hope more than conscious enough." For moments at least they unite speaker, audience, and landscape. The "I" becomes "we" in "June," "thou and I" in "July," and in "August" the "you" is dominant. The apparent integrative movement is facilitated by spatial perspective. These lyrics carry narrator and audience into particular landscapes.

The landscapes of summer are pastoral, surrounding the characters with familiar details of natural harmony along the Thames valley. The binding action of the shepherd in "August" metaphorically expresses the tenor of these idylls, which enclose a variety of natural activity within a static construct. The speaker invites auditor and reader to see, behold, rest, and hear. Sense response is purified by reduction: "All little sounds" (bees, barley-mowers, sheep-bells, and weir) are "made musical and clear" (*CW* 4:187). These landscapes, remarkably similar to idyllic scenes from the tales and *News from Nowhere*, seem to epitomize pastoral peace, but the narrator's response betrays a search for a vision that falls short of mature pastoral. The speaker, experiencing the double vision of real pastoral, wishes to negate its "civilized," conscious aspect and attain unconscious unity with what he observes.

Again the shadowing effect is expressed in a number of ways, e.g., "No thought of storm the morning vexes yet" ("June," l. 7; *CW* 4:87). This unwilling negation is temporal. More important is spatial qualification. In "June" the speaker also reveals his urban consciousness by praising the landscape's isolation:

> See, we have left our hopes and fears behind
> To give our very hearts up unto thee;
> What better place than this then could we find

> By this sweet stream that knows not of the sea,
> That guesses not the city's misery,
> This little stream whose hamlets scarce have names,
> This far-off, lonely mother of the Thames?   (*CW* 4:87)

Compelling though the descriptions are in these poems, they represent escape for the narrator into benign, maternal nature. Their meditative value is their unexpected revelation that peace, quietness, and happiness (words repeated in all three lyrics) release antithetical feelings in the speaker. The concluding stanzas again include rhetorical questions implying that total unconsciousness is impossible. It is a "rare happy dream" ("June," l. 18; *CW* 4:87).

This recognition of discrepancy between wish and reality becomes in the succeeding lyrics a kind of qualified acceptance of double vision. The truer pastoral vision emerges as the speaker rejects illusion's power while recognizing its inevitability. In "September" he says:

> What vision wilt thou give me, autumn morn,
> To make thy pensive sweetness more complete?
> . . . .
> Look long, O longing eyes, and look in vain!
> Strain idly, aching heart, and yet be wise,
> And hope no more for things to come again
> That thou beheldest once with careless eyes!   (*CW* 5:1)

The direct cause of disillusionment is the psychological separation of speaker and auditor, the continuous theme of that "delicate" and "outspoken" autobiography Mackail finds in the interludes. But the natural setting is more than backdrop. It is the agent of rehabilitation of the "careless eyes." Without its role as mirror and antithesis, the human relationship would lack dimension or outlet.

The strongest lyrics are those which face the failure of the relationship. After the October lyric, the second-person pronoun is vague. The speaker seems to address himself. The situation invites the introspection of despair, yet it is precisely here that vision becomes "extraverted." The movement into darkness and final light parallels the cycle of the tales and framework, utilizing nature as prism. "October" and "November," the darkening phase, are inspired by the face of nature hidden by spring and summer's vitality. The "year grown old, / A-dying mid the autumn-scented haze" ("October," ll. 2–3; *CW* 5:122), provides a vision of mutability; and in "November," the best of the lyrics, nature guides what Bodkin calls the poet's descent into hell. Of Morris she says what we have seen to be true of the characters of the autumn and winter tales. The Icelandic journals and these *Earthly Paradise* passages "show the nature of the need he felt—to experience, at least in symbol, such hardness, terror, and desolation as probe a man even to those innermost places where fears lurk." [5]

The setting of "November," urban and enclosed, "returns" the speaker to his accustomed environment. From the literal and metaphoric distance of civilized closure he looks within and without to probe his relationship with nature. Meditation here takes the form of debate. The movement begins with internal questioning, turns to the "real" world for unsuccessful refutation, and returns to the narrator's response. Instead of solipsistic progression, we find confirmation of vision.

The speaker's struggle is perceptual. In the first stanza he struggles with the temptation to cease looking:

> Are thine eyes weary? is thy heart too sick
> To struggle any more with doubt and thought,
> Whose formless veil draws darkening now and thick
> Across thee, e'en as smoke-tinged mist-wreaths brought
> Down a fair dale to make it blind and nought?
> Art thou so weary that no world there seems
> Beyond these four walls, hung with pain and dreams?
>   (*CW* 5:206)

For the first time the illusionary veil is overtly identified with consciousness, doubt, and thought. Its comparison with smoke suggests a fall of man and nature, the latter associated with man's activities. Implied is a purer, more physical state of man and nature which would release the speaker from introspection into simple rest. The stanza concentrates on subject, not object, assuming the control of human vision, however negative.

To deny the chaos of introspection, the speaker turns in the next stanza to "Look out on the real world"—significantly a midnight, winter landscape that reverses the connotations of the daylight world of the spring and summer lyrics. He seems to wish away the "doubt and thought" of complex civilization by viewing nature in its stark, cosmic simplicity. Yet his consciousness automatically dictates romantic illusion. Although there are "no images, / No hopes of day," he tries to imagine that

> the moon,
> Half-way 'twixt root and crown of these high trees,
> Turns the dead midnight into dreamy noon,
> Silent and full of wonders.

Both this stanza and the last utilize the concluding couplet for a question. Neither seems rhetorical in the sense of implying a satisfying answer. Both are searching; form and content fuse to suggest the insoluble antitheses of man's vision. The answer to the question, "Is it not fair?" is both positive and negative. The ideal of permanent beauty, created by the poet's eye, is there, but so is the reality of permanent flux, "the changeless seal of change." It is the unexpected dark side of simplicity.

Both discoveries receive powerful statement in the opening line of the last stanza: "Yea, I have looked, and seen November there." November is simultaneously real landscape, ideal beauty, and symbol of "the dread eternity." The speaker's recognition of nature's complexities forces acceptance of his own in a way that the benign seasons could not. Dreamer of dreams, man yearns for permanence. Facing its "void patience," he cherishes his own "out-stretched feverish hands" and "restless heart."

The imagery of darkness also dominates the next two lyrics, a city midnight again in "December," and in "January," the "murky ending of a leaden day" (*CW* 6:65). Again also, celestial light in "December" reveals a classical starkness reminiscent of Arnold. The turn to human resources of "November" is intensified here at the still point of winter. It can hardly be called hope, but it is an insistence on life and a dependence on vision as its vehicle. The rhetoric of "December" still expresses doubt, but temporarily the interrogative form becomes declarative:

> O thou who clingest still to life and love,
> Though nought of good, no God thou mayst discern,
> Though nought that is, thine utmost woe can move,
> Though no soul knows
>   wherewith thine heart doth yearn,
> Yet, since thy weary lips no curse can learn,
> Cast no least thing thou lovedst once away,
> Since yet perchance thine eyes shall see the day.
>
>   (*CW* 6:1)

"The day" comes in the concluding lyric, where stark imagery is most compelling. It is high noon, the hour of romantic vision in the tales and of realistic perception for the Wanderers. The predicative sentences of the first stanza reveal the "new world" with images divested of fantasy: *empty, rain-washed, bare, leafless, void, lonely*. Although the imagery is totally visual, its denotative force looks forward to Morris's assessment of Icelandic song where "your ears might hear / Earth's voices as they are indeed." [6]

Using winter's "barrein ground" as mirror, the speaker accepts and employs double vision. Seeing the winter world, he records its clarity. Converting illusionary vision into the vision of memory, he projects perception into the future: "Shall it not hap that on some dawn of May / Thou shalt awake, and . . . See nothing clear but this same dreary day, / Of all the days that have passed o'er thine head?" (*CW* 6:175). The questions acknowledge the impossibility of prophecy, but they strongly assert the power of memory to retain both pleasure and pain and to stir in man the same wish for continuity that the seasons embody. Certainly this conclusion is tenuous. It must be in order to contain total vision. It also might seem melancholy, but only if defined as the elegiac melancholy experienced by Colin Cloute "as he satte in secrete shade alone." The solitary singer of pastoral elegy can say, "The God of Shepherds, Tityrus, is dead" or "O! trustlesse state of earthly things." In *Adonais* Shelley says that "grief returns with the revolving year." At the point of descent into this recognition of changeless change, "No sonne now shines." At the point of "return," however, light re-emerges. For the idle singer it is not the conventional promise of individual immortality but the light of human consciousness itself.

The Wanderers of the framework are a chorus who mirror the experience of the lyric poet. Their aesthetic journey through the changing year, while it effects fatigue, also affirms the continuity of human memory. As they perceive the ages of man implied in the tales, they respond with initial pain—rekindling of "wild hope"—that, gradually blended with aesthetic pleasure, produces distance.

The locus of the framework, with its ordered enclosures, natural beauty, and communal feasts, is a picture of the possibilities of civilization. Its medial location in time and space may suggest a Palace of Art, but it is too temporary and too communal to function in that way. In fall and winter the Wanderers hear the sea of flux even while they enjoy safety:

> They sat within the city's great guest-hall,
> So near the sea that they might hear the fall
> Of the low haven-waves when night was still.
> But on that day wild wind and rain did fill
> The earth and sea with clamour, and the street
> Held few who cared the driving scud to meet.
> But inside, as a little world it was,

> Peaceful amid the hubbub that did pass
> Its strong walls in untiring waves of rage,
> With the earth's intercourse wild war to wage.
>   (*CW* 5:157)

The sounds of nature are augmented by aesthetic experience to remind listeners of reality:

> Yet of the world's woe somewhat was within
> The noble compass of its walls, for there
> Were histories of great striving painted fair,
> Striving with love and hate, with life and death,
> With hope that lies, and fear that threateneth. (*CW* 5:157)

The tales, like the feasts that provide occasion for their repetition, give pensive "nourishment." What is thus created in the listeners is escape not from life but from self: "each deemed himself not quite alone" (*CW* 5:157), and

>   they might sit and praise
> The calm, wise heart that knoweth how to rest,
> The man too kind to snatch out at the best,
> Since he is part of all, each thing a part,
> Beloved alike of his wide-loving heart.   (*CW* 5:205)

The communal identification of elegy, the effect of "return," finally unites man with "the very skin and surface of the earth on which man dwells" and with the communal consciousness of the "art of the people." The intimation of rebirth is still distant in *The Earthly Paradise*, but its sources are both natural and social. The old tales are like "feathery seed" that are "borne across the sea to help the need / Of barren isles" (*CW* 4:3). The narrator repeats the figure to his contemporary audience at the end of the dying year. The book itself, the "old garden" with potential to make "fresh flowers spring up from hoarded seed" (*CW* 6:333), signals the narrator's "return." Art is solace not because it insulates the artist or audience from reality but because it recalls man's and nature's "eternal recurrence" (*CW* 22:11). As the seeds bring new life, they remind man again of the rhythmic disparities of all life—individual, cultural, natural—but they also affirm the memory of human tradition as the primary resource of "Earth the Healer, Earth the Keeper" (*CW* 9:184). In the cycle of cultural rehabilitation, the narrator serves only to initiate insight. By separating the reader from the familiar construct of reality and returning him again, the pastoral poet provides a context for evaluation.

The Earthly Paradise is a unique work. Never before or after its publication did Morris bring together all the elements that created its complexity. Yet it prophesies the search for a higher, simpler civilization, the dream that would inform his works until the end of his life. For Morris, more than any other Victorian, the vision of utopia is literally rooted in the familiar earth and the cultural heritage of England. In an era when the past provided epic heroes, architectural grandeur, or a Gothic landscape that never was, Morris directed his pastoral vision toward the historical realities of English country life. He peopled his Arcadia with simple men, like the medieval Cotswold laborer whose cottage was "a work of art and a piece of nature"; and he rejected the dramatic settings of "great wastes" and "terrible untrodden mountain-walls" for the pastoral scale of the "little land" that had sustained its people for centuries: "all is measured, mingled, varied, gliding easily one thing into another: little rivers, little plains, swelling, speedily-changing uplands, all beset with handsome orderly trees; little hills, little mountains, netted over with the walls of sheep-walks; all is little; yet not foolish and blank, but serious rather, and abundant of meaning for such as choose to seek it: it is neither prison nor palace, but a decent home" (*CW* 22:17).

Finally, the discovery of Morris's pastoral world is the fresh recognition of what was already present in the "continuous life of the world of men." [7] Its revelation is the "idle" work of the poet; but its "continuous life" depends upon the culture that symbolically embodies the kingdoms of Rome and Arcady. Through this dialectical potential of modern civilization the poet's vision of an Earthly Paradise is both threatened and nourished.

INTRODUCTION

1. "How I Became a Socialist," *The Collected Works of William Morris,* ed. May Morris, 24 vols. (London: Longmans, 1910–1915), 23:279. Hereafter cited as *CW* with volume and page number.

2. Biographical studies are the most numerous, dating from J. W. Mackail, *The Life of William Morris,* 2 vols. (1899; 2nd ed., London: Longmans, 1901), the standard biography; the *Collected Works,* edited by Morris's daughter May Morris, is important for introductions and biographical material; see also May Morris, *William Morris, Artist, Writer, Socialist,* 2 vols. (Oxford: B. Blackwell, 1936), a later collection of Morris's work with his daughter's commentary. Shorter appreciations are too numerous to detail.

3. Especially important studies include Margaret Grennan, *William Morris: Medievalist and Revolutionary* (New York: King's Crown Press, 1945); and E. P. Thompson, *William Morris: Romantic to Revolutionary* (London: Camelot, 1955). Source studies include Oscar Maurer, Jr., "William Morris's *The Earthly Paradise:* The Composition, Sources, and Critical Reception," Diss. Yale 1935; and Ralph A. Bellas, "William Morris' Treatment of Sources in *The Earthly Paradise,*" Diss. Kansas 1961.

4. After almost three lean decades of Morris scholarship, three books were published in 1967 alone: Philip Henderson, *William Morris: His Life, Work and Friends* (New York: McGraw-Hill, 1967); Paul Thompson, *The Work of William Morris* (New York: Viking, 1967); and Ray Watkinson, *William Morris as Designer* (New York: Reinhold, 1967). Lewis's essay, still one of the best on Morris, was published as "William Morris," *Rehabilitations* (London: Oxford Univ. Press, 1939).

5. Although retreat is a pervasive assumption in Morris

criticism, its most famous expression occurs in Douglas Bush, *Mythology and the Romantic Tradition in English Poetry* (1937; rpt. New York: W. W. Norton, 1963), p. 326: "And this man of immense and versatile creative energy was the mild-eyed melancholy lotos-eater who spent part of that energy in composing an immense mass of verse most of which cannot appeal to modern readers after they have passed twenty." Its most recent expression occurs in Philip Henderson, p. 96, who feels that the fear, despair, and passion of the *Earthly Paradise* period were "in later life . . . channelled . . . into public causes, but this process had not yet begun."

6. See Karl Litzenberg, "William Morris and the Reviews: A Study in the Fame of the Poet," *Review of English Studies*, 12 (1936), 413–28. Litzenberg notes that "the first three parts of *The Earthly Paradise* had been reprinted a total of seven times before the fourth part was sent to press" (p. 420). Attack of this popular work concentrated on Morris's pose as idle singer: "Morris may have been wrong about all this; but his reviewers were not content to call him wrong and pass on to his skill as a story-teller. Instead, they argued the merits of his theory of life" (p. 425).

7. Quoted in B. Ifor Evans, *William Morris and His Poetry* (London: G. G. Harrap, 1925), p. 153.

8. Lewis, p. 45.

9. *The Autobiography of William Butler Yeats* (New York: Macmillan, 1953), p. 87.

10. Carl G. Jung, "On the Relation of Analytical Psychology to Poetic Art," *Contributions to Analytical Psychology*, trans. H. G. and Cary F. Baynes (London: Routledge and Kegan Paul, 1928). Rpt. in *Modern Continental Literary Criticism*, ed. O. B. Hardison, Jr. (New York: Appleton, 1962), p. 287.

11. "The Happiest of the Poets," *Essays and Introductions* (New York: Macmillan, 1961), pp. 53–64.

12. The term *pastoral* was first applied to Morris by Mackail in describing *News from Nowhere* (2:243, 295). Northrop Frye

calls the same work a very pure example of the Arcadian utopia in "Varieties of Literary Utopias," *Daedalus*, 94 (1965), 342–44.

13. "Two Kingdoms of Force," *Massachusetts Review*, 1 (1959), 89. For the extension of these views, see *The Machine in the Garden: Technology and the Pastoral Ideal in America* (New York: Oxford Univ. Press, 1964). Other helpful works on the pastoral include William Empson, *Some Versions of Pastoral* (Norfolk, Conn.: New Directions, 1960); and several works by Renato Poggioli: "The Oaten Flute," *Harvard Library Bulletin*, 11 (1957), 147–84; "The Pastoral of the Self," *Daedalus*, 88 (1959), 687–99; "Naboth's Vineyard or the Pastoral View of the Social Order," *Journal of the History of Ideas*, 24 (1963), 3–24. Pastoral interpretations of individual poets include John Lynen, *The Pastoral Art of Robert Frost* (New Haven: Yale Univ. Press, 1960); John W. Stevenson, "The Pastoral Setting in the Poetry of A. E. Housman," *South Atlantic Quarterly*, 55 (1956), 487–90, 492–500; and George Mills Harper, *Yeats's Quest for Eden*, Dolmen Press Yeats Centenary Papers, 9 (Dublin: Dolmen Press, 1965).

14. Lynen, pp. 11–12.

15. Lewis, pp. 39, 49.

CHAPTER ONE 〜〜〜〜〜〜〜〜〜〜〜〜〜

1. William Blake, Preface to *Milton*, in *The Complete Writings of William Blake*, ed. Geoffrey Keynes, rev. ed. (London: Oxford Univ. Press, 1966), p. 481; and John Ruskin, *The Works of John Ruskin*, ed. E. T. Cook and Alexander Wedderburn, Library Edition (London: George Allen, 1905), 18:457.

2. May Morris, *William Morris: Artist, Writer, Socialist*, 1:193.

3. Ibid., 2:16.

4. Mackail, *Life*, 1:239.

5. The passages from the Apology of *The Earthly Paradise* are from *CW* 3; *The Life and Death of Jason* is in *CW* 2; and *News from Nowhere* is in *CW* 16.

6. *Life*, 2:243.

7. *The Poetical Works of Matthew Arnold*, ed. C. B. Tinker and H. F. Lowry (London: Oxford Univ. Press, 1950), pp. 248–49.

8. *The Works of Thomas Hardy*, Wessex Edition (London: Macmillan, 1912), 1:414–16.

9. Ruskin, *Works*, 18:133–34.

10. Ibid., pp. 508–10, 512.

11. Thomas Henry Huxley, *Collected Essays*, 9 vols. (New York: D. Appleton, 1898), 3:159.

12. *Works of Lord Macaulay*, Albany Edition, Essays and Biography (London: Longmans, 1898), 2:616.

13. *Collected Works of John Stuart Mill*, vol. 10, *Essays on Ethics, Religion and Society*, ed. J. M. Robson (Toronto: Univ. of Toronto Press, 1969), p. 381.

14. *The Works of Thomas Carlyle*, Centenary Edition, ed. H. D. Traill, 30 vols. (New York: Scribners, 1896–1901), 5:2.

15. *Past and Present* (1898) in ibid., 10:207.

16. Ibid., p. 160.

17. Ibid., pp. 273–74, 276.

18. Yeats, *Autobiography*, p. 89.

19. Huxley, 1:136–37.

20. Ibid., 3:86.

21. Letter to T. C. Horsfall, Oct. 25, 1883, *The Letters of William Morris to His Family and Friends*, ed. Philip Henderson (London: Longmans, 1950), p. 190.

22. Ibid.

CHAPTER TWO

1. Mackail, *Life*, 1:132

2. Letter to Andreas Scheu, Sept. 5, 1883, *Letters*, ed. Henderson, p. 186.

3. See Northrop Frye, *Anatomy of Criticism* (New York: Atheneum, 1966), pp. 33–66 and 131–239. Of special importance is the section entitled "The Mythos of Summer: Romance," pp. 186–206.

4. *The Hero with a Thousand Faces* (New York: World, 1956), p. 30. Cf. Frye's description of the quest, p. 187: "The complete form of the romance is clearly the successful quest, and such a completed form has three main stages; the stage of the perilous journey and the preliminary minor adventures; the crucial struggle, usually some kind of battle in which either the hero or his foe, or both, must die; and the exaltation of the hero."

5. *Anatomy*, p. 33.

6. Preface to the Second Edition of *Lyrical Ballads* (1800), *The Poetical Works of William Wordsworth*, ed. Ernest de Selincourt (Oxford: Clarendon Press, 1944), 2:386–97.

7. Campbell, p. 44. These qualities can also be expressed as order and chaos, or as Frye describes them, the apocalyptic and demonic worlds.

8. Ibid., p. 20.

9. The edition consulted was *Beowulf and the Fight at Finnsburg*, ed. Fr. Klaeber (Boston: Heath, 1950).

10. *Patterns in Comparative Religion*, trans. Rosemary Sheed (New York: Sheed and Ward, 1958), p. 379. Quoted by Edward B. Irving, Jr., *A Reading of Beowulf* (New Haven: Yale Univ. Press, 1968).

11. "Utopia, The City and The Machine," *Daedalus*, 94 (Spring, 1965), p. 277.

12. *The Enchafed Flood, or The Romantic Iconography of the Sea* (New York: Random House, 1950), p. 8.

13. *Anatomy*, pp. 306, 304.

14. *Mimesis: The Representation of Reality in Western Literature*, trans. Willard R. Trask (Princeton, N.J.: Princeton Univ. Press, 1953), pp. 142, 139.

15. Auden, pp. 13–14.

16. See Robert Langbaum, *The Poetry of Experience: The Dramatic Monologue in Modern Literary Tradition* (New York: Norton, 1957), pp. 57–58.

17. Mackail, *Life*, 1:132. Mackail notes that "Browning himself . . . was one of the earliest and the most enthusiastic admirers of this volume" (p. 133).

18. *Eras and Modes in English Poetry* (Berkeley: Univ. of California Press, 1964), p. 162. See also R. A. Foakes, *The Romantic Assertion* (New Haven: Yale Univ. Press, 1958), pp. 51–79.

19. Langbaum, pp. 53–56.

20. John M. Patrick, "Morris and Froissart: 'Geffray Teste Noire' and 'The Haystack in the Floods,' " *Notes and Queries*, N.S. 5 (1958), 425.

21. Printed by Caxton in 1485, *The Morte Darthur* was presumably written between 1469 and 1470 by the "Thomas Maleore Knyght" who spent most of his last years in prison. Froissart's *Chronicles of England, France, Spain, and the Adjoining Countries, from the Latter Part of the Reign of Edward II, to the Coronation of Henry IV* were composed earlier, apparently between 1357 and his death, near 1400.

22. Charles Moorman, *The Book of Kyng Arthur: The Unity of Malory's Morte Darthur* (Lexington: Univ. of Kentucky Press, 1965), p. 73. See also D. S. Brewer's introductory discussion of "The Tragedy of the Honorable Society" in his edition of *The Morte Darthur*, Parts Seven and Eight, York Medieval Texts (London: Edward Arnold, 1968), pp. 23–35.

23. The mimetic tendency, discussed by Frye and Auerbach, is reflected in both the direct style and "tragic" dimension of these writers, especially Malory, who employs the traditional notions of Fate, the wheel of Fortune, and the rise and fall of great men.

24. The rapid immersion in the situation of the speaker is assisted by Morris's omission of a scenic frame in an earlier draft (*CW* 1:xix–xx). It is not helped by the use of a past-tense "narration" by the poet, though the effects are as negligible as they are in Browning's "Childe Roland," where the sense of mental and physical activity overshadows the technicality of tense. See Langbaum's discussion of Browning's poem, pp. 192–99.

25. Cf. Malory XVIII, Chapter 25 (Brewer, pp. 78–79). Just before the Mellyagraunce scandal is narrated, Malory pauses for editorial comments on spring, love, and change. He idealizes old love, in harmony with the seasons, and makes Guene-

vere and Launcelot models of this paradise lost: "Therefore, like as May month flowereth and flourisheth in every man's garden, so in like wise let every man of worship flourish his heart in this world: first unto God, and next unto the joy of them that he promised his faith unto." The "virtuous love" of the old days grew and lasted many years, but Malory likens "love nowadays unto summer and winter: for, like as the tone is cold and the other is hot, so fareth love nowadays. And therefore all ye that be lovers, call unto your remembrance the month of May, like as did queen Guenevere, for who I make here a little mention, that while she lived she was a true lover, and therefore she had a good end."

In handling the whole Guenevere scandal in Books XIX and XX, Malory makes it clear that Guenevere and Launcelot are in fact lovers, but he refuses to judge as much as Morris. Instead he grants them the immunity of idealization. When he takes Launcelot to the Queen's chamber for the second meeting the poem alludes to, he says: "For, as the French book saith, the queen and sir Lancelot were togethers. And whether they were abed other at other manner of disports, me list not thereof make no mention, for love that time was not as love is nowadays" (Brewer, p. 103).

26. Stanza 85, *CW* 1:9. We might note also the parallel between nature's colors and heaven's. The blue of the sky echoes the blue cloth which seems "heaven's color." In antithesis, the red color of the other cloth, suggesting hell, is converted to the imagery of blood and heat—both associated with lust, adultery, and the purgatorial fire that is prepared for Guenevere by her captors.

27. Langbaum, p. 146.

28. *The Alien Vision of Victorian Poetry* (Princeton N.J.: Princeton Univ. Press, 1952), p. 29.

29. Curtis Dahl, "Morris's 'The Chapel in Lyoness': An Interpretation," *Studies in Philology*, 60 (July, 1954), 482–91.

30. Mumford, pp. 281, 277.

31. "The Second Coming," *Collected Poems* (New York: Macmillan, 1956), pp. 184–85.

CHAPTER THREE ∿∿∿∿∿∿∿∿∿∿∿∿

1. All references are from S. T. Coleridge, *Biographia Literaria*, chaps. 12 and 13, ed. J. Shawcross, 2 vols. (1907; rpt. London: Oxford Univ. Press, 1967).

2. W. B. Yeats, "The Symbolism of Poetry," *Essays and Introductions,* p. 159.

3. Carl G. Jung, "On the Relation of Analytical Psychology to Poetic Art," pp. 274–75. The following references to Jung are from this selection, pp. 274–87.

4. Frye, *Anatomy*, p. 55.

5. Virgil, *The Pastoral Poems,* trans. E. V. Rieu (Harmondsworth, Middlesex: Penguin Books, 1949), x:32; ix:11–13.

6. The text consulted here is *Kalender of Shepherdes*, including the edition of Paris 1503 in facsimile and a reprint of Pynson, 1506, ed. H. O. Sommer (London, 1892), 2. Morris's interest in medieval calendars is confirmed by his daughter, who said "he could not get enough of these in his head" (May Morris, 1:400).

7. An example is *The Zodiake of Life* (1565), trans. Barnaby Googe, "wherein are conteined twelve severall labours, painting out moste lively, the whole compasse of the world, the reformation of manners, the miseries of mankinde, the pathway to vertue and vice, the eternitie of the Soule, the course of the Heavens, the mysteries of nature, and divers other circumstances of great learning, and no lesse judgement." For excellent commentary on this genre and on medieval attitudes toward nature, see Rosemond Tuve, *Seasons and Months: Studies in a Tradition of Middle English Poetry* (Paris: Librairie Universitaire, 1933).

8. Nils E. Enkvist, *The Seasons of the Year: Chapters on a Motif from Beowulf to the Shepherd's Calendar,* Commentationes Humanarum Litterarum xxii, 4 (Helsingfors, Finland, 1957), p. 30. Cf. Tuve on the *Georgics* and *Eclogues*, pp. 26–35.

9. See Mary Parmenter, "Spenser's Twelve Aeglogues Proportionable to the Twelve Monethes," *Essays in Literary History*, 3 (1936), 190–217; and Paul E. McLane, *Spenser's Shepheardes*

Calender: A Study in Elizabethan Allegory (Notre Dame, Ind.: Univ. of Notre Dame Press, 1961).

10. Sommer, *Kalender of Shepherdes*, 2:9.

11. Morris's admiration of Spenser is reflected in the publication of a Kelmscott edition of the *Shepheardes Calendar* on Oct. 14, 1896, just eleven days after Morris's death.

12. Edmund Spenser, *Shepheard's Calendar*, ed. C. H. Herford (London: Macmillan, 1932), p. 2.

13. Ibid., p. 4.

14. May Morris, 1:543.

15. *The Machine in the Garden*, p. 23.

16. The list of favorite books is included in May Morris's introductory notes to *CW* 22:xiii; she recalls family reading in the same section, xviii–xix.

17. See, for example, E. R. Curtius, *European Literature and the Latin Middle Ages*, trans. W. R. Trask, Bollingen Series, 36 (New York: Pantheon, 1953), pp. 183–202; A. Bartlett Giamatti, *The Earthly Paradise and the Renaissance Epic* (Princeton, N.J.: Princeton Univ. Press, 1966), pp. 11–86; J. J. Wilhelm, *The Cruelest Month: Spring, Nature, and Love in Classical and Medieval Lyrics* (New Haven: Yale Univ. Press, 1965), pp. 35–60; and H. R. Patch, *The Otherworld According to Descriptions in Medieval Literature* (Cambridge, Mass.: Harvard Univ. Press, 1950), passim.

18. Giamatti, p. 15. Giamatti's discussion has provided valuable background for this survey of the garden.

19. The following discussion will in no way be a history of the paradise motif, which is full, long, and incorporates additional themes and *topoi*, e.g., the mountain. Patch and Giamatti are especially thorough, and Maud Bodkin's discussion of the Paradise-Hades archetype is relevant. A full survey should consider the sources and development of paradise literature in different cultures (Patch), and it would necessarily follow the expansion of the paradise garden of early pagan and Judeo-Christian models into classical and pastoral gardens, the Venus gardens of late Latin epithalamia, the Edenic paradises

of medieval Christian allegory, the love-pleasance of medieval romance, and finally the true and false paradises of Renaissance epic (Giamatti).

20. *The Odyssey*, trans. Robert Fitzgerald (Garden City, N.Y.: Doubleday, 1961), IV:564–68, p. 81.

21. *Hesiod, The Homeric Hymns and Homerica*, trans. H. G. Evelyn-White, Loeb Classical Library (Cambridge, Mass.: Harvard Univ. Press, 1936), *Works and Days*, 113–16, p. 11.

22. Marx, *The Machine in the Garden*, p. 22.

23. Giamatti, pp. 11–12.

24. John Ruskin, "Of Classical Landscape," *Modern Painters*, vol. III, part IV, chap. 13, *Works*, 5:235–36.

25. All references are from the idylls of Theocritus in *The Greek Bucolic Poets*, trans. J. M. Edmonds, Loeb Classical Library (London: William Heinemann, 1923).

26. Renato Poggioli, "The Oaten Flute," p. 151.

27. From a lecture entitled "The Early Literature of the North—Iceland," probably first delivered at Kelmscott House, Hammersmith, Oct. 9, 1887, in *The Unpublished Lectures of William Morris*, ed. Eugene D. LeMire (Detroit: Wayne State Univ. Press, 1969), pp. 184–85.

28. Poggioli, "The Oaten Flute," p. 150.

29. T. P. Harrison, ed., *The Pastoral Elegy* (Austin, Tex.: Univ. of Texas Press, 1939), p. 3.

30. The term is Poggioli's, developed in "The Pastoral of the Self," pp. 687–99.

31. Erwin Panofsky, "*Et in Arcadia Ego:* Poussin and the Elegiac Tradition," *Meaning in the Visual Arts* (Garden City, N.J.: Doubleday, 1955), p. 296.

32. *The Pastoral Art of Robert Frost*, p. 11.

33. *Studies of the Greek Poets*, 2nd Series (1876), (London: Adam and Charles Black, 1902), 2:258–365.

34. Bruno Snell, "Arcadia: The Discovery of a Spiritual Landscape," *The Discovery of the Mind: The Greek Origins of European Thought*, trans. T. G. Rosenmeyer (Cambridge, Mass.: Harvard Univ. Press, 1953), p. 290.

35. This attitude is reflected to some degree in W. P. Mustard's *Classical Echoes in Tennyson* (New York: Macmillan, 1904), and is more central to his "Later Echoes of the Greek Bucolic Poets," *American Journal of Philology*, 30 (1909), 245–83. The Victorian interest in Theocritus is also explored in J. W. Mackail, *Lectures on Greek Poetry* (London: Longmans, 1910), pp. 208–38; and in Robert T. Kerlin, *Theocritus in English Literature* (Lynchburg, Va.: J. P. Bell, 1910). Virgil's unfavorable comparison with Theocritus is partly a result of Virgil's misinterpretation by John Conington, whose 1858 edition of *The Works of Virgil* (London: George Bell and Sons, 1898) condemned his work as "unreal," "palpable and avowed imitation," and a "corruption of literature."

CHAPTER FOUR

1. Mackail, *Life*, 1:188.
2. Quoted by Max A. Wickert, "Form and Archetype in William Morris, 1855-1870," Diss. Yale Univ. 1965, pp. 113–14. British Museum Add. MS 45305, fol 121.
3. Cf. *Ancient Mariner*, part I, stanza 7:

> The ship was cheered, the harbour cleared,
> Merrily did we drop
> Below the kirk, below the hill,
> Below the lighthouse top.

4. John Arnott MacCullouch, ed., *The Mythology of All Races* (Boston: Marshall Jones, 1930), 2:59.
5. Yeats, *Collected Poems*, p. 244.
6. *Biographia Literaria*, chap. 14.
7. Philip Ziegler, *The Black Death* (London: Collins, 1969), pp. 111–12.
8. Yeats, "Song of the Happy Shepherd," *Collected Poems*, pp. 7–8.
9. Letter of Katherine Tynan, March, 1888. *Letters of W. B. Yeats*, ed. Allan Wade (New York: Macmillan, 1955), p. 63.

10. Epilogue of *The Earthly Paradise, CW* 6:327; italics mine.

11. *Anatomy*, p. 202.

12. Quoted in Bellas, "William Morris' Treatment of Sources in *The Earthly Paradise*," p. 31.

13. See T. McAlindon's fine article, "The Idea of Byzantium in William Morris and W. B. Yeats," *Modern Philology*, 64 (May, 1967), 307–19.

14. Morris's interpretation of Byzantine culture, important for its metaphoric value, also sheds light on his choice of historic setting for the Prologue. See Mackail, *Life*, 1:178–79. Mackail speaks of the inherited tradition of the Byzantine Greeks of the fourteenth century and notes that "the collection of minor poetry known as the Anthology owes its final form to a Byzantine scholar who was ambassador to Venice at the time of Edward III's accession to the crown of England, and was probably still alive when Chaucer was born" (p. 179).

15. References from the Prologue, *CW* 3, and Yeats, "Sailing to Byzantium," *Collected Poems*, pp. 191–92.

16. See Wickert, pp. 105–6.

17. *The Chronicles of Froissart*, trans. John Bourchier, Lord Berners, ed. G. C. Macaulay (London: Macmillan, 1904), chap. 121, p. 93; chap. 50.

18. *The Enchafèd Flood*, p. 7.

CHAPTER FIVE

1. Mackail, *Life*, 1:177.

2. Ibid., 1:178–82.

3. *Form and Meaning in Medieval Romance*, Presidential Address of the Modern Humanities Research Association, 1966 (Cambridge: MHRA, 1966), pp. 10–13.

4. Henderson, p. 106.

5. Abbie Findlay Potts, *The Elegiac Mode* (Ithaca: Cornell Univ. Press, 1967), pp. 38–39.

6. Ibid., p. 49. See also Martha H. Shackford, "A Definition of the Pastoral Idyll," *PMLA*, 19 (1904), 583–92.

7. The method is also characteristic of Tennyson in the early poems as well as the more ambitious *Idylls*. Speaking of "Oenone," Douglas Bush says, "For the general mode of treatment, the placing of a miniature epic in a luxuriant natural background, Tennyson was indebted to the Alexandrian idyll and epyllion, especially to his favorite Theocritus" (p. 204).

8. Walter Pater, "Poems by William Morris," a review of *The Defence of Guenevere, Jason,* and *The Earthly Paradise*, part I, in the *Westminster Review*, 90 (1868), 300–12. Quoted here from recent reprint in Peter Faulkner, ed., *William Morris: The Critical Heritage*, The Critical Heritage Series (London: Routledge and Kegan Paul, 1973), pp. 84–85.

9. *Kalender of Shepherdes*, ed. Sommer, p. 10, ll. 5–18.

10. Spenser, *Shepheard's Calendar*, p. 84.

11. Frye, *Anatomy*, pp. 163–239.

12. Spenser, XII:19–20, p. 85.

13. Spenser XII: 97–102, pp. 87–88.

14. Ibid., ll. 149–50, p. 89.

15. Yeats, "Lapis Lazuli," *Collected Poems*, p. 292.

16. A. Dwight Culler, *Imaginative Reason: The Poetry of Matthew Arnold* (New Haven: Yale Univ. Press, 1966), p. 5.

17. *The Metamorphoses of Ovid*, trans. A. E. Watts (Berkeley: Univ. of California Press, 1954), pp. 5–10.

18. Richard Wilbur, "Statues," *The Poems of Richard Wilbur* (New York: Harcourt, Brace, and World, 1963), p. 83.

19. Eleanor T. Lincoln, ed., *Pastoral and Romance*, (Englewood Cliffs, N.J.: Prentice-Hall, 1969), p. 3.

20. Frye, *Anatomy*, pp. 43–44.

21. Ibid., p. 200.

22. Enkvist, *Seasons of the Year*, p. 27; Tuve, *Seasons and Months*, p. 12.

23. Frye, *Anatomy*, p. 198.

24. "Dolfinus a Wise Emperoure," a story in Brunet's 1858 edition of *Le Violier des Histoires Romaines*, a reprint of an early French translation of the *Gesta Romanorum;* "Li Contes Dou

Roi Coustant L'Empereur," a thirteenth-century French romance in an 1856 edition; "The Devil with the Three Golden
Hairs," a folk tale from the Grimm collection; and a story in
Thorpe's *Northern Mythology* (1851). The first three sources are
discussed by both Bellas and Maurer. Maurer adds the last.

25. Cf. Morris's translation, *CW* 17:313–24, with the original
in *Nouvelles Françoises en Prose du XIIIe Siècle*, ed. L. Moland and
C. D'Héricault, Bibliotheque Elzevirienne (Paris: Chez P. Jannet, 1856).

26. See E. Faye Wilson, "Pastoral and Epithalamium in
Latin Literature," *Speculum*, 23 (1948), 35–57. Contributions of
the pastoral to the other classical form include natural setting,
introduction of rural deities, and references to the Golden
Age.

27. Maurer, p. 41.

28. Subtitle of the tale of Jovinian: "Of too much pride; and
how the proud are frequently compelled to endure some notable humiliation." In an 1876 edition of *Gesta Romanorum*, trans.
Charles Swan, rev. Wynnard Hooper (rpt. New York: Dover,
1959), p. 100.

CHAPTER SIX ∿∿∿∿∿∿∿∿

1. Lecture entitled *The Lesser Arts*, first published in 1878,
CW 22:11.

2. Frye, *Anatomy*, p. 193.

3. Tuve, *Seasons and Months*, p. 35. Cf. Enkvist, *The Seasons
of the Year*, p. 38.

4. Virgil, *The Pastoral Poems*, ed. Rieu, VII:47–48. Hereafter
cited in the text by eclogue and line.

5. *The Greek Bucolic Poets*, ed. Edmonds, XIII:1–4. Hereafter
cited in the text by idyll and line.

6. It is interesting that Lempriere, unquestionably familiar
to Morris (May Morris in *CW* 3:xviii–xix), details the symbolic
equation of Psyche and the soul. Morris instead identifies

Psyche with body's beauty and gives spiritual attributes to Cupid.

7. Frye, *Anatomy*, p. 193.

8. This is one of the supernatural details admired by Bush for its naturalness. Morris changes the original speaking tower to the spirit of a once-living character similar to Psyche. See *Mythology and the Romantic Tradition*, p. 319n.

9. Quoted by Maurer, p. 55.

10. "The Writing on the Image" (ii), "The Watching of the Falcon" (ii), and the two Venus tales of vol. iv.

11. Maurer, p. 48.

12. The "negative formula" is mentioned by Patch, *The Otherworld . . . in Medieval Literature*, p. 12. It is interpreted by Giamatti, *The Earthly Paradise and the Renaissance Epic*, p. 85, as an attempt to "express the inexpressible." Giamatti suggests that "in order to reflect in limited, recalcitrant words what they see directly with the mind's eye, the poets must resort to a technique which says what the site and nature of the good life are *not*, as well as to descriptions of what it is. And this very spectacle, of words striving through traditional images and the negative formula to encompass an inner ideal, stylistically mirrors those central themes of earthly paradise literature—the place's desirability and inaccessibility."

13. "Romanticism and Classicism," *Speculations* (1924; rpt. New York: Harcourt, Brace, n.d.), p. 117.

14. Bush, p. 319.

15. William Wordsworth, *The Prelude, or Growth of a Poet's Mind*, ed. Ernest de Selincourt, 2nd ed., rev. Helen Darbishire (Oxford: Clarendon Press, 1959), pp. 141, 143.

16. Note the reference to Psyche at the conclusion of "Pygmalion," where the image tells her maker that Venus said:

> Now herewith shalt thou love no less
> Than Psyche loved my son in days of old;
> Farewell, of thee shall many a tale be told (*CW* 4:207).

CHAPTER SEVEN

1. Mackail, *Life*, 1:201.

2. "The Grettis Saga," published in April, 1869, and the "Saga of Gunnlaug Worm-tongue," Jan. 1969, in the *Fortnightly Review*. Mackail, *Life*, 1:201.

3. Maurer, pp. 15–16. According to Mackail, Morris wrote "Bellerophon" in March of this same year (1:201).

4. Enkvist, *Seasons of the Year*, pp. 3, 5.

5. "Journey to Iceland," *The Collected Poetry of W. H. Auden* (New York: Random House, 1945), p. 8.

6. *Life*, 1:201.

7. *Mythology and the Romantic Tradition*, pp. 318–19.

8. He adds, in this letter to Swinburne, "Acontius I know is a spoony, nothing less, and the worst of it is that if I did him over a dozen times I know I should make him just the same" (*Letters*, p. 31).

9. Hallett Smith, "Pastoral Poetry," *Elizabethan Poetry* (Cambridge, Mass.: Harvard Univ. Press, 1952), pp. 3–4, 8.

10. Bush, p. 317.

11. Spenser, argument for II, p. 17; italics mine.

12. See "The Early Literature of the North—Iceland," a lecture first delivered in 1887, in *Unpublished Lectures*, ed. LeMire, pp. 179–98. Morris has this to say of the mythology of the Germanic tribes: "it is really much akin to that of the classical peoples: but as was likely to be from the simplicity of the people the Gods are more obviously than in other mythologies the reflexion of their worshippers: good-tempered and placable though as fierce as you please, with no liking for or indeed endurance of servility and no complaisance for cowardice or yielding, kind to their friends and hard to their foes, it must be said that the Norse Gods are distinctly *good-fellows*, and really about the best that mankind has made. In one point they are very specially a reflex of the men; that though [they] are long-lived they are not immortal, but lie under the same

fate as mankind. The day is to come when the forces of evil that they have chained and repressed shall at last break loose, and the good and evil of man's age and the Gods who have ruled over it shall meet in mortal conflict at last, and after fierce battle destroy each other" (pp. 188–89).

13. J. N. Swannell, *William Morris and Old Norse Literature*, a lecture to the William Morris Society, Dec. 18, 1958 (London: WMS, 1961), p. 14.

14. Jung, "On the Relation of Analytical Psychology to Poetic Art," pp. 273, 279.

15. Coleridge, *Biographia Literaria*, chap. 14.

16. In this volume, light is repeatedly associated with Hercules, Aslaug, and Bellerophon. It is first employed, however, in the tales of Vol. III to describe Rhodope and Kiartan. In Vol. III light reveals primarily selfish distance from others, especially with Rhodope. In Vol. IV its meaning more closely resembles that of the Beowulf poet, who announces his hero's courage and detachment from self with the image.

17. *Unpublished Lectures*, ed. LeMire, p. 163.

18. Campbell, *Hero with a Thousand Faces*, pp. 71, 72.

19. The communal value of art accounts for another positive connotation of light in the framework, the recurrent "firelight" that provides setting for the winter tales.

20. *Letters*, p. 30.

21. Although the stories, part of the original plan, were written earlier, they received major revision in the spring of 1870. See *Letters*, p. 35.

22. Yeats, "The Happiest of the Poets," *Essays and Introductions*, p. 63.

CHAPTER EIGHT

1. "A Prayer for My Daughter," *Collected Poems*, p. 187.

2. Isabel G. MacCaffrey, "Lycidas: Poet in a Landscape," *The Lyric and Dramatic Milton* (New York: Columbia Univ. Press, 1965), rpt. in *Pastoral and Romance*, ed. Lincoln, p. 127.

3. See Potts, *The Elegiac Mode,* p. 37.

4. Maud Bodkin, *Archetypal Patterns in Poetry* (1934; rpt. London: Oxford Univ. Press, 1963), p. 122.

5. Ibid., p. 127.

6. Envoi to *The Eyrbyggja Saga* (1870).

7. *News from Nowhere, CW* 16:132: "and now we do, both in word and deed, believe in the continuous life of the world of men, and as it were, add every day of that common life to the little stock of days which our own mere individual experience wins for us: and consequently we are happy."

selected bibliography

Arnot, Robert Page. *William Morris: The Man and the Myth.* New York: Monthly Review Press, 1964.

Auden, W. H. *The Enchafèd Flood, or The Romantic Iconography of the Sea.* New York: Random House, 1950.

Auerbach, Erich. *Mimesis: The Representation of Reality in Western Literature.* Trans. Willard R. Trask. Princeton: Princeton Univ. Press, 1953.

Bellas, Ralph A. "William Morris' Treatment of Sources in *The Earthly Paradise.*" Diss. Univ. of Kansas, 1961.

Bodkin, Maud. *Archetypal Patterns in Poetry.* 1934; rpt. London: Oxford Univ. Press, 1963.

Buckley, Jerome. *The Victorian Temper.* New York: Vintage, 1964.

Bush, Douglas. *Mythology and the Romantic Tradition in English Poetry.* 1937; rpt. New York: W. W. Norton, 1963.

Campbell, Joseph. *The Hero with a Thousand Faces.* New York: World, 1956.

Curtius, E. R. *European Literature and the Latin Middle Ages.* Trans. Willard R. Trask. Bollingen Series, 36. New York: Pantheon, 1953.

Dahl, Curtis. "Morris's 'The Chapel in Lyoness': An Interpretation." *Studies in Philology,* 60 (July, 1954), 482–91.

Empson, William. *Some Versions of Pastoral.* Norfolk, Conn.: New Directions, 1960.

Enkvist, Nils E. *The Seasons of the Year: Chapters on a Motif from Beowulf to the Shepherd's Calendar.* Commentationes Humanarum Litterarum, XXII, 4. Helsingfors, Finland, 1957.

Evans, B. Ifor. *English Poetry in the Later Nineteenth Century.* 2nd ed., rev. London: Methuen, 1966.

——. *William Morris and His Poetry.* London: G. G. Harrap, 1925.

Faulkner, Peter. *William Morris and W. B. Yeats.* Dublin: Dolmen Press, 1962.

————. *William Morris: The Critical Heritage.* London: Routledge and Kegan Paul, 1973.

Foakes, R. A. *The Romantic Assertion.* New Haven: Yale Univ. Press, 1958.

Froissart. *The Chronicles of Froissart.* Trans. John Bourchier, Lord Berners (1523–25). Ed. G. C. Macaulay. London: Macmillan, 1904.

Frye, Northrop. *Anatomy of Criticism: Four Essays.* 1957; rpt. New York: Atheneum, 1966.

————. "Varieties of Literary Utopias." *Daedalus,* 94 (1965), 323–47.

Gent, Margaret. " 'To Flinch from Modern Varnish': The Appeal of the Past to the Victorian Imagination." *Victorian Poetry,* Stratford-Upon-Avon Studies, 15 (London: Edward Arnold, 1972), 11–35.

Gesta Romanorum. Trans. Charles Swan. Revised Wynnard Hooper. 1876; rpt. New York: Dover, 1959.

Giamatti, A. Bartlett. *The Earthly Paradise and the Renaissance Epic.* Princeton: Princeton Univ. Press, 1966.

The Greek Bucolic Poets. Trans. J. M. Edmonds. Loeb Classical Library. London: William Heinemann, 1923.

Grennan, Margaret R. *William Morris: Medievalist and Revolutionary.* New York: King's Crown Press, 1945.

Harper, George Mills. *Yeats's Quest for Eden.* Dolmen Press Yeats Centenary Papers, 9. Dublin: Dolmen Press, 1965.

Harrison, T. P., Jr., ed. *The Pastoral Elegy.* Austin: Univ. of Texas Press, 1939.

Helmholtz-Phelan, Anna A. *The Social Philosophy of William Morris.* Durham, N.C.: Duke Univ. Press, 1927.

Henderson, Philip. *William Morris: His Life, Work and Friends.* New York: McGraw-Hill, 1967.

Hesiod, The Homeric Hymns and Homerica. Trans. H. G. Evelyn-White. Loeb Classical Library. Cambridge, Mass.: Harvard Univ. Press, 1936.

Hoare, Dorothy M. *The Works of Morris and Yeats in Relation* to *Early Saga Literature*. Cambridge: The University Press, 1937.

Houghton, Walter E. *The Victorian Frame of Mind, 1830–1870*. New Haven: Yale Univ. Press, 1957.

Hunt, John Dixon. *The Pre-Raphaelite Imagination, 1848–1900*. Lincoln: Univ. of Nebraska Press, 1968.

Johnson, E. D. H. *The Alien Vision of Victorian Poetry: Sources of the Poetic Imagination in Tennyson, Browning, and Arnold*. Princeton Studies in English, 34. Princeton: Princeton Univ. Press, 1952.

Jung, Carl G. "On the Relation of Analytical Psychology to Poetic Art." *Contributions to Analytical Psychology*. Trans. H. G. and Cary F. Baynes. London: Routledge and Kegan Paul, 1928. Rpt. in *Modern Continental Literary Criticism*. Ed. O. B. Hardison, Jr. New York: Appleton, 1962.

Kalender of Shepherdes (1503; 1506). Ed. H. O. Sommer. 2 vols. London: K. Paul, Trench, Trubner, 1892.

Kerlin, Robert T. *Theocritus in English Literature*. Lynchburg, Va.: J. P. Bell, 1910.

Langbaum, Robert. *The Poetry of Experience: The Dramatic Monologue in Modern Literary Tradition*. New York: W. W. Norton, 1957.

Lewis, C. S. "William Morris." *Rehabilitations*. London: Oxford Univ. Press, 1939.

Lincoln, Eleanor Terry, ed. "Introduction." *Pastoral and Romance*. Modern Essays in Criticism. Englewood Cliffs, N.J.: Prentice-Hall, 1969.

Lindsay, Jack. *William Morris, Writer*. London: William Morris Society, 1961.

Litzenberg, Karl. "William Morris and the Reviews: A Study in the Fame of the Poet." *Review of English Studies*, 12 (1936), 413–28.

Lynen, John. *The Pastoral Art of Robert Frost*. New Haven: Yale Univ. Press, 1960.

McAlindon, T. "The Idea of Byzantium in William Morris and W. B. Yeats." *Modern Philology*, 64 (May, 1967), 307–19.

MacCaffrey, Isabel G. "Lycidas: Poet in a Landscape." *The Lyric and Dramatic Milton.* New York: Columbia Univ. Press, 1965. Rpt. *Pastoral and Romance.* Ed. Eleanor T. Lincoln. Englewood Cliffs, N.J.: Prentice-Hall, 1969.

Mackail, J. W. *Lectures on Greek Poetry.* London: Longmans Green, 1910.

———. *The Life of William Morris.* 2 vols. 2nd ed. London: Longmans Green, 1901.

Malory, Sir Thomas. *The Morte Darthur.* Parts Seven and Eight. Ed. D. S. Brewer. York Medieval Texts. London: Edward Arnold, 1968.

Marx, Leo. *The Machine in the Garden: Technology and the Pastoral Ideal in America.* New York: Oxford Univ. Press, 1964.

———. "Two Kingdoms of Force." *Massachusetts Review,* 1 (1959), 62–95.

Maurer, Oscar, Jr. "William Morris's *The Earthly Paradise:* The Composition, Sources, and Critical Reception." Diss. Yale Univ., 1935.

Miles, Josephine. *Eras and Modes in English Poetry.* Berkeley: Univ. of California Press, 1964.

Moorman, Charles. *The Book of Kyng Arthur: The Unity of Malory's Morte Darthur.* Lexington: Univ. of Kentucky Press, 1965.

Morris, May, ed. *William Morris: Artist, Writer, Socialist: Unpublished and Hitherto Inaccessible Writings.* Oxford: B. Blackwell, 1936.

Morris, William. *The Collected Works of William Morris.* Ed. May Morris. 24 vols. London: Longmans Green, 1910–1915.

———. *The Letters of William Morris to His Family and Friends.* Ed. Philip Henderson. London: Longmans Green, 1950.

———. *The Unpublished Lectures of William Morris.* Ed. Eugene LeMire. Detroit: Wayne State Univ. Press, 1969.

Mumford, Lewis. "Utopia, The City and The Machine." *Daedalus,* 94 (1965), 271–92.

Mustard, W. P. *Classical Echoes in Tennyson.* New York: Macmillan, 1904.

————. "Later Echoes of the Greek Bucolic Poets." *American Journal of Philology*, 30 (1909), 245–83.

Nouvelles Françoises en Prose du XIIIe Siècle. Ed. L. Moland and C. D'Héricault. Bibliotheque Elzevirienne. Paris: Chez P. Jannet, 1856.

Palingenius, Marcellus. *The Zodiake of Life.* Trans. Barnabe Googe (1576). Introd. Rosemond Tuve. New York: Scholars' Facsimiles and Reprints, 1947.

Panofsky, Erwin. "*Et in Arcadia Ego:* Poussin and the Elegiac Tradition." *Meaning in the Visual Arts.* Garden City, N.Y.: Doubleday, 1955.

Parmenter, Mary. "Spenser's Twelve Aeglogues Proportionable to the Twelve Monethes." *Essays in Literary History*, 3 (1936), 190–217.

Patch, H. R. *The Otherworld According to Descriptions in Medieval Literature.* Cambridge, Mass.: Harvard Univ. Press, 1950.

Patrick, John M. "Morris and Froissart: 'Geffray Teste Noire' and 'The Haystack in the Floods.'" *Notes and Queries*, N.S., 5 (1958), 425–27.

Perrine, Laurence. "Morris's Guenevere: An Interpretation." *Philological Quarterly*, 39 (1960), 234–41.

Poggioli, Renato. "Naboth's Vineyard or the Pastoral View of the Social Order." *Journal of the History of Ideas*, 24 (1963), 3–24.

————. "The Oaten Flute." *Harvard Library Bulletin*, 11 (1957), 147–84.

————. "The Pastoral of the Self." *Daedalus*, 88 (1959), 687–99.

Potts, Abbie Findlay. *The Elegiac Mode: Poetic Form in Wordsworth and Other Elegists.* Ithaca: Cornell Univ. Press, 1967.

Shackford, Martha H. "A Definition of the Pastoral Idyll." *PMLA*, 19 (1904), 583–92.

Smith, Hallett. "Pastoral Poetry." *Elizabethan Poetry: A Study in Conventions, Meaning, and Expression.* Cambridge, Mass.: Harvard Univ. Press, 1952.

Snell, Bruno. "Arcadia: The Discovery of a Spiritual Landscape." *The Discovery of the Mind: The Greek Origins of European*

Thought. Trans. T. G. Rosenmeyer. Cambridge, Mass.: Harvard Univ. Press, 1953.

Spenser, Edmund. *Shepheard's Calendar: Containing Twelve Eclogues Proportionable to the Twelve Months.* Ed. C. H. Herford. London: Macmillan, 1932.

Stevenson, John W. "The Pastoral Setting in the Poetry of A. E. Housman." *South Atlantic Quarterly,* 55 (1956), 487–500.

Stevenson, Lionel. *The Pre-Raphaelite Poets.* Chapel Hill: Univ. of North Carolina Press, 1972.

Swannell, J. N. *William Morris and Old Norse Literature.* Lecture to the William Morris Society, December 18, 1958. London: William Morris Society, 1961.

Thompson, E. P. *William Morris: Romantic to Revolutionary.* London: Camelot, 1955.

Thompson, Paul. *The Work of William Morris.* New York: Viking, 1967.

Tuve, Rosemond. *Seasons and Months: Studies in a Tradition of Middle English Poetry.* Diss. Bryn Mawr College. Paris: Librairie Universitaire, 1933.

Vinaver, Eugène. *Form and Meaning in Medieval Romance.* Presidential Address of Modern Humanities Research Association, 1966. Cambridge: MHRA, 1966.

Virgil. *The Pastoral Poems.* Trans. E. V. Rieu. Harmondsworth, Middlesex: Penguin, 1949.

Watkinson, Ray. *William Morris as Designer.* New York: Reinhold, 1967.

Wickert, Max A. "Form and Archetype in William Morris, 1855–1870." Diss. Yale Univ., 1965.

Wilhelm, J. J. *The Cruelest Month: Spring, Nature, and Love in Classical and Medieval Lyrics.* New Haven: Yale Univ. Press, 1965.

Wilson, E. Faye. "Pastoral and Epithalamium in Latin Literature." *Speculum,* 23 (1948), 35–57.

Yeats, William Butler. *The Autobiography of William Butler Yeats.* New York: Macmillan, 1953.

————. *Collected Poems.* New York: Macmillan, 1956.

————. *Essays and Introductions.* New York: Macmillan, 1961.

————. *Letters of W. B. Yeats.* Ed. Allan Wade. New York: Macmillan, 1955.

index